A Treasury of World

Antiques

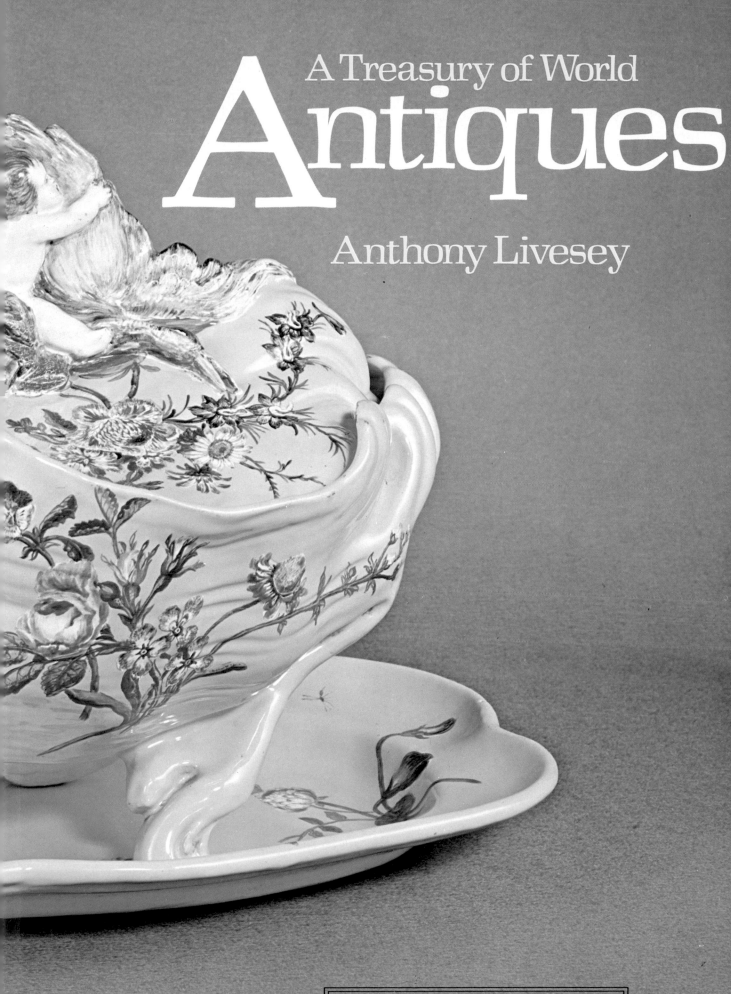

A Treasury of World
Antiques

Anthony Livesey

This edition produced exclusively for

WHSMITH

**This edition published exclusively for
W H Smith**

All rights reserved. No part of this publication may be reproduced,
stored in a retrieval system, or transmitted, in any form or by any means,
electronic, mechanical, photocopying, recording or otherwise, without
the permission of the Hamlyn Publishing Group Limited

Published by
The Hamlyn Publishing Group Limited
London · New York · Sydney · Toronto
Astronaut House, Feltham, Middlesex, England

Third impression 1981

Copyright © The Hamlyn Publishing Group Limited 1979

ISBN 0 600 30482 5

Printed in Italy

Title page photograph: a French
porcelain *terrine*, made in Marseilles
in the 18th century. Reunion des
Musées Nationaux.

Contents

Introduction

Many books have been written on the subject of antiques. Some are of great scholarship and breadth; others are shorter works, often specializing in a limited field; still others are illustrated books with lengthy captions. The purpose of this work is to take the reader through the styles and articles of western European and American antiques from the 16th century (when "modern" antiques may be said to begin) to the end of the Second World War. In this way it is hoped the reader will gain the essential knowledge which will enable him to appreciate the products of the past, to date them accurately, to distinguish between the genuine and the fake; he will also have learnt where and how to buy antiques, how to display, preserve and repair them. Perhaps most important of all, the reader will then, it is hoped, be in a position to decide in which area of antiques he wishes to collect. As we shall see, collecting is largely dependent on specializing and it is therefore essential that the reader should be fully aware of the advantages and hazards that attend the various fields.

It will be appreciated that, while the scope of the book has been made as wide as possible, certain aspects of the history of antiques have had to be omitted. To have included every possible form of antiques from every country in the world, from the earliest times to the present day, would, in a work of this length, have reduced the coverage of individual forms to frivolous brevity. Certain antiques have therefore been excluded. Thus, references to the products of antiquity, the works found in the Middle East, in Greece and Rome, have been omitted. Few have survived and those which have are safely housed in museums. Pieces seldom if ever come up for sale and, even if they did, they would be of stupendous price. They may be seen in many museums, how-ever, and readers would be wise to study them there whenever possible.

Also excluded, save where they affect western styles, are the styles of the East – of Japan, China, south-east Asia and India. These are fascinating but specialized areas and readers seeking information about their antiques must regrettably look elsewhere.

It has again been necessary to exclude certain individual fields. Paintings and watercolours cannot fall within the scope of this book. The history of painting is truly an enormous subject and has been written on over the years most copiously. However, the visual arts have had a profound effect on every field of craftsmanship – on the design of furniture, silver and metalware, jewellery and even toys. As a result, even though the visual arts are not covered here as such, information will be provided about the great styles, Baroque, Rococo and the rest, which originated in painting and architecture and were then adopted by the various craftsmen.

Finally, some smaller, highly specialized areas have likewise been omitted. Stamp collecting is indeed a fascinating and rewarding pastime, but it is of interest to the collector only rather than to the general reader. The same is true of book collecting. There is an abundance of literature on both these subjects but space prevents more than their mention here.

We have attempted to arrange the book in the manner most convenient for the reader. Some works take individual themes, such as furniture, and treat them from the beginnings to the present day in strictly chronological order, then in further chapters treat silverware, metalware, jewellery and so on in the same way. This is not a satisfactory arrangement in many ways. It must be remembered that artifacts (they were not, of course, considered "antiques" at the time of

Opposite:
Selection of English Georgian silverware.

6

their production) of every sort are made at the same time. Thus, while in Elizabethan times the English were producing diverse pieces of oak furniture, they were also producing armour, jewellery, toys and so on, and the favoured styles of the time affected all these products. It is therefore easier for the reader to get a feeling for a style or period if all these subjects are discussed together.

The chapters are therefore arranged by century, beginning with the 16th century and ending in the middle of the 20th. Each chapter begins with a description of the styles which dominated that century. Thus the 16th century begins with an account of the Italian Renaissance style, and covers Mannerism and the School of Fontainebleau; the 20th century discusses the styles known as Art Nouveau and Art Deco.

In each chapter the first specific subject to be discussed is furniture. This arrangement has been chosen because of the vital importance of furniture in everyone's life. Furniture is understandably the most popular area of antiques. Anyone who cares to study the shelves of a public library will see that books on furniture far outnumber those on any other form of antique. The beds we sleep in, the tables we eat at, the chairs we sit in – these are part of our everyday lives, and the question

of how they have been adapted and modified over the centuries provides some of the most revealing clues we have as to our ancestors' manner of living. Furniture also dominates a study of antiques because of its abundance. Even the most modest 16th-century home would have a stool, some form of bed and some sort of chest in which to keep things. In later centuries homes were, of course, more generously furnished and by the beginning of the 20th century there was such an abundance of pieces of furniture in the drawing room as to amount to clutter. Those interested in furniture (and that must surely include almost everyone interested in antiques at all) will readily be able to buy pieces to suit their pocket. It is not so easy in other areas. Jewellery, for example, is almost by definition costly, although even here, as we shall see, judicious searching will sooner or later unearth a bargain.

After furniture, the order becomes less rigid. In helping the reader to gain an understanding of a particular century the pieces are discussed in the order of importance which obtained at the time. To the 16th-century nobleman, for example, armour was of considerable importance and therefore logically follows closely after furniture; by the following centuries, however, furniture keeps its predominance but weaponry has become rather more

peripheral. This may be further illustrated by the example of toys. Playthings for children were produced in the 16th century but with little thought for the child's needs. The Renaissance concentrated on the mature, the universal man of achievement; and women and children were less highly regarded. By the 18th century, however, Europeans had accepted the need for toys to be an aid to a child's development; playthings therefore became more abundant, and so in the 18th-century chapter playthings are given extra coverage.

The book is designed to be read straight through, from beginning to end, so that the reader can see how one style led to another, how the production of chairs and tables developed with the invention of new techniques, how the shape and nature of glassware changed over the years and so on. Each chapter is nevertheless an independent entity in itself. It will therefore be quite possible for the reader to refer to a single century, should it be of especial interest to him, and there find an account, complete in itself, of the trends of the time.

What is an antique?

A definition of what is and what is not an antique is of necessity an arbitrary one. In the strictest sense and as defined by the great auction houses and high-

Left:
A fine example of an early 16th-century *cassapanca*, or combined chest and seat. Made of walnut, it is typical of the majestic furniture of the Renaissance.

Below:
A plain but elegant sugar caster of 1773; a fine example of the qualities of English Georgian silver.

Right:
The distinctively American tallboy, or high chest of drawers. This example was made in Boston in the 1740s. H. F. duPont Wintherthur Museum, Delaware.

9

quality sale rooms, such as the annual Grosvenor House Antiques Fair in London, an object may only be called an antique if it is at least 130 years old. The reader, however, need not pay too much regard to this definition. It is, after all, mainly the view of professional societies and some dealers, not of the owners of antique shops and stalls. Furthermore, to keep strictly to the 130-year definition would mean that in 1980 no piece made after 1850 could properly be termed an antique. This, for the general reader or the person anxious to furnish his home with pleasing but not modern pieces, is patently an absurd limitation. It would exclude not only almost all Victorian furniture, some of which is now once more recognized to be attractive, but also the many beautiful pieces made in the Art Nouveau and Art Deco styles. It would further exclude many pieces of high quality produced in the USA (for it is mainly in the last 130 years or so that an individual, national style evolved in that country; previously craftsmen had tended to copy European trends), as well as the revolutionary designs in furniture and other artifacts which emanated from Germany and America in the 1930s. Within the scope of this book the strict definition has been ignored; instead the year 1945 has been chosen as the dividing line between antique and modern. This is an equally arbitrary definition, but it is also a more useful one. Items from the Art Deco period (the 1920s and 1930s), for example, are no longer found in everyday shops; they are found in antique shops, on stalls and at auctions and they are sold as antiques. Because of this, and because breakages have made them less plentiful than hitherto, they are now generally more expensive than they were at the time of their manufacture. Anyone investing in a piece of Art Deco furniture or glassware would rightly consider he was buying an antique, since he would have legitimate expectations of its rising in value. After 1945, however, a different picture emerges. Furniture very similar to that of the early post-war years is still produced and can be bought in modern furniture shops and elsewhere. There is little difference in value or appearance between, say, a set of china

produced in 1950 and another set produced in 1970. A further point makes the year 1945 a valid dividing line. Let us suppose that someone wishes to buy a set of china, though not a modern one; let us further suppose that he knows nothing about the history of antiques and cannot tell one style from another. A knowledgeable friend or agent buys on his behalf a set of Art Deco china, complete, in perfect condition and sold to him at a fair price. There can be little doubt that under those conditions he would have made a good investment, and that the value of his purchase, in strictly financial terms, would increase. Buying a product made since 1945, however, would be a matter of speculation and guesswork. He may have bought china which in coming years will still be regarded as attractive; on the other

Above:
A Victorian watch – large enough to be hung on the wall of a coach. Good 19th-century clocks and watches can be at least as reliable as modern timepieces of equivalent price. Private collection.

Right:
A *bonheur-du-jour*, made in France in about 1770 by Martin Carlin and covered in Sèvres porcelain. This piece reached a record price in a saleroom in the late 1960s.

Above:
A selection of Victorian games; these can offer an incredibly rich field for collectors. The Museum of London.

Below:
A wineglass of about 1720, inscribed with the words "Prosperity to Ireland". Antiques can provide fascinating insights into the history of the times in which they were produced.

hand he may not, since only time will reveal the taste of future generations. This must not be taken to mean, however, that collectors should avoid anything produced since 1945; far from it, as we shall see in the last chapter. It means, nevertheless, that he is speculating in a modern product rather than investing in an antique.

The question of taste

In the fictitious example given above, how likely would it have been for the speculation in modern china to have turned out to be wise? This brings us to the elusive question of "taste". It has been described as "a disinterested enthusiasm for the best", and this is certainly as good a definition as any for the great works of art, whether in architecture, literature, music or the visual arts. But why can we immediately tell on entering a person's home whether or not the owner has "good taste"? The answer lies not only in the objects themselves but in harmony: whether the selection and arrangement of his furniture and ornaments are pleasing when they are all seen together.

Two points deserve to be made here. It was once said with some truth that it took three generations to amass a fortune and three generations to squander it. In some ways it was also true that it took three generations to acquire good taste. A child, however

instinctively he may have been attuned to things of beauty, started at a disadvantage if his youth was passed in unsympathetic surroundings. His son, however, would have been brought up in more attractive surroundings and his grandson reaped the advantages of what would have been called a cultured background. This, or something very like it, was true in the past. Today, however, with greater social and financial equality, no-one is barred from cultural awareness. It is true that few own ancestral homes and their contents accumulated over the centuries, but we can all now visit such places and see at close hand the masterpieces of architecture, painting and furniture of the past. Museums, too, are open to all, so that today anyone interested in antiques has many opportunities for study, and the "three generations" theory can no longer be said to apply. We can all, indeed, acquire "good taste" today.

The second point concerns the taste of others. Patronage today, in consequence of taxation and other factors, has passed from the individual to the state – some would say with disastrous results. Patronage is essential to art. It can be simply speculation, but it is usually more than that. It is reasonable to suppose that the artists of even the early cave paintings were perhaps excused other duties such as hunting – surely an early example of patronage. Through the centuries wealthy and discerning art lovers have encouraged and financed artists of talent, and indeed made their work possible. Today few can afford to perform this crucial service; the state, which has filled the void, must do so indiscriminately to ensure that no potential talent is overlooked. Much of the art that is encouraged and financed today is thus regrettably of inferior invention. Is that important, however? It matters, of course, that qualified and gifted guardians of great works, whether museum curators or private owners, should pass on the traditions of taste to future generations, but it matters less if other collectors have a taste of their own. The point is important, for it is crucial when buying antiques to be guided by one's own judgment; results cannot but be disastrous if the collector merely apes the preferences of others, copying furniture or wall decorations which he has seen else-where. The reader of this book will evolve his own preferences, his own taste; whether or not they are the preferences of other collectors essentially does not matter. Collecting should be enjoyable and the results pleasing to the owner; that is all.

Some aids

Before setting out in search of antiques the collector may wish to equip himself with some tools to assist him in judging the age of an antique and in detecting fakes. It should be noted here that no-one should be unduly depressed if he finds he has inadvertently bought a piece which is not what he supposed it to be. Perhaps every year and certainly every decade the art market is disconcerted to learn that a painting or other work which it had attributed to a certain artist is in fact the work of someone else. This occurs despite the professionalism and extensive knowledge of the attributors, and despite the sophisticated equipment at their disposal. It is far more forgivable, therefore, for the general collector to be at some time (though not always deliberately) duped. Indeed, it will almost inevitably occur even to those with great expertise and it should never be allowed to discourage or depress.

The more sophisticated techniques are quite impractical for the general collector. The carbon-14 test, for example, is serviceable when dealing with works from antiquity but it has a very wide error margin which debars it from use with later antiques (it can hardly be helpful to be told, for example, that a table was made somewhere between 1700 and 1900).

One or two simpler, inexpensive items are of more help. A magnifying glass is virtually essential, especially when looking at such things as silver stamps or studying wood to look for minute evidence, such as tool marks, to establish its age. Any reasonable magnifying glass will serve although it is often helpful to use an attachment on a headband or on one's glasses, since this will permit the collector to use both hands, moving the object from side to side and from angle to angle.

A light source is also helpful. Many of the older shops are crowded and

ill-lit and it is not always possible to take pieces into the daylight. There are many products of convenient size on the market, but the beginner might decide to make do at first with a good-quality torch. Later he may decide to invest in something more sophisticated. Many authors advocate the use of an ultra-violet light, which on ceramics will reveal the use of additional pigment to the original, as newer pigments appear as black under ultra-violet light. There are highly effective and elaborate examples; there are also simple light tubes with an extension cord which fits into the pocket.

The novice collector might be well advised not to invest in anything more than the above until he has decided in which field he is going to work, since more sophisticated equipment may be helpful in examining, say, ceramics and not wood, or the other way round. In any event, the collector is himself the best equipment: the first requirement is sharp eyesight, to which magnifying glasses and light sources are merely aids; thereafter he requires a retentive memory and a knowledge of what to look for and where to look for it. There are no inventions which can aid him in those areas.

Buying antiques

Antiques may be found in all manner of places; sometimes they may be obtained for nothing. Even judicious

An English Victorian drawing-room; the accumulation of pieces makes it easy to understand how it is that there are so many antiques still available for sale today.

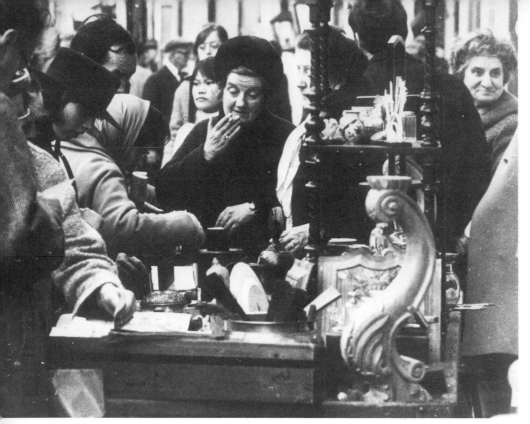

Bargain-hunters searching the stalls in the street market of Portobello Road, London.

searching in the banks of the Thames at low tide, for example, can result in the discovery of Roman and Saxon coins, since London was one of the earliest settlements. It is even possible to find artifacts in dustbins, skips and in rubbish tips. Realistically, however, antiques must be bought and there are a number of ways of doing this.

The first, and in many ways the most useful, especially for smaller items, is the street market. These may be found in all the major cities of the western world, including those of the USA. Paris and Amsterdam, for example, both have a world-famous "flea market" where almost anything can be bought, from second-hand welling-ton boots to dubious magazines, from china to the military uniforms of defunct regimes. London is one of the better equipped cities in this respect, the markets at the Portobello Road and in Bermondsey being among the most famous. Markets are often sit-uated on streets where the shops also deal in antiques, so that the collector is presented a wide range of material to consider. Another advantage of mar-kets is that they are in the open, so that pieces may be examined in daylight. Furthermore, since most markets are held on only one day in the week, the rent for a stall is considerably less than the rent and rates for a shop and pieces are probably offered for sale at a slightly lower price than elsewhere.

There is yet another advantage. As with shop owners, stall holders tend either to specialize or to offer a wide selec-tion of unrelated objects; since, how-ever, there are many more stalls than shops the quantity of goods on display is much greater.

Buying at a stall calls for some sensi-tivity. Antique dealers are in the main intelligent and friendly people; they need the first quality in order to buy respectable stock and the second in order to deal with the buying public. It is therefore helpful to establish a *rapport* with a dealer (a fairly natural process, since both the collector and the dealer have interests in common), although clearly this is less easy for the tourist. A bargain over the price of a piece may be struck, but the golden rule is never to haggle. It is a surprising quirk of nature that a shopper entering a shop to buy a bar of chocolate either buys it or rejects it as being too expen-sive; with antiques it is often otherwise. The potential buyer will frequently try to "beat down" the price, sometimes by a truly greedy proportion. It must never be forgotten that the dealer has had to invest money in his wares; sometimes they may have remained on his stall unsold for many weeks. Moreover, he has his overheads to meet – his rent, petrol, insurance and road tax for his car (an essential for a dealer), as well as other necessities of his trade such as cleaning fluids, paint, paint removers and so on. Even more important than this is his investment of time. He may well drive hundreds of miles in a week and will certainly have spent many hours repairing and re-storing pieces before putting them on display. He is, as is any dealer, perfectly entitled to a legitimate profit and the collector who haggles too much is likely to find his efforts counter-productive: sometimes the dealer will simply refuse to sell the piece to that particular person. On the other hand, it is perfectly proper to ask if the dealer can make a slight reduction in his asking price. It would not be un-reasonable, if a piece were priced at £10, to get it in this way for, say, £9. The request will either be accepted or rejected, the purchase made or not; either way, the arrangement can be amicably arrived at and future deals made in a similar manner.

Nineteenth-century American shop signs for a maker of nautical instruments and a tobacconist; in recent years such pieces have become highly collectable.

Above:
A medium-price silver auction in progress in London, at Phillip's, Son and Neal.

Right:
An 18th-century satinwood games table; most items now classed as antiques were designed to be used, and can still give the owners much pleasure today.

Many items on display in a street market will not be in perfect condition; the dealer will be quite as aware of this as the collector and will in most cases already have adjusted his price accordingly. The collector is naturally at liberty to point out this defect, but again it is counter-productive to make much of it; the piece, after all, has not been offered as being in perfect condition. Successful dealing at street markets is therefore to a great extent a matter of manners. Dealers usually spend a great deal of time arranging their stalls so that pieces appear to their best advantage; they will have arrived at the market early for this purpose and got out of bed long before the customer. Hardly anything, therefore, infuriates the dealer more than to have a customer pick up pieces from his stall, study them and then replace them in a different place. Far from achieving a rapport with the dealer, collectors who do this are likely to become involved in acrimonious dispute. Nor will the collector be endeared to the dealer if he treats the wares roughly. This is particularly true of items such as boxes and Victorian photograph albums which have hinges, often in a frail condition.

All of the above applies equally when dealing in antique shops. And indeed, perhaps civility is even more necessary in shops, since they are fewer in number and every time a collector has irritated a dealer he will have disproportionately reduced his sources of supply. It is unnecessary to dwell further on this point, beyond saying that developing a pleasant relationship with dealers will be of inestimable value to the collector.

Another important source for the collector of antiques is the auction room. These establishments are to be found in all cities and most towns of any size. National and provincial newspapers carry notices as to when and where auctions are to be held. They vary greatly in the quality of the items offered and prices reached. At the great sale rooms, such as Sotheby's in London, pieces will go for thousands, often hundreds of thousands, of pounds. In the smaller auction rooms – and this is especially true of those in provincial towns – lots will be far cheaper. Often a lot will go for less than £10; occasionally even for £1 or so.

Viewing (that is, the freedom to walk around the lots on display and study them at leisure) is usually allowed on the day before the auction. It is very much in the collector's interest to attend on that day. In the first place,

moving around the auction room while the auction is actually in progress is discouraged; more often than not the auctioneer will forbid it. In any event, it is highly distracting to those bidding. Secondly, the viewing day gives the collector an excellent opportunity to study the lots at his leisure and to come to a rational, unhurried decision as to how much he is prepared to pay.

This last is important, for a fever all too easily seizes the collector and he can find he has paid more than he ever intended or wished. One solution to this is to buy a catalogue on the viewing day. This will describe the lots (often a lot will comprise a variety of pieces and collectors must reconcile themselves to acquiring a number of things they do not want in order to get one that they do) and the collector can then mark the lots which interest him and, after consideration, work out the top price to which he is prepared to go.

It is useful in this respect to give an approximate sum, but if bidding reaches his highest figure, the collector is advised to stop at once. Auctions take on a personality of their own: on some days the entire stock will go for less than the collector expected, on others for more. It is therefore quite possible to find that what has been estimated to be worth " £10 – £12 " in fact goes for £20. In the fever of bidding it is all too easy to go up to £20. True he will have acquired a piece he wished to possess, but after doing this on a number of lots on an expensive day he may have overspent his budget by £50. Therefore, having decided at leisure the previous day what he is prepared to pay, he should not exceed that figure when actually bidding. If the piece is unique, it will in any event go for a considerable sum; if it is not, he can console himself that he will come across another example of a similar piece in the future.

While it is advisable to attend the auction, it is not essential. It is a common practice to leave a maximum bid with a porter, who will then bid on the day. If the bid is successful, however, the porter will expect a reasonable tip.

It is advisable to arrive early at an auction. This enables the collector to have a further, albeit brief, look at the lots before bidding starts; it will also enable him to get a seat (standing for the full length of an auction is an extremely tiring experience), ideally one near the auctioneer and the lots on offer. A cheque book and means of identification are also necessary if the collector is not known in that particular auction room.

A bid may be given in almost any way – a nod of the head or shouting out – but the usual and most convenient is to raise the catalogue; this can be easily seen by the auctioneer, who will undoubtedly be grateful for this.

Bidding rises by units. In Britain most auctioneers take bids of 50p up to £10; then units of £1 up to £20; thereafter the bidding rises by £2, £3, £3, £2 up to £100 – that is to say, £30, £33, £36, £38. At greater sums the usual increase is by £5 above £100 and by £25 above £1000. This information, or whatever variant is used, is usually printed on the programme but if in doubt the collector should seek confirmation on the viewing day so that there can be no mistakes when he comes to bid.

Another rewarding source of antiques is the antiques fair. These have become increasingly popular since the Second World War, particularly so in Britain. Some are mounted for charitable purposes, others as business ventures. As with street markets, dealers hire a stall for the day or the evening as the case may be. Admittance may be free; at most a modest charge will be asked. These fairs will be advertised in local newspapers. When buying at antique fairs the suggestions given for buying at street markets also apply, but with one difference. Antique fairs often provide such a rich (though often expensive) supply of goods that, during the early hours of the fair, professional dealers are likely to be in evidence in great numbers; local people, too, will attend and the crush often makes viewing difficult. Later in the day the number will have decreased. True, items in which the collector might have been interested may have been sold, but it will then be possible to view the remaining pieces more closely and at your leisure. Moreover, many of the stall holders may not be exhibiting at another fair for some time; they may have shops to attend during the week or be restricted in the distance they are willing to travel. During the later stages of a fair they are therefore usually prepared to make a significant

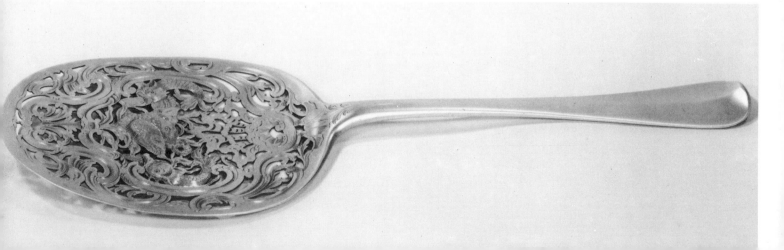

reduction in their asking price, since they may feel it is better business to make a sale than to have to take a great many pieces home.

Rather different rules apply with what are called jumble sales. These are local affairs organized for charity. The bulk of items on display comprise second-hand clothing, unwanted sports equipment and so on, items of no interest to the collector. Often, however, there is a stall for china and silver and, in order to secure something of value it is essential to queue to be among the first at that stall. Etiquette prohibits any bargaining at a jumble sale; it has been organized for charity, the stall holders are unpaid and overworked, the prices extremely modest. It is an accepted rule that the purchaser pays the asking price (ideally in the exact change asked) or refrains from buying.

Another source which has appeared since the Second World War is the charity shop. These are located in many cities throughout England, the USA and elsewhere. Items of interest can often be found in these shops, but they will seldom be bargains. The shop was established to make as much money as possible for the charity in question; the prices asked will therefore be the maximum that they have been advised they can expect. If a piece would make a valuable addition to a collection, however, the collector will hardly object that he is obliged to pay a full rather than a knock-down price.

Sometimes the entire contents of a house will be offered for sale. The conditions under which this occurs are numerous, but usually it follows the death of the owner. An elderly lady, for example, may have left her home and its contents to a nephew; the nephew may already have a home of his own and prefer to raise capital by selling rather than inheriting a second

Above:
A tinware tray painted with *chinoiserie* decoration of the English Regency period of the early 19th century. Royal Pavilion, Brighton.

Left:
A silver fish slice, made by Paul de Lamerie in 1741.

home and a second set of furniture, china and glass. These sales are popular with dealers and competition is likely to be stiff; nevertheless, individual pieces often go for very reasonable sums. For example, a single lot might comprise all the vases in the house – perhaps ten or more. It is unlikely that a local person would wish to acquire so many and, unless there is a dealer present who handles vases, a lot such as this will often be knocked down for a few pounds.

It is always worth while studying the advertising columns of newspapers. Single items of considerable value, such as pianos, are often offered in this way, as are collections of silver, jewellery, furs and so on. This source is, however, of interest mainly to the collector of specialized pieces, such as items associated with a distinguished historical figure. The advertisement may offer, for example, a number of

pieces connected with Nelson or Washington; if this is the field in which the collector is working he should obviously contact the vendor without delay.

Finally, specialized fields, such as coin collecting, usually have a publication of their own, appearing monthly, quarterly or sometimes annually. Some of these publications are printed to a high standard; most are designed to be merely serviceable and are copies of typed sheets, stapled together. The antique book market, for example, relies heavily on this kind of advertising. Pieces of interest will be offered and the prices stipulated. In many instances, too, an offer to exchange one piece for another will be made; this can often be helpful when making a collection.

It should be noted in passing that all these sources are also available to the collector who wishes to dispose of his

property. To place an advertisement in a newspaper is cheap and there is no need to pay commission. Stall holders and shop owners will make an offer on pieces but, however scrupulous, they will naturally need to make a profit. Usually the best and safest way is to put the piece or collection in an auction. By the time a collector comes to sell his property he will have a very good idea of its current value; he will know, after all, what he paid for individual pieces and will have a shrewd idea of how much it has increased in value through inflation, especially if the collection is complete. Nevertheless, if in doubt most reputable auction houses will be prepared to give an estimate of its value. The vendor may also put a reserve figure on his lot; a figure below which the piece is withdrawn from the sale. The vendor will be obliged to pay the auction house a percentage fee (usually around ten per-

Left:
A pair of porcelain figures, probably modelled by Kändler at Meissen in about 1740. Victoria and Albert Museum, London.

Right:
An English bracket clock of about 1700, probably the work of John Martin. The case is decorated with marquetry. Victoria and Albert Museum, London.

Below right:
An oak armchair of 1550, from England or Scotland; chairs are probably the most important antiques of any period, but examples as early as this one can rarely be bought. Victoria and Albert Museum, London.

Below:
A French chair of the end of the 16th century, covered in leather. Musée des Arts Decoratifs.

Above:
Two highly ornate pieces of English silver in the Rococo revival style of the 1830s.

Left:
A crowded antiques shop specializing in metalware, but even so revealing an enormous diversity of goods. Portobello Road, London.

Opposite:
A pair of early 19th-century parchment candle-shades on adjustable stands. American Museum, Bath.

cent) but at least he is sure that his property will not inadvertently be disposed of for a trivial sum.

The tourist

It is perhaps worth making a point, obvious but often overlooked, in the case of tourists. The great museums throughout Europe and the USA, and the private collections, their locations, times of opening and the nature of their contents may all be had from information offices, cultural attachés at embassies and elsewhere in the tourist's home country. It is highly recommended that the tourist should equip himself with this information before leaving. This will save him many valuable hours when he arrives at his holiday centre. In many cases, such as the National Trust properties in Great Britain, a comprehensive ticket at a reduced fee may be had beforehand, entitling the tourist to visit all the properties owned by the National Trust.

Fakes and disguised antiques

We have noted how possible it is, even for someone whose student years and entire working life has been devoted to a specialized area of the arts, to be deceived as to the nature and authorship of a piece. Before discussing this further, however, it may be useful and encouraging briefly to consider the reverse side of the coin: since dealers can themselves be taken in, it is still possible for the knowledgeable collector to find bargains. Furniture especially is not always what it seems. For example, during the 1920s, 1930s and occasionally earlier there was a common habit of applying a dark brown varnish to furniture, especially chairs, tables and chests. It was quickly painted on and gave a brighter, newer look to old furniture. Oak was often stained an even darker colour in an attempt to make it look Jacobean. This unfortunate practice was extensively employed and even today many attractive pieces of lighter wood may be rediscovered by the simple though time-consuming process of stripping. This is one of the reasons why, when considering a piece of furniture, the col-

lector should pay as much, if not more, attention to its design as to its colour, for design is a great aid in establishing its date of origin.

There are many products on the market for stripping wood and other articles. Naturally, some are better than others and some more suitable for one kind of object than another. Until the collector has acquired sufficient expertise, he should always seek advice before beginning the restoring process. Dealers, as we have noted, are in general friendly people, willing, even anxious, to share their knowledge and the experiences they have had in restoration work. Much can be learnt by being on friendly terms with a shop owner and by seeking his advice.

Many so-called antiques are in fact cunningly disguised fakes. In this respect furniture is the most notorious. There are a number of reasons for this. In the first place, most collectors prefer furniture, so there is a large market; secondly, furniture now attracts high prices; and, thirdly, it is easier to work in wood than in metal or precious

Left:
A spectacular piece of English furniture from the Restoration period, at the end of the 17th century. Restoration furniture has suffered badly from fakes and reproductions. Marquess of Northampton, Castle Abbey.

Below left:
An English chair of the mid 18th century, made of mahogany and stained and carved in rustic style. Victoria and Albert Museum, London.

Below right:
English 18th-century Chippendale style chair of mahogany.

stones. It must be remembered, however, that wood is at the same time one of the easiest materials for judging its age. It shrinks with time and, because it is soft in comparison to other materials, it scars and therefore reveals tool marks and evidence of wearing. Wear marks, at the back of chairs where they have been handled, and on the back of the rear legs if they have been repeatedly dragged to new positions, are small but significant indications of their age. Furthermore, wood discolours with age. Thus, while furniture is relatively easy to fake, it is also the area in which fakes may be most readily detected.

It has been calculated that during the period between 1660 and 1700 there could not have been more than 50,000 families in the whole of England who could have afforded the kind of Restoration furniture that is now everywhere in great demand. Yet every year more is sold and transported from England to the USA and the Arabian gulf than could possibly have been produced in the whole of that period. Some for-

geries are so lacking in skill that even an untrained eye can detect them; others, however, are cunningly executed and pose difficulties even to the most discerning expert.

A large amount of high-quality, handcrafted imitation period furniture is now constructed and openly sold as such. Unfortunately, some of this later reaches less scrupulous vendors in the "antique" market, and may be sold as original. While these pieces may satisfy aesthetic requirements they are clearly to be avoided by anyone buying as an investment.

There are no easy rules to follow in distinguishing true from false; even the most experienced dealer can sometimes be deceived. Most dealers handle a vast range of wares and their very lack of specializing inherently leads to incomplete knowledge, even when a piece is guaranteed in good faith. It can take a lifetime to learn all there is to know even about one aspect of antiques and few experts would claim to have attained this happy position.

There are, nevertheless, some simple

Above:
A French *canapé* or settee dating from 1770. Musée des Arts Decoratifs.

Below right:
A simple but attractive late 17th-century English honey-pot. City of Stoke-on-Trent Museum and Art Gallery.

Opposite above:
English hunting prints, such as this etching made by H. Alken in 1823, are both attractive and popular.

Opposite below:
A late 19th-century French desk and an English rosewood chair on display in a spacious English saleroom. T. R. G. Lawrence and Son, Crewkerne, Somerset.

indications which enable the collector to avoid the more obvious traps. A background knowledge of the piece's period and history is vital. Much is merely a matter of common sense. If the collector were told that a chair was made in about 1640 and then noticed a label describing it as "Restoration" (a period starting in 1660), suspicions would immediately be aroused; the dealer is clearly unsure or ill-informed. The collector must be able to distinguish between one wood and another and have an understanding of how pieces were made at different times in history. It is only with this knowledge that he can detect the mis-information, whether deliberate or otherwise, in a dealer's description of a piece. For example, a table with gilded legs and made with laburnum veneer, offered as the work of a craftsman of 1600, would then be seen immediately to be impossible. The question of detecting forgeries and reproductions is discussed in detail in the chapter on the 18th

Above left:
An American side chair of the 1830s, and made of hickory and maple. These were reasonably priced and made in considerable numbers.

Above:
A typical Victorian rosewood balloon-backed dining chair.

Left:
A mid 20th-century chair designed by the architect Mies van der Rohe.

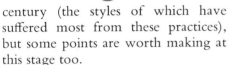

century (the styles of which have suffered most from these practices), but some points are worth making at this stage too.

In addition to newly constructed furniture, many forgeries consist of parts of genuine pieces fused with others and grafted on to newer wood. This is the most usual practice of the accomplished forger. His basic problem is that an original surface can never be copied exactly. This is one of the aspects that an expert considers to establish authenticity. Again, any cut edge will show clearly to the practised eye, as will a freshly planed surface and the slightest discrepancy in grain; methods of joining also provide valuable clues. Another procedure, often more successful from the forger's point of view, is to build a new piece from a plain item of inferior but antique timber, which can be altered or embellished. A simple tripod table, for example, can be converted into something more elaborate, and if well done this may be extremely difficult to detect.

It is desirable to be able to differentiate between antique and modern methods of veneering. In the early years veneers were only cut with a saw. Evidence of forgery might therefore appear in the "cut", in that a sawcut looks completely different from a knife cut.

It should also be possible to discover whether a piece has been simply renovated or actually forged, and indeed whether the renovation was done in the past or whether it is a modern "improvement". Although not a forgery in essence, a modern renovation will markedly affect both the present value and the future resale price of a piece. Consider elaborate oak pieces. Unless such a piece possesses an unquestionably authentic pedigree, its validity should be questioned sceptically. When renovated (or forged) with little knowledge on the part of the renovator, incongruities might occur, such as the presence of a basket of apples carved at the bottom of the piece instead of at the top as was the rule with early 17th-century decoration.

Oak needs especial scrutiny since, of all woods, it is the easiest to fake. All that essentially needs to be done to a thick block of oak to give it apparently Tudor cracks is to damage the surface with a hammer. Remember, too, that walnut finishing in the early 17th century was done in clear oil varnish; shellac varnish only evolved in the following century. Many forgers attempt to resurface a poor quality antique piece with a covering of shellac; this is then rubbed in to produce a semblance of patina (the texture of old age) which will pass off for a more ancient finish. This practice should be watched for with care. Moreover, various chemicals can today be used to produce a convincing appearance of seasoning and weathering.

Metals, too, show signs of age. Scars from use or abuse will be evident,

Above:
An English earthenware teapot dating from about 1756. Victoria and Albert Museum, London.

Above left:
A Venetian ewer of the 16th century, in millefiore glass. British Museum.

as will the techniques of manufacture. Metals will also oxidize and patinate. Ceramics and stone, on the other hand, neither shrink nor patinate and the collector must rely on detecting signs of genuine wear and of the method of manufacture.

If a collector inadvertently buys a piece that is later established as a fake he should not despair. All dealers make this mistake, not once but usually many times in their career. Moreover, all is not lost. In the first place, the collector will, with any luck, learn from his mistake. He is also, of course, free to offer the piece for resale. In such cases it will be in the collector's interest to offer it for what he now knows it to be, rather than try to recoup his outlay by continuing the deception. In the antique business a general reputation for integrity is important – and it can be quickly lost. In any event, he will in all probability get a reasonable price for the piece. If he was deceived by it in the first place, it is certainly of reasonable appearance; many people, when furnishing their homes, will happily settle for a reproduction or imitation, knowing it to be so, rather than pay a far higher price for an original. There are also antique dealers who actually collect fakes (famous fakes command a high price) and it is always possible for the collector to go to one of them.

The subject of fakes, imitations and "marriages" is an extensive one; many long books have been written on the subject and the collector is advised, when he has determined on the field in which he wishes to work, to apply himself to further reading. It will save him money and heartache to gather as much information as possible before he makes his first purchase. His best safeguard, however, will cost him nothing. Genuine pieces have a certain, intangible "look" about them; all their components – their colour, materials, method of manufacture, their overall appearance in fact – seem "right"; the fake, unless of consummate skill, will always make the trained eye look again more carefully. This is another reason why the collector cannot be advised too strongly to study reputable works in museums; it is never time wasted. The owner of a general antique shop or the person wishing to furnish and

Top:
A porcelain group made at Nymphenburg in Germany in about 1766. Victoria and Albert Museum, London.

Above:
A French porcelain teapot of 1754, painted in blue, flesh tones and gilt. Victoria and Albert Museum, London.

English roll-top desk and chair made of mahogany. The chair is in Hepplewhite style.

Left:
An early 19th-century porcelain bowl, touched with gold. It was made in Limoges in about 1810. Musée Nationale Adrien-Dubouché, Limoges.

Below:
English salt-glazed stoneware jugs of the 19th century.

decorate his home must acquire as much knowledge as he can over the widest possible field; the collector, however, will usually specialize.

There are a number of reasons for this. In the first place, as we have seen, it is only by specializing, and thereby reducing one's field of operations, that it is possible to acquire sufficient knowledge to detect fakes, to pick out bargains and make worthwhile investments. Again, different areas of antiques appeal to different personalities. As we shall see, watch- and clock-collecting can be an absorbing pastime, but its appeal will be greatest to those with at least some interest in machinery; military uniforms, medals and decorations will appeal to some; 18th-century silver to others. It is also advisable to give careful consideration to the practical aspects before selecting an area in which to make a collection. For example, collections as they grow require housing; it would be impractical to make a collection of 16th-century oak furniture if the collector had limited space at his disposal. Moreover, collections become of greater interest and value the more comprehensive they are; it is a pity and may even represent a financial loss if the collector tires of his choice and is obliged to sell the collection prematurely in order to raise capital for some other collection. Ideally, the collection should remain an absorbing interest for many years, if not a lifetime.

There are several important points to consider when deciding what antiques to collect. Space, and therefore the average size of the pieces, is clearly a prime consideration. Those with little available space will have to limit themselves to smaller items, such as stamps, coins or snuff boxes, which can be housed in drawers and special cabinets. Secondly, the collector should obviously have an interest not only in antiques as such but in the world from which they emanate. It would be self-defeating, for example, to decide on making a collection of medals if one had no interest in military history and little knowledge of the wars and campaigns for which they were struck. Finance, too, must be taken into account. Some areas of antiques can be extremely expensive – in general items of jewellery are high in price and, if

money is a consideration, the collection would be slow in growing, even though Victorian jewellery offers considerable scope for finding bargains. There would also be the expense of insurance.

No-one, however, should refrain from forming a collection simply because he has little space available and is restricted in the sums he can invest. There are many areas where neither need be a consideration. Prices tend to rise but even with limited means collections can be made of such items as cigarette cards, fans, surgical instruments and craftsmen's tools, model soldiers, old photographs and photograph albums, prints, picture frames and valentines; the options are virtually limitless.

Having decided on what to collect, ever further specialization is to be

Above:
The ribbon and medal of the Most Distinguished Order of St Michael and St George; these have been awarded since 1818. Such pieces are available from specialist shops and auctioneers.

recommended. Coin collecting may serve as an example. This field is extremely popular and has become increasingly so with the growing number of limited issues of pattern coins. The two main considerations that establish a coin's value are its condition (a series of symbols is used to define this) and its rarity. It would be pointless, however, merely to start a collection of coins in good condition (they would have no relationship one to another) or of great rarity (they would be extremely expensive and hard to find). Collections must have an identity of their own, which will not be achieved by indiscriminately collecting any sort of coin; rather, a collection of coins of a certain period, a certain metal, a certain nation, monarch or dynasty should be made. Suppose the collector decided on 17th-century English coins; he would then concentrate his reading and study in that period and build up a collection which would soon be comprehensive and an entity in itself. Furthermore, there is nothing to prevent his later extending his range, collecting for example 18th-century English coins, or French coins or those of north America, colonial or modern.

This rule of specializing within an area applies to all antiques. Collections of stamps, silver, jewellery and so on all gain from being taken from a particular period or style.

Some collectors, however, may not wish to specialize in this way. They may feel it too restricting and prefer making a collection of more variety. How, then, are they to make a collection which will "hang together", which will comprise pieces which logically belong in a group? This problem may be overcome by selecting a subject and then collecting anything related to it, no matter how disparate the individual pieces. In this way the collector might settle, for example, on the American navy; he could make his collection of such items as early navigational instruments, pieces from broken-up vessels, cooking utensils and cutlery used by the crews, medals, uniforms and so on. The items would cover a wide field but would be held together by their common theme.

Alternatively, items connected with a famous historical figure can make an

Opposite above:
A piece of Art Nouveau costume jewellery, made by René Lalique.

Opposite below:
A snuffbox, intended for the table rather than the pocket. The main interest of this piece is that it is a very early example of Sheffield plate, dating from about 1750.

Below:
A collection of early American painted tinware, from Pennsylvania; such pieces require great expertise in cleaning and handling. American Museum, Bath.

A Victorian silver inkstand.

intriguing collection. The collector should first select a figure in whom he has interest – perhaps a soldier, statesman or artist. It is surprising how many pieces may be found for such a collection. The advantages in choosing an 18th- or 19th-century figure are considerable. In the first place, the pieces may in most cases be properly termed antiques, since they will have acquired a sufficient age; on the other hand, their relative modernity will ensure that many items still survive, while the lives of the people chosen are probably well documented, which will help the collector in tracking down pieces.

A good example to illustrate this would be Abraham Lincoln, the American president, or Benjamin Dis-

raeli, the British prime minister. In the case of Disraeli, a collection might be formed of items such as these. A bust (terracotta busts in perfect condition are rare) may be found in an antique shop or on a market stall, as may articles authenticated as his, such as spill vases and china. A letter in his handwriting and signed by him would be a useful addition to a collection, as would a photograph. In the latter case it should, of course, be housed in a frame of the period. A sketch or watercolour of Hughenden Manor, his country home, would be attractive; so would contemporary caricatures. Newspaper cuttings would legitimately extend the field; and also photographs and caricatures of his political allies and his

opponents. Jugs and other memorial ware bearing his image are also abundant. Disraeli was also a novelist, so a collection of his works (ideally, of course, first editions) would be a valuable acquisition. With a figure relatively recently deceased, detective work can also bring rewarding results. The collector will need to know as much as possible about his subject's life. In the case of Disraeli, he will know that he died childless and left Hughenden Manor to a nephew; later the house was sold and is now owned by the National Trust. In such cases, the collector can easily find out when it was sold and the name of the auctioneer who disposed of its contents. Thus he may possibly be able to acquire, or at least to study, a copy of the auction catalogue. He should then visit all the antique shops in the area in which the sale took place, for in such cases the smaller, less expensive items are often bought by local residents for their personal use; a generation or two later many of the pieces (pens, lamps and so on) will have been superseded by more modern devices. The descendants of the original purchasers do not always throw such things away; often they will part with them to the owners of antique shops – almost always to those in the locality. It is therefore well worth while visiting these shops; often pieces belonging to the person in question can be found in this way and they will often be well authenticated. The collector

A mid-Victorian meat-dish cover, in electroplate. Collection of John Blair.

Opposite:
A Staffordshire figure of the British Prime Minister W. E. Gladstone, made in 1873. Private collection.

Above:
A selection of "Favrile" glasses by the American glassmaker Tiffany, from the last years of the 19th century.

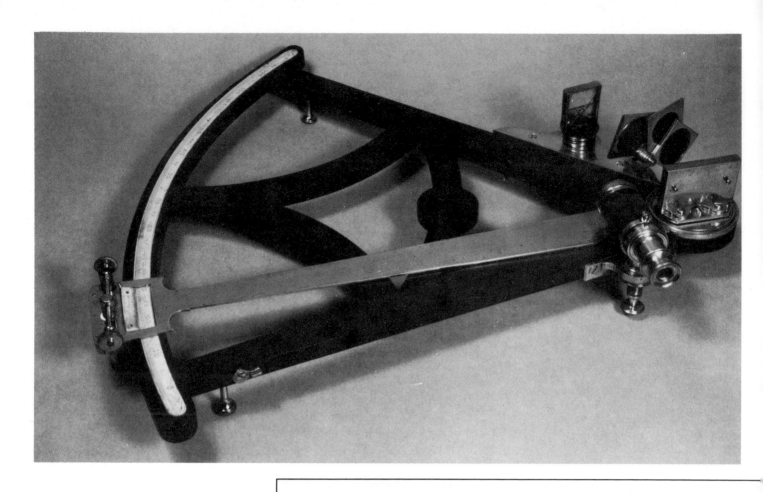

Above:
Collections of coins and medals can be both fascinating and rewarding: this bronze medal, carrying a portrait of Albrecht Dürer, was made in 1528.

Top:
A late 18th-century ship's sextant; such a piece might form part of a collection based on the life of Captain Cook. National Maritime Museum, London.

Right:
A selection of English early 19th-century card cases, in tortoise-shell, mother-of-pearl and silver filigree. Gloria Antica, London.

can find additional confirmation in this respect if he has managed to acquire a catalogue of the sale. In this way silver, china, vases and all manner of items, big and small, may be added to the collection.

In passing it may be observed that such a collection would almost certainly increase in financial value. A figure as distinguished and fascinating as Disraeli or Lincoln is of interest to many people; advertisements often appear in national newspapers offering to purchase items associated with such prominent men. An extensive collection would readily find a purchaser.

Looking after the collection

Two further points need to be made concerning collecting antiques. By their very age, they often need some repair or restoration; they were, after all, originally made to be used and the effects of wear are almost always present. The beginner should never regard the question of restoration complacently. Some points will readily

spring to mind – no-one, it is hoped, would use a nail of modern manufacture on an old piece of furniture, for example; but restoration is skilled work and requires not only dexterity but a thorough knowledge of the way the piece was originally made. As with so many aspects of antiques, there are numerous books on the market specializing in restoration; anyone contemplating carrying out his own restoration work would be well advised to read as deeply in this field as possible. Again, with any luck he will have made friends with one or two experts and should seek their advice. Until he has acquired sufficient knowledge, however, and later with intricate and delicate work, it may be best to employ a professional restorer of repute to do the work for him. This will often save money in the end, for even a small error such as an inadvertent tool mark, can drastically reduce the value of a piece. Nor would anyone wish to risk damaging an antique in this way.

The second point concerns display-

ing a collection. We have spoken earlier of taste and it is here that it is put most to the test. It is mainly a matter of common sense. Surely no-one would wish to put a pair of 18th-century silver candlesticks on a scrubbed pine table; the association would be wrong, the effect disturbing. Both pieces separately might be attractive; together they would conflict. It follows, therefore, that the background to the display is as important as the display itself. Thus, a collection of 19th-century china, for example, should be displayed on a cabinet of the same period. This is a cardinal rule when displaying antiques; any collector who doubts it need merely arrange a few pieces deliberately in conflict one with another to see how damaging this is to the appearance of individual items. A collector who does not immediately find a cabinet or display case to his liking should, as a temporary expedient, devise as plain a background as possible.

Display cases have increased in price in recent years, both because of the

A collection of Edwardian English cigarette cases for ladies; smoking for women was a new fashion at that time.

growing popularity of collecting and also because antique dealers themselves need them for their shops and stalls. They can still be had, however, although often in need of repair. Some collectors will prefer to make, or have made, their own. In such instances it is best to study closely a display case to one's liking in a shop or elsewhere; often permission can be obtained to take a photograph. The display case should then be produced in a manner as near to the original as possible, using the same kind of wood and so on. The result will of course be a "fake" but the piece will at least be to the size and shape of the collector's preference.

The same applies where collections are stored rather than displayed. Coins are often kept in specially grooved drawers, a considerable number of which can fit into a chest. In the case of stamps, albums are a necessity since stamps will discolour if exposed to light for long. The same point must also be borne in mind with such items as watercolours: discoloration may occur if they are placed on a wall which is exposed to bright sunlight.

One further point must be made before we turn to the 16th century and the early antiques. It is a truism of the antique business that "today's junk is tomorrow's antique". This point is

further discussed towards the end of the book, but as the collector goes from stall to stall, from shop to shop, from auction to auction hoping to add to his collection, he might at the same time look out for other pieces, a second collection as it were, pieces which, although of modern manufacture, are of intrinsic interest and attractive execution. Many items such as tins and boxes fall into this category; they may in 20 years be both of financial value and historical interest. We shall see how this has occurred with pieces of Art Deco china, mass-produced in the 1920s and 1930s and today, less than half a century later, keenly sought. Some surprising items now worth collecting are discussed at the end of the book.

The new collector is embarking on a fascinating project. He will inevitably encounter disappointments and frustrations; he will on occasion buy unwisely, and will sometimes decide not to buy and realize later that he should have. These are undeniable aspects of collecting antiques, but they are rarer than the moments of delight in coming across a bargain or the piece which he has long required to complete a collection. Whatever else may be said of collecting antiques, one thing is generally agreed upon: it ought to be, and usually is, great fun.

The 16th Century

Introduction

The 16th century provides in essence an introduction to what may be termed "modern" antiques. Earlier civilizations – notably the Chinese, the Egyptians, the Greeks and Romans – produced an abundance of statuary, pottery, glass and other pieces, often of exquisite beauty. Their surviving items are almost without exception in the great museums; they seldom if ever come on the market and would, in any case, be beyond the means of all but the very richest. They certainly repay study in the museums, however, where they are usually displayed in logical order and to the best advantage.

With the fall of the Roman Empire, western Europe descended into the "Dark Ages", a period of superstition, fear and endless wars. Survival was the prime concern and artistic output, though at times astonishing in its range and beauty, was limited. Then, in 15th-century Italy, there occurred a seemingly spontaneous eruption of artistic output, to which has been given the name Renaissance (from the French word meaning "rebirth"). The term is general and loose, but it denotes the rebirth of classical, humanist values which first appeared under the prosperity and relative stability of the Italian city-states. The Renaissance lasted into the 16th century and was a period of brilliant accomplishments in scholarship, in literature and the arts. Great painters abounded: Leonardo and Michelangelo in Florence, Raphaël in Rome, Correggio in Parma, and Titian and Giorgione in Venice. Stimulated by new contacts with the Arab world, scholarship concentrated on Latin and Greek manuscripts, a scholarship which permeated the poetry of Petrarch and others. Libraries were established and academies flourished. The great patrons of the time – the popes, the doges of Venice, and powerful families such as the Este of Ferrara and the Gonzaga of Mantua – gave bountiful support to scholars, poets, artists and craftsmen. These patrons vied with one another in the possession of silver, glass, tapestry and the personal adornments of costume and jewellery. The concept of the Renaissance man, with emphasis placed on the individual, aspired to the universal man of genius as exemplified by the towering achievements of Leonardo. From this concept developed the courtier: educated, polished and widely accomplished, whose descendant in later centuries would be the cultivated man of society.

By the 16th century these currents had spread throughout Europe, where they developed in local forms. In contrast to the imagination shown in the arts of Italy and France, the northern countries placed emphasis on visual realism, often depicted with sombre restraint. The acceptance of the Italian Renaissance in the north was largely the work of a few men, notably Albrecht Dürer. He sought to transplant the reborn arts of the south into his native German soil and to this end made two journeys to Italy to study the mathematical principles of perspective and proportion, and to fathom the mystery of classical beauty. Through his work, and that of others like him, the concepts of the Renaissance spread throughout Europe.

New universities were established in France, Spain, England and notably in Germany. Architecture flourished and the invention of printing in the 1450s gave a further spur to learning. Thus the humanist scholarship of men such as Erasmus in the Netherlands and Sir Thomas More in England reached a newly enlarged readership.

These developments were to have a crucial effect on the production of antiques. Kings and princes were no longer content with armour that was merely protective or furniture that was

43

Above:
Early Tudor oak chest, showing Gothic decoration. Victoria and Albert Museum, London.

Left:
An early Tudor oak trestle stool.

Opposite:
An English chest of about 1500, with the so-called linenfold decoration very popular in English furniture of this date.

no more than functional: the armour must now be decorated and styled, the furniture comfortable and pleasing to the eye. Glass, silver, wall-hangings – all developed from the purely functional to the decorative during the course of the 16th century. This process occurred in different ways in different countries, not merely through local characteristics and taste but in large measure through political and religious forces. It is a truism that the nature and development of antiques can be fully understood only with an appreciation of the historical forces operating at the time. The England of the 16th century may serve as an example. Henry VIII lured Italian Renaissance artists to England and patronized them at his court, in part so that he could outshine his rival, François I, the king of France. When he broke with the Church of Rome in 1534, however, links with Italy were greatly curtailed and England sought security by closer

ties with the Low Countries. Thus, by the end of the century and the reign of his daughter, Elizabeth I, the greatest influence was Dutch, not Italian.

Two further points must be briefly mentioned as significant in the development of antiques. The first is that art movements have a life cycle of their own: they start as a reaction against a current style, progress to their full flowering, then begin to decline and are themselves replaced. In this way the artistic style known as Mannerism developed as a rejection of the classicism of the High Renaissance. It began in Italy and flourished there from about 1520 until about 1580, emerging in Florence with Pontormo and Rosso Fiorentino and in Rome with Parmigianino. They painted figures of great elegance, elongated and in seemingly uncomfortable postures, often in crowded compositions. By the end of the 16th century Mannerism had in turn given way to the Baroque.

In 1526 François I of France decided to remodel his château at Fontainebleau. There were at the time few French painters and decorators to his taste. The king, therefore, attracted to his court Italian masters – among the most notable were Rosso Fiorentino, Francesco Primaticcio and Niccolò dell'Abbate – to decorate his château; he thereby established what has come to be known as the First School of Fontainebleau. The Mannerist works produced by these artists were a mixture of their Italianate style, their French surroundings and the northern influences to which they were now exposed. Thus a local form of Mannerist painting and decoration developed from causes which had nothing to do with art. Likewise production at Fontainebleau ceased not because fashion changed but because the religious wars intervened. Thus political, military and social events affect the development of art forms and in turn antiques.

By bearing these briefly-described movements in mind, we can now turn to the various branches of antiques during the years 1500 to 1600. As we have seen, these years provide an introduction to what was to come later. It is true that he would be a fortunate collector indeed who found much from this century at a reasonable price, but it would be difficult to understand future developments without understanding these early years.

Furniture

Furniture design has reasonably clearly defined ages since the Renaissance. In this respect, English design is the easiest to follow. Put at its most simple, there are three ages up to the early years of the 19th century. The first is that of oak, which lasts up to and including the mid-17th century. This is followed by walnut, which encompasses the late 17th century and the early 18th; followed by mahogany, through most of the 18th century from about 1720. The period from 1800 until 1830 is generally given the name "Regency", even though the dates do not absolutely coincide with the regency of the future George IV. These terms are admittedly vague, so that when we speak, for instance, of "Victorian" furniture we do not necessarily mean precisely 1837 to 1901 (the years of Victoria's actual reign), but they are a useful if imprecise guide.

Since furniture is essentially utilitarian, it is an area of where a knowledge of history is of special importance. It is far easier to understand why a particular piece was made in the way it was if we also know something of the social life of the time. A thorough knowledge of the development of furniture may not be necessary but, if it is wanted, help is readily available. Much furniture is on display in museums and books on the subject abound. So much information is available that a collector wishing to specialize in, say, chairs will have no difficulty in acquiring information to meet his needs. An additional source of information is the museums, which frequently provide lectures on such subjects.

Right:
The *Galerie François I*er at the Château of Fontainebleau, decorated between 1533 and 1540 by Rosso Fiorentino.

Right:
Back stool, with the back legs extended upwards to give support. City Museum and Art Gallery, Birmingham.

Opposite:
French armchair, with the arms terminating in rams' heads. Both the seat and back are upholstered in velvet. Frick Collection, New York.

Below:
Chair of the early 16th century, with solid panels beneath the seat and arm rests. Victoria and Albert Museum, London.

Suffice it here to say that the history of 16th-century furniture is largely moulded by political factors. In England, for example, the feudal system lasted into the century; fortunes were quickly made but also quickly lost. The powerful acquired as much property and land as they could as opportunity afforded, but they were principally motivated by a determination to hold on to what they already had. Their homes, therefore, were as strongly fortified as possible. Furniture was sparse and was designed for two purposes: it was strictly utilitarian but it also had to be movable in the event (frequent at the time) of fire or attack. The owners of these fortress homes displayed their wealth not in furniture but in wall hangings – especially banners – and accumulations of silver and gold. During the reign of Henry VIII, homes gradually became more com-fortably furnished. During the reign of Elizabeth I, when the Tudor dynasty began at last to feel secure, far greater attention was paid to furnishings and comfort. This change from fortress to comfortable home may be illustrated by the moat; although a common feature at the beginning of the century, it had by the reign of Elizabeth I been replaced by the formal garden.

The dominating item in any study of furniture is the chair. Primitive man squatted or lay on the ground; no doubt he sat on boulders or fallen tree trunks. In time he employed primitive devices, and the chair is one of the earliest recorded pieces of furniture. Later it became adapted to represent, in the form of a throne, a symbol of authority. The chair fulfils a number of duties. It is not only used at meals; it is used when people read or write and when they sit together in conversation.

Chairs are also an especially valuable guide to changes in style, since it is usually the chair which exhibits a new trend first.

The 16th century saw many changes and innovations in the production of chairs. Until the Reformation they had been decorated, when decorated at all, on ecclesiastical models, with markings like the arch shapes on cathedral and church doors. This was done by chipping or carving in low relief; pieces were often decorated with bright colours. Richly upholstered chairs now make their appearance and, after 1550, differently shaped chairs appear. Two are especially important. The folding or "Savonarola", a product of the Italian Renaissance, was light and easily portable. Genuine examples are extremely rare but the design was much copied in Victorian times. The second was the "back" stool. These were developed, as so much has been, because of a change in social manners. In the 16th century meals for the first time were no longer taken by all members of the household together, including the servants. A separate room for dining became common in large households, instead of the raised dais at which all ate, with the table close to the wall. The master of the house now sat at one end of the table, his wife at the other. Guests and other members of the family sat on stools on either side of the table. Previously these stools had not needed a back support, since this was provided by the wall; but now that the table was placed in the centre of the room alternative support had to be found. This was achieved by continuing the back legs of the stool upwards. These uprights were then joined together by two rails or a panel, thereby forming a back.

Backless stools remained common in other parts of the house and were used either as ordinary chairs or as footstools. The most common stool of the time was the five-board seat. This was made of five sections of flat wood; two upright at either end (usually with a large, inverted "V" cut out at the bottom), one each at the front and back and a fifth on top to form the seat. The boards were secured together by wooden pegs or iron nails.

A significant development of the 16th century was the abandonment of the panels beneath the arms and seat of a chair. So long as these were kept, the legs and arm supports, being part of the frame, were necessarily straight; once they were discarded, as they were with the development of the *caquetoire* sometime before 1550, the arms could be curved to support the elbows. The chairs also became, of course, much lighter.

Next in importance to the chair was the bed. So long as whole families lived in one room, the bed was usually tucked into a corner where it would take up as little space as possible. As more rooms became available, the heads of the household had their own sleeping quarters and so the bed was brought into prominence. It was no longer placed along a wall, but with only its head against it and its length projecting into the room. As the bed grew in importance – it was customary for royalty to give audiences and for ladies of rank to receive visitors from their beds – elaborate and costly materials displaying the owner's wealth were draped from a canopy which

49

hung from the ceiling. After 1500 bedposts and carved headboards were introduced. From that date, too, the curtains around the bed began to be supported from the bedhead itself.

The emphasis placed upon the costliness of bed furnishing and decoration meant that the wooden framework was itself less regarded than hitherto. It comprised a wooden frame, with holes through the sides at regular intervals. Ropes were then passed through the holes both from side to side and lengthways, and on this support was laid the mattress, usually filled with straw but, in richer households, with wool and, in the richest of all, sometimes with swansdown.

The great importance which the nobility now gave to their beds led to further developments. In most cases the master of the house considered that he needed an attendant, with him throughout the night, but he did not wish his attendant to have a bed of

equal size, for that would have occupied much of the space which his personal bedchamber now gave him. The problem was solved by the invention of the truckle-bed, a lightly-framed bed built low off the ground which could, during the day, be placed out of sight beneath the master's bed. Soon these truckle-beds were being used by those in more humble abodes.

The third most important item of 16th-century furniture was the chest, although it began to lose favour towards the end of the century. Its popularity stemmed from its versatility, for it served both as a seat and as a place for keeping things. Some chests were decorated on top with different coloured woods so as to serve as chess boards; the "five-board" variety were often carved in low relief; one of the most popular decorations on the front panel was medallion heads.

The earliest chest had been made by hollowing out a tree trunk and then

Above:
A 16th-century Venetian *cassone*; its carvings are based on designs by Mantegna. Museo del Castello Sforcesco.

Opposite:
Painted leather table desk of the 1520s, belonging to Henry VIII. Victoria and Albert Museum, London.

giving it durability by banding it with iron. In time chests were made of planks and the ironwork gradually developed into decoration. They were sometimes placed at the foot of a bed as a receptacle for linen.

During the course of the 16th century the chest was largely superseded by the court cupboard, presumably so-called from the French word meaning "short". These had been known for many years, especially in Germany, but they now came into general use. A Spanish and Italian version of the 16th century was in essence little more than a sideboard: a closed compartment with a flat top on which plate might be displayed. In England and northern Europe, a popular version had a wholly open lower part and, above, a small closed compartment in the middle of the otherwise open shelf. In the latter part of the century the wholly enclosed cupboard became more common.

Tables were among the most massive pieces of furniture in this century and, as with other large pieces, they were often decorated with the now general processes of inlay (a decorative pattern of metal or ivory laid into the wood) and marquetry (a similar decoration, applied as a veneer). By the end of the century it had become accepted that any piece which might be seen by people of quality should not only be serviceable but also a thing of beauty. Until the 17th century tables were generally merely tops made of oak resting on trestles. These were not in the shape of modern trestles – in the form of a capital letter "A" – but usually comprised three perpendicular sections joined in a triangle, facing outwards at either end of the table. Sometimes these supports were carved in the form of heraldic beasts.

From this developed the framed table, with a fixed leg at each of the four corners, joined together by rails. A further development was the draw table, which has a movable leaf at either end; when these leaves were fully pulled out, the centre piece dropped into place between them, to form a useful extension.

Chests with drawers made their appearance during the 16th century, but they were still not in general use until well into the next century. However, cabinets with drawers were being produced, usually with a number of small drawers for keeping documents, jewellery and other valued items. The drawers were generally enclosed by two doors and the whole cabinet usually placed on a table. Desks were also made, but they were in fact little more than a box covered with a sloping lid, joined at the top by an iron hinge. Many however, were carved and decorated with inlay of coloured woods.

By the end of the century the home had been completely transformed. In about 1500 the panelled construction called wainscot had been introduced; by the end of the century it was in general use. Picture frames became ornately carved and looking-glasses would soon be used for wall display. For centuries after the fall of the Roman Empire, Europeans had tolerated sparse and uncomfortable furniture. In the years between 1500 and 1600 all this changed. People of culture and wealth now looked, not merely for furniture which would make their daily lives more comfortable but for furniture which would be pleasing to the eye. The scene was thus set for the enormous advances in every type of antique which the skills of the ensuing centuries would provide.

Above right:
Early Tudor bed, with elaborate carving on the head-board and foot-posts.

Right:
German panelled room of the early 16th century, with the bed located in the corner. Dithmarscher Landesmuseum, Meldorf, Holstein.

Opposite above:
Oak draw-table of the late 16th century, with leaves for extension and gadrooned underframe.

Opposite below:
French dresser. The panels represent Jupiter, Juno, Mercury and Venus, and are inspired by the decorations at Fontainebleau. Musée de Lyon.

Above:
French dresser in the Renaissance style, with two doors and two drawers. Musée des Arts Decoratifs, Paris.

Opposite above:
An English late 16th-century interior, heavily panelled and furnished in oak. Geffrye Museum, London.

Opposite below:
Elizabethan draw-top table, with typical bulbous legs. Victoria and Albert Museum, London.

Silver

To the collector silver has many advantages. It is generally both attractive and functional. Furthermore, the variety of articles made in silver is considerable; it includes not only pieces for the table – knives, forks and spoons, salt cellars and pepper pots, tea and coffee pots – but items such as snuff boxes and card cases, figures and ornaments. It has the further advantage, in England at any rate, of usually being stamped to indicate that it has been tested by an assay office. The different features of the stamp, which can soon be memorized, makes silver much easier to date than, say, glass. It must always be kept in mind, however, that forging marks was a common practice, not only to make the piece

appear older and more valuable but also in early years as a deceit by silversmiths to avoid paying the required duty, of which the stamp was evidence. The Victorians were particularly adept at forging and it takes experience to acquire the skill to detect these falsifications. Silver is a good investment in the long term but the market price can fluctuate dramatically in the short.

Silver as a token of payment is known to have been in use from about 4500 BC in Babylon and since then it has been in ornamental as well as practical use. In western Europe, however, silverwork first flourished as an art form after AD 313, when Christianity was given official recognition. From that date beautifying churches to the glory of God became the prime concern of craftsmen, and it remained so for 1000 years or more.

By the Renaissance the best goldsmiths and silversmiths were established in one of two places. Many were in Spain, where, after the country's unification in 1492 and with the beginnings of its priceless plunder of South America, the profligate aristocracy was able to indulge its taste for splendour. The other centre was Italy, where the great patrons were the Papacy in Rome and the Medici family in Florence. From these centres, where superb church plate was made, the craftsmanship spread throughout Europe. Augsburg became an important centre for silver work, as it was for jewellery. Antwerp, by the 16th century a flourishing trading city, also had high standards of its own and even rivalled Rome. Style was everywhere influenced by the great painters, but above all by the sculptors of the time. Indeed, some of the greatest artists of the 16th century, notably Benvenuto Cellini and Antonio Gentili, were themselves making pieces in silver. The motifs – human forms, animals, birds, fish and grotesques – used at that time have been copied and elaborated upon ever since.

For the general collector silver, as with so much else of the 16th century, is hardly available. Nevertheless, it is a wise as well as enjoyable task to view as closely as possible great pieces from this century in museums and private collections open to the public. Pieces such as the Great Salt (highly decorated

century. Necklaces once again became popular, and were often given as part of a dowry and might later pass to a daughter on her marriage, perhaps to a foreigner; in this way jewellery moved from country to country, and styles could be examined, copied and improved upon. New techniques were also being developed. It is from this date that the brilliance of a stone was greatly enhanced by polished surfaces that would reflect light.

So great was the demand for jewellery that young men who wished to become painters were often apprenticed first to goldsmiths. It was a normal part of an artist's training and Hans Holbein the Younger, to name but one, designed jewels for the English court. Unfortunately, the passion for jewellery became such that all sense of moderation was often abandoned. Portraits of the time, particularly from Tudor England, show the habit to have been so extravagantly indulged that good taste and sense of balance were lost. Nor was this true of women alone. Men were even more elaborately adorned: Henry VIII wore far more jewellery than did any of his six wives.

Centres for making jewellery to meet this demand were numerous in 16th-century Europe, and Italian Renaissance styles spread rapidly. In Germany Augsburg and Nuremburg were especially famous, as were Munich and Basle. Many goldsmiths' shops existed in Prague, under the patronage of the discerning Rudolph II. François I of France was an outstanding patron and, as we have seen, brought many masters from Italy to work at Fontainebleau. The English court also welcomed numerous French, Italian and Flemish goldsmiths, first to gratify Henry VIII's love of jewellery and then Elizabeth I's, for whom jewellery seems to have been almost an obsession. Indeed, her affection for pearls was so great that she had no scruples about buying hundreds of false ones to have sewn on her dresses. Spain, by now the richest country in Europe, was another important centre of jewellery production. Spanish jewellery of the time is notable for its rich colour and extensive use of filigree and enamel decoration. It was also distinguished by its abundance of religious themes, such as crosses and

and designed to be placed on the table to denote the place of honour) have the irrefutable quality of great craftsmanship. It is only by studying such early pieces that the collector will appreciate the silver of later centuries and acquire the skill to differentiate between the real and the bogus, the superb and the second-rate.

Jewellery

Jewellery production during the Renaissance and the 16th century greatly increased to satisfy the desire of Euro-pean princes for personal display. In Italy the great families – Este, Medici, Sforza and others – vied with one another in their magnificence, as did the kings and queens of England, France and Spain. Those at court emulated, though were careful never to outshine, their sovereigns. Moreover, with the passing of the feudal system a rich bourgeoisie arose which also sought to display its wealth to the world through personal adornment. The quality of workmanship also greatly improved during the 16th

ANNO ·ÆTATIS·   · SVÆ·XLIX ·

Above:
A portrait of Henry VIII by Holbein,
showing the king's elaborate use of
jewellery.

Opposite:
French Renaissance design for a piece
of costume jewellery. Bibliothèque
Nationale.

Above:
English glass goblet of about 1578. It comes from the workshop of Giacomo Verzelini, who introduced Venetian skills of glass-making to England. Fitzwilliam Museum, Cambridge.

Right:
Late 16th-century Venetian wine glass, with baluster stem and elegant side decorations. Victoria and Albert Museum, London.

Opposite:
Venetian milk-glass dish, designed to give the impression of a net. Victoria and Albert Museum, London.

pendants on which sacred subjects were intricately carved.

Glass

Glass is so commonplace a thing that it is easy to forget what a remarkable and versatile substance it is. An artificial product, it is formed by fusing together mixtures of the silicates of potash, soda, lime, magnesia, alumina and lead in various proportions. The earliest glass was, of course, produced with less sophistication. It is not known how it first came to be made, but many romantic though unfounded accounts survive. What is known, however, is that stone beads with a glass glaze dating from about 4000 BC have been discovered in Egypt. It was to be many centuries, however, before glass vessels were made. These early examples were made by "wrapping" the molten glass around shaped clay and then, when the glass was cold, removing the clay. This was the method in use from about the 15th century BC until the beginning of the Christian era, when it was discovered, almost certainly in Syria, that by dipping a hollow iron tube into a hot mass of glass and then blowing through the other end of the tube the substance could be fashioned into various shapes. This revolutionary discovery was to remain the principal method of glass production until the advent, in modern times, of mechanical methods of manufacture.

Even by the 16th century, however, more sophisticated techniques had been discovered, including a means of purifying the substance. For this we are indebted to the Italians. Already before AD 1000 glass was being made in Venice. At the end of the 13th century all Venetian glass-furnaces, which in those days were a serious source of fire outbreaks, were removed to the nearby island of Murano, which thereafter flourished as the greatest glass-making centre in Europe. By the time of the Renaissance its craftsmen were especially renowned for their marvellous sense of colour – dark blues, greens and red being the most favoured. Many pieces were lavishly decorated.

By the 16th century output had greatly increased and chalices, cups, goblets, bottles and glasses were produced in centres throughout Europe. New techniques evolved, including

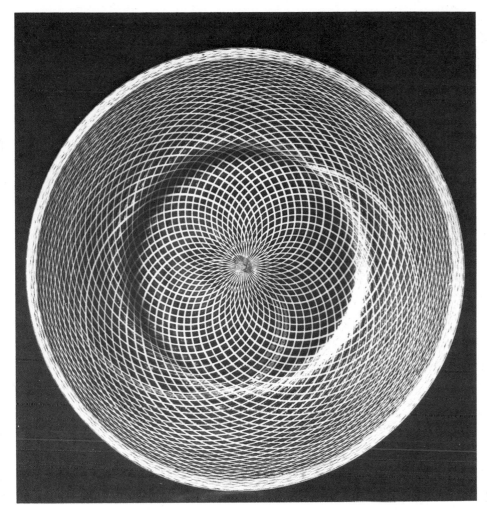

that of covering transparent glass with threads of milky white glass, and of producing opaque glass covered with an abundance of thin, crack-like lines to contrast with the parts of the object left smooth and transparent. Mirrors made of glass appear for the first time in the 16th century; previously they had been of highly polished silver or steel. Other items which make their first appearance in glass include medicine bottles, test tubes and various other pieces for medical and scientific use.

Modern glass-making thus sprang from Italy, but different local administrations even within Italy adopted quite different attitudes to the craftsmen. For example, at Altare, a famous town at the time but now almost defunct, the craftsmen were permitted, even encouraged, to travel far afield, taking their skills with them; at Murano, on the other hand, craftsmen were forbidden to leave under threat of heavy penalties. Nevertheless, some did escape and they and artists from other centres settled in cities throughout Europe. France was one of the first to benefit,

and in England Giacomo Verzelini, one of the most gifted glassmakers of the time, supplied the inspiration for an English glass industry after he arrived there in 1571. His especial expertize was for decorating his work with engravings done with the point of a diamond. Many other Venetians settled in the Spanish Netherlands. The Venetian style was to last throughout the 17th century, but towards the end of the 16th century Renaissance styles gave way to the Baroque and glass products, like so many others, became extremely ornate.

A surprising number of 16th-century pieces survive. The majority are, of course, in museums (the British Museum has, among much else in glassware, a magnificent collection of Spanish glass) and these make rewarding study for the beginner. As with silver and jewellery, the sheer quantity on display may at first be confusing and it is wise to study a little at a time. Museums arrange their pieces in logical order and the beginner will soon grasp the history of glass.

Clocks

Collecting clocks and watches can be a rewarding pastime, but they have certain drawbacks that other antiques do not have. Some clocks strike only hourly; others also strike the half-hour and still others the quarter as well. Once the collector has a clock, or at most two, in every room of his home the problem of noise arises. The potential collector should first give thought as to whether he and his family are prepared to tolerate this. Furthermore, clocks are a subject in which art and science meet. The collector should have some interest in mechanics or be prepared to acquire at least a rudimentary understanding of how clocks work. This is a necessary skill if he is accurately to judge the age, quality and efficiency of a piece. Moreover, repairs are today extremely expensive and the collector who can perform his own makes a great saving. For this reason the beginner might be advised only to buy clocks which are in working order. Sometimes, of course, a clock case may be so attractive or unusual as to justify buying it for its own sake but, if outlay

is a consideration, the collector should delay investing in defective clocks until he can carry out his own repairs.

It is beyond the scope of this book to describe in detail the mechanical aspects of clocks. It is a specialized subject and numerous books are available if this is the field in which the collector wishes to work. The fundamental knowledge is not difficult to acquire. There are also societies, including local, provincial societies, throughout the western world; members have similar interests and their knowledge will be helpful to the beginner.

Mechanical clocks have been made for centuries – certainly since 1400 – but few have survived from before 1600. They have been made in a great variety of faces and shapes, but since about 1600 they have fitted into one of six general categories: lantern clocks, bracket and mantle clocks, long case clocks, carriage clocks, wall clocks and, lastly, any other decorative clock. These will be described in the chapters dealing with the centuries in which they made their first appearance. Thus, although in 1582 Galileo discovered

Above:
Table-clock made in about 1540 in either England or Germany. The clock is spring-driven. British Museum.

Opposite above:
German wall-clock of about 1550 similar to English lantern-clocks, even down to the pivoted side panels. British Museum.

Opposite below:
German drum-clock of 1576, attributed to Paulus Grimm. The dial has eight concentric bands, and provides astronomical information. British Museum.

the great time-keeping potential of the pendulum, a discovery which was to revolutionize the accuracy of clocks, it was not until the 17th century that the pendulum became widely employed and so it will be described in the next chapter. A few lantern clocks (so-called because they look like ships' lanterns) were made in the 16th century. They were hung on walls from a bracket, were made of brass or other metal and had a bell at the top for striking. Early examples were so inaccurate, however, that they had to be checked against a sundial repeatedly. Later refinements remedied this and they remained popular throughout the 17th century. Few genuine examples come on the market today and the collector should be warned that imitations were later made in great number.

In the 16th century, and more especially the 17th, a growing number of people could afford to buy timekeepers. The industry grew rapidly, although more so in some countries than in others. England produced hardly any clocks at this time but in Germany, particularly the cities of Augsburg and Nuremburg, there was considerable output. England, therefore, had to "import" clockmakers. Thus, Henry VIII's horologist, Nicholas Cratzer, was a native of Bavaria.

The value of an antique clock is enormously increased if the name of the maker can be established. This is usually simple with English work after 1698 since an Act of Parliament of that year ordered all clockmakers to inscribe their name and the town of manufacture on the clock; this is generally found on the clock face. The name of the artist who designed the clock case is also important, for frequently he was a different artist from the clockmaker. Holbein, for example, designed cases for some of Cratzer's work.

A further reason for the increase in production from the middle of the 16th century onwards, was the invention, some time late in the 15th century, of the clock spring. This invention made possible the portable clock and, eventually, the watch. This was to be perfected in the Victorian age, the watches of that period being in general more accurate than many of similar value produced today.

By the end of the 16th century, therefore, clocks had developed into more accurate timekeepers and were being produced in greater numbers than ever before. The scene was set for the great advances, both mechanical and aesthetic, of the following century.

Armour and weapons

By the 16th century armour was used principally for tournaments and parades; designs and appendages became more elaborate than ever before. Plate armour was intended to present a smooth surface so that the opponent's weapon would glance off it. Yet, since armour was as much a symbol of wealth and prestige as was jewellery, it now had to be decorated. This was usually achieved by etching. The design was first painted on with a mixture of resin and wax; acid was then administered to the uncovered areas. When this had eaten into the surface, the coating was removed and the design stood out against the areas into which the acid had burned. As skills such as these developed, the armour itself became progressively more elaborate. The Germans, for example, created extrava-

gant designs, including helmets in the shape of grotesque and intimidating faces. Henri II of France had one of the most renowned workshops in Europe. There the decoration and design of armour reached its highest point, the more elaborate pieces displaying scenes from mythology or classical history. Armour was in consequence extremely expensive – even in the Middle Ages a plain mail shirt was worth the equivalent of a dozen or so cows – and today, on the rare occasions on which complete suits come on the market, is beyond the purse of most individuals. Magnificent examples, however, are on display in European museums and in the great houses.

Weapons, however, are more readily available and naturally less expensive. At the beginning of the 16th century swords were still heavy and large, designed for combat; by the end of the century they were much lighter. Those made for wear at court were often intricately designed and, particularly in the case of daggers, richly embellished with jewels. Hunting, one of the great royal pastimes of the 16th century, provided another source of weaponry,

Above left:
German white stoneware tankard of 1559. Decorations, in low relief, show scenes from the life of Christ. Museum Roseliushaus, Bremerl.

Above:
Large dish of maiolica (tin-glazed earthenware). It was made in Italy in about 1530. Museum für Kunst und Gewerbe, Hamburg.

Opposite left:
English decorated suit of armour made in 1590 by Jacob Holder for the Earl of Cumberland. Metropolitan Museum of Art, New York.

Opposite right:
Sword, dagger and knife of about 1590, with hilts of blued and chiselled steel. They were made for the guards of the Elector of Saxony. Victoria and Albert Museum, London.

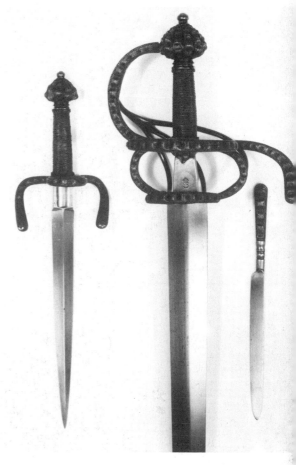

and special knives and spears were produced to meet the demand. It should not be forgotten that, while Europe was a great centre of weapon design and production, many other parts of the world produced elaborately, often exquisitely designed examples. The Turks, the Persians, the Indians, the Chinese, the Japanese, all had their own individual styles and examples may be found in the sale rooms and in shops which specialize in weaponry. As with most antiques, however, it is a specialized field and the novice collector should be wary of mass-produced replicas, many of which were made in the 19th century.

Firearms, on the other hand, were still in a primitive stage of development. Guns were already in use in the second half of the 14th century, but they were crude indeed and often more dangerous to the firer than to the fired upon. Moreover, they were grossly inaccurate and usually did no more than frighten the enemy's horses. In the early 16th century firearms became serviceable and accurate, and they were also frequently finely decorated, with ivory and brass inlays on the butt, lock and barrel.

Coins

Coins are thought to have begun to supplant barter as a means of exchange in the Middle East in about 700 BC. Some 500 years later they were in regular use and even the ancient Britons are known to have made them. Sizeable hordes as well as individual examples, usually made of tin, are still sometimes found. From ancient Greece to the 14th century AD coins were made either by casting or by hammering, the latter being the more practical and common method. In the 16th century milled coins began to appear; these were coins made with the help of a machine. The primitive "mill and screw press" was used in the reign of Elizabeth I for a few coins. It proved uneconomic, however, and the idea of using machines was not revived until the reign of Charles I. English 16th-century coins are therefore mostly hammered; they may be seen in numerous museums. Medals to commemorate great events had long been struck and the 16th century provides notable examples, in particular those celebrating the defeat of the Spanish Armada in 1588. They are now, however, extremely rare.

Metalware

Metalware provides a wide range of choices for the collector, with the fireplace providing some of the most interesting pieces. The Romans were so advanced technologically that they dispensed altogether with fireplaces, using instead a form of central heating or, in smaller homes, movable charcoal braziers. With the collapse of the Roman Empire, however, these techniques were lost. The tribes which took over the territory previously held by the Romans were unsophisticated; they built their homes of wood rather than stone and usually had one room only, with a central hearth upon stone blocks, where the fire served both for heating and cooking. Logs for the fire were held in by brackets of iron, which are known as firedogs. The central hearth disappeared with the return of stone-built houses, when it became possible to build fireplaces with chimneys against a wall.

Firedogs were still used and by the 16th century they were decorated; by the following century they were to be embellished with brass overlay or, in rare cases, even with solid silver. These and the great iron firebacks placed behind the fire to avoid burning the wall are among the most attractive and impressive pieces of 16th-century metalwork.

The growing use of metal was of particular importance in the kitchen. Roman expertise had been lost in this as in so many areas and kitchen equipment remained primitive until the end of the 15th century. It was not until the 17th century that great advances were made (towns then started to grow rapidly, with an increasing demand for equipment) but even in the 16th century there are signs of the beginning of modern living. There were tough, durable utensils, pewter spoons and

Firedogs with the arms of Henry VIII and Anne Boleyn. They date from the 1530s.

used to put the loaves into the back of the oven and to remove them when baked.

Lighting devices were still primitive in the 16th century. Candles were extremely expensive and used only by the Church and the nobility; everyone else relied on methods known to the Middle Ages, such as a form of taper made by dipping dried rushes into fat. Small items of metalware – utensils, pot hooks, mortars and pestles – are rarely, and larger items almost never, available for sale today and the collector must generally be content to await the 17th century to find pieces if he is making a collection of metalware.

Toys

Toys have been made since ancient times. It would seem that even primitive people were aware of, even if they barely understood, the importance of toys in the child's progress to adulthood. If we think of modern toys it is clear how they help develop a child's mind and aptitudes: building blocks are said to stimulate the imagination, and miniature tools, such as dolls' brushes and brooms, are an aid to acquiring adult skills. Children imitate their elders and their toys reflect this. A girl plays with her doll in imitation of her mother playing with an infant; boys look to such toys as soldiers and toy trains in imitation of adult male employment.

Toys have been found in all cultures. They were known in the East, in Egypt and Africa and in both north and south America as well as in Europe. The most common of these early toys are animals, although balls are numerous (some even contained small stones to form primitive rattles), as are decorated figures, the earliest form of doll. These may now be seen in museums.

Both the Greeks and the Romans had toys. Few have survived but vases and reliefs testify to their original abundance. They were made in a great variety of materials, including bone, bronze and lead, leather and wood. Many were made of clay. These toys often reflect an idealized hero, so that, in Greek times as today, soldiers were especially popular. During the Middle Ages toys appear to have been less plentiful. This may be because few

plates and some brass and copper cooking pots. The poor continued to make do with wooden platters. The central piece of equipment for all was a large, round pot or cauldron in which water or stews could be heated. Soon the cauldron came to be hung from a chain above the fire, a considerable advance since the chain could be lengthened or shortened and the degree of heat applied to the cauldron thereby adjusted. Developments in roasting equipment belong more properly to the next chapter, but brick ovens were certainly known in the 16th century. They were large and situated next to the fire for baking bread; spade-like implements with long handles were have survived from the time; another explanation, not entirely contradictory, is that since medieval women were held in considerably lower regard than they had been in Roman times, the needs of childhood were similarly considered unimportant. But there is no doubt that toys were made during those centuries: some indeed, such as clay and tin figures of knights, have survived and paintings of the time often show children playing with toys. Patricularly revealing in this respect is Pieter Brueghel's *Children's Games* (1560), in which children are depicted playing with spinning tops and other toys, as well as wrestling and climbing trees.

The Renaissance and the 16th century saw a considerable development in the production of toys although, as with so much else, it was not until the 18th century that Europeans paid adequate attention to the needs and wants of children. In fact, the Renaissance did not produce as imaginative an output of toys as might be expected; perhaps, it has been suggested, because emphasis was put instead on the flowering culture of mature man. The main development of the 16th century came as toy makers began to organize themselves into guilds. Germany was the leading area, with Nuremburg the pre-eminent centre. This pre-eminence has been partially explained by two facts: there was an abundance of wood from the great German forests and the long winter nights provided the peasants with leisure. At this time toys were in general made for the home market, little being exported; and toys, therefore, have a distinct flavour of their country of origin. An Elizabethan doll, for example, richly attired in the costume of the period, is as easy to identify as English as is a portrait of an Elizabethan lady.

During the 16th century, however, toys began to be exported, principally from Germany. Toys for royal children, often made of silver and elaborately decorated, were no doubt commissioned, but the wood carvings and cheaper items were taken about Europe by what would today be called travelling salesmen. England was an important market, especially for Dutch dolls, which were very popular at the time. Another popular item was the

peep-show, a cabinet in which movable figures might be seen against a painted background, sometimes enhanced by the use of mirrors. Royal and aristocratic families often had their own, more sophisticated versions. Other toys popular in the 16th century include hobby-horses, tops and small windmills. Towards the end of the century puppet shows were also popular. Apart from museums and private collections where surviving material may be seen, an alternative means of appreciating the nature and variety of these early toys is to study the portraiture of the time. Paintings which include children, and especially groups of children, tell us much about their playthings.

Swedish doll of the 1590s; the clothes imitate the fashions of that date. She has a papier-mâché head and shoulders, and a leather body.

69

The 17th Century

Introduction

During the two centuries that ended in 1599 the western world witnessed a spectacle of unparalleled drama. The Renaissance made its appearance on the Italian stage with force; the humanism of its thought, rooted in the classicism of ancient Rome, swept through the dark ways of medieval conservatism. Its effect was to liberate men from the stifling feudalism of the Middle Ages.

It was a time of renewal; the Renaissance marked the rebirth of man's innate urge to create, and it encouraged him to see himself again as the central figure in the drama of history, as he had during the golden age of ancient Greece.

When Martin Luther nailed his 95 theses to the door of a church in Wittenberg in 1517 and thus began the Reformation, he unknowingly started a process that would bring the Renaissance to an end. The Reformation overwhelmed the Christian communities of northern Europe, and the sack of Rome by Spanish soldiers shook the Church of Rome to its foundations.

The Catholic Church launched the Counter-Reformation, although the price was heavy. Where during the Renaissance there was joy and a sense of excitement, radical thinking and universal compassion, now there was austere piety and a sense of turning inwards, of renewed conservatism.

The results of the decrees of the Council of Trent (the body set up by the Catholic Church to define dogma and re-establish its authority) were far-reaching and diverse. Though there was no special dictatorship of the arts, learning was stifled. The Church sought not to condemn the humanism of the Renaissance but to reinstate respectability in religious art. Perhaps most important of all, the Council of Trent led to an enhancement of the prestige of the Vatican. The Counter-Reformation marked the final eclipse of the Renaissance, but it created a new feeling of confidence in the Papacy and this was reflected, eventually, in a new desire for expression in art. The resulting development in the arts became the Baroque Age, which lasted very roughly from 1600 to about 1720.

The period known as the Age of Baroque has always caused problems for the art historian. It has been the subject of controversy, defined and re-defined by successive generations. The word Baroque has been used in so many different ways and to describe so many different works of art that it is probably true to say that any art historian could give it an accute definition, but one with which no other historian would agree.

Some say it is derived from the Portuguese word *barroco*, a "mis-shapen pearl". To others the word signifies the people's art, because it comes from the Latin *baro*, meaning common man. It has even been suggested that baroque is a derivation from the Latin *verruca*, which translated means wart, or again *burag*, a Persian word for hard soil containing small stones.

In a sense the meaning of the word itself is of little consequence. What is important is that the Baroque is generally agreed to distinguish a particular period of cultural endeavour, defining a specific period of Western art development. Defined in *The Oxford English Dictionary* a characterized "by exuberance and extravagance", it embraces a multitude of complex styles.

Any reference to the Baroque Age must consider that this period was rooted in Mannerism, and eventually evolved into the Rococo style. Mannerism introduced the Baroque Age and was gradually eclipsed by it. Rococo witnessed the decline of the

Right:
An early 17th-century English oak chair; its decoration was inspired by Renaissance motifs.

Baroque and set the stage for the
rationalism of the 18th century.

The Counter-Reformation began as
a reassertion of the pre-eminence of the
Church of Rome in matters of man's
spiritual relations with God. Initially
it maintained a stern though insecure
attitude towards painters, stonemasons
and wood-carvers, and a ferocious
treatment of heretics. European artists
and craftsmen in turn responded with
a combination of unconscious acceptance of the strictures of the age and a
conscious attempt to rebel against such
unnatural restraints. The result was a
style of art which has come to be
known as Mannerism. As the word
implies, the works of art produced
during this period seem artificial, with
a studied affectation.

In many ways the early Baroque
movement evolved in opposition to
the style, method and outlook of
Mannerism. It sought to move forward
yet it hoped to achieve this by looking
backward to the High Renaissance.
The movement spread across national
frontiers and evolved many different
styles and artforms.

Unlike Mannerism, the Baroque
was purposeful; it experimented vigor-
ously with the world. Baroque was as
dynamic as Mannerism was static: it
flowed and pulsated with a sense of
energy. Its creators sought to defy the
ordinary limitations of the materials
they were using.

Baroque architecture is characterized
by a sense of exuberance. It is ornate
but never stifled by its ornamental
features. Buildings constructed in the
Baroque style seem to flow; they have
grace and grandeur, revelling in the

curved line, the informal spiral. They appeal as much to the emotions as to the intellect. Architects sought to arouse a sensation of astonishment and to give the impression of grand scale.

Furnishing revelled in the ornate abandon of the Baroque style. Cabinets, chairs, tables, all seemed to stagger under the weight of their decoration; bronze, marble and heavy crops of wood carvings covered the furniture of the period.

Towards the end of the 17th century the Baroque gradually evolved into a style even more sensuous: Rococo. Where Baroque furniture still revealed the fundamentals of its construction, the Rococo style set out to conceal its manner of construction and to disguise its inner form. Art became an almost purely visual experience: every line was softened to a point of oblivion; shapes were contorted for pure effect. Visual proportion was sacrificed to the sensual delight of writhing form and plastic shape. Rococo was joyfully decadent and it persisted until the middle of the 18th century.

English furniture

The last years of Elizabeth I's reign were marked by a distinct richness of colour and design. Chairs, for example, upholstered in a variety of warm colours, were immensely popular at the time, often appearing with richly designed cushions. By the time of James I ornaments such as capitals, pilasters and pediments were added for purely decorative effect. The Civil War years (1641–49) resulted in a heavy cutback in furniture production, and the furniture that followed was markedly simpler. It was generally sombre in aspect, with dark leather coverings most commonly in use.

Until the Restoration of the monarchy in 1660 furniture in England was almost all made of oak, except for a few rural pieces which were fashioned in one of the fruit woods.

Of the major categories of oak furniture to be found in most homes during the 17th century, the principal piece was the chest. In country and rural areas, Elizabethan chests continued to be made throughout the 17th century although from the reign of James I onwards the style and character of the chest changed considerably.

Chests exchanged their solid strength for more sophisticated carving; joinery and panelling improved and greater use was made of ornamentation. Mitring of mouldings became popular, and the old-style lockplate gave way to a small metal shield which was placed over the keyhole.

It was not until the early 17th century that chairs came into general use, and most of these were now equipped with arms. In great demand at this time were turned chairs; these had posts and rails which were "thrown" by a turner on a lathe, rather than being made by a joiner. These were made in a variety of woods such as elm, yew and ash, depending on the predominant wood in the locality. During the Commonwealth the so-called York-shire and Derbyshire chairs came into fashion; these had a broad top rail in the back, and no spindles, and they

Above:
The State Bedroom at Chatsworth House, Derbyshire, decorated in the English Baroque style of the William and Mary period.

remained popular until the end of the 17th century. Many of these had a hollowed-out seat-board on which a cushion was placed.

Early 17th-century oak tables were still generally cumbersome, squat and heavy, but in about the mid-1620s a smaller type of oak table came into use. It was light in construction and often included a set of drawers. The legs were turned in ball and knob forms and the feet were vase-shaped. The gate-leg table with drop leaves was also introduced at about this time. There were several types, differing in the number, type and style of leg and stretcher employed.

Left:
Portuguese bed of the 17th century, made of Brazilian hardwood. Collection of D. Clesta Cabral, Evora.

Below:
Spanish table from the early 17th century. Hispanic Society of America, New York.

Above:
Early 17th-century court cupboard, inlaid with semi-precious stones. Victoria and Albert Museum, London.

Above right:
English carved oak bookcase of about 1675. Dyrham Park, Gloucestershire.

Right:
Simple oak stool of the 17th century. Similar stools were found in both England and America.

Top:
English centre table in the Baroque style of 1680. It is made of cedarwood and the top is inlaid with ebony. Collection of N. V. Stopford-Sackville.

Above right:
English cabinet of about 1690, decorated with Japanese motifs.

Above:
English looking glass in a gilt frame, of about 1680. Collection of the Marquess of Exeter.

It was not until the middle of the 17th century that chests of drawers came into prominence, and shortly after the Restoration they became available in large numbers. They were often ornate, as if the English carpenter had decided to expand his creative energy on these particular pieces of furniture rather than on other, more mundane wooden artifacts. The result was some of the richest workmanship in wood ever undertaken in England. Rich carvings adorned the front of the piece, even to the point of covering the corner posts and the frames of the panels. The use of ivory and bone inlays in picturesque decoration is an entirely English creation during the 1660s.

The Baroque style in furniture design arrived somewhat late in England. Its introduction occurred with the Restoration of Charles II, who brought with him from exile on the Continent a taste for elegance and comfort. The influence of this was far-reaching, and led to a decline in the use of oak and a corresponding increase in popularity of such woods as walnut, in high fashion on the Continent. There were other changes. Marquetry became fashionable and soon the development of skills in veneering led to a blossoming of this type of carpentry. Bold, floral designs superseded the old sombre styles.

Chairs grew taller and adopted arched backs; legs were elaborately carved, perhaps with two cherubs supporting a crown. Armchairs developed wider seats, some employing rich upholstering in velvets. A whole new range of woods became popular; ebony, laburnum and even olive were used with increasing frequency.

In other ways, too, England broke new ground. As the East India Company established safer and faster trade routes to the East, so a vast range of exotic imports arrived to spur the imagination of artists, carpenters and the great families who patronized them. Thus, lacquered cabinets from China soon led to the development of the so-called japanning in England. By about 1700 the deliberate use of lacquered surfaces on all types of furniture had reached the level of a craze, and it was soon being copied in both Europe and America.

With the arrival of Huguenot refugees from persecution in France in the 1680s, it was not long before English furniture began to reflect many of the Continental ideas on design that had been flourishing in Holland and France for the previous decade. English carpenters quickly absorbed every innovation and began to produce a fresher, more stylized and more ornate type of furniture which eventually became known as "Queen Anne" style.

French furniture
The characteristic gift for elegance is shown clearly in the furniture produced in France during the 17th century. Ensconced at the Gobelins

Right:
One of a pair of English carved, gilt and painted armchairs, c.1685. The front stretcher is decorated with putti blowing trumpets. Marquess of Exeter.

Below:
English walnut day-bed, c.1685. Victoria and Albert Museum, London.

Left:
English cabinet on matching stand, veneered with parquetry (inlay of varying colours and grain of a single type of wood). It was made in about 1680. Royal Academy of Arts, London.

Below left:
French chair of the late 17th century. Its broad low seat and high upholstered back are typical of the furnishing of Versailles. Musée des Arts Decoratifs.

Below:
English upholstered armchair of walnut, c.1680. Collection of the Duke of Buccleuch.

Right:
A triangular chair made of ash. It dates from the England of the Cromwellian period. Leonard Lassalle.

Below:
Florentine table top, of about 1635. The mosaic is by Domenico Benotti. Palazzo Pitti, Florence.

factory in Paris, or the Louvre itself, the king's carpenters, joiners and turners concentrated on the manufacture of the most precious examples of their art and their outpourings can still be seen at Fontainebleau, the Louvre, Saint Germain and at other mansions owned by Louis XIV and the French princes. Next in line to the royal family stood the great ministers of state, who also received a handsome tribute from the hands of the woodworkers. Farther down were the nobility; they imitated the court's styles according to their means but were often obliged to fall back on second-rate purveyors and on less precious materials. Their furniture is

Above:
Late 17th-century French cupboard, with veneers of pewter, brass, tortoise-shell and contrasting woods. Such veneers are known as boullework, after their inventor André Charles Boulle. Musée des Arts Decoratifs.

Opposite above:
The *Salon de Mars* in the Palace of Versailles.

Opposite below:
French stool from Versailles, with heavily carved legs and upholstered seat. Château de Versailles.

none the less in the same style as the king's, all blazing with splendour.

In the homes of the bourgeoisie we find a curious range of styles, some going back to the plain, undisguised furniture more typical of the early 17th century, during the reign of Louis XIII. Such pieces as the diamond-pointed and panelled door cupboards, known as cabinets in Gascony, were in common use among the gentry, rich traders and the military. They used the walnut bureau surmounted by a painted writing desk; not for them the ornately carved and richly gilded cabinets which embellished the rooms of the great.

For the aristocracy, though, nothing was too rich or too grand. Mouldings were carved in a fantastic wealth of elaborate designs; veneers made from the finest available woods, whether homegrown or imported from west or east, were used to surface stronger timber or to provide material for ingenious inlays. Surfaces were also painted, gilded or lacquered in a great range of brilliant colours. Furniture groaned beneath the weight of solid gold and silver ornamentation, sometimes inlaid with precious stones, ebony, ivory or mother-of-pearl. All this characterized the finest tables, beds, cupboards and cabinets from the workshops at the Louvre and the Gobelins, where splendid pictorial tapestry wall-hangings were produced. The intention was nothing less than to create a blaze of splendour round the brilliance of the Sun King, Louis XIV.

Louis XIV had a grandiose dream: to surround himself with gold, the only material that could truly reflect the splendour of his own godlike quality. Yet to cover every piece of furniture in solid gold was an impossibility, even for such a monarch as the Sun King. Failing this, he demanded silver; where this too eventually became impossible, baser metals or gilded wood were substituted. Even silvered wood was used.

How all this was achieved technically is worthy of note. First the untreated wood was coated with size and then given one thin coat after another of white mixed with skin glue, followed by a coat of yellow and a compound of seven or eight glutinous materials applied in the form of an *assiette* or skin. When all this had been done there remained the careful laying on of gold or silver leaf and a final burnishing. Louis's furniture was sometimes silvered, as were many of the caryatids that supported the tables on which the cabinets were placed.

The opulence, the sheer sumptuousness of the French Baroque period reached its climax in Louis's great palace at Versailles. This mighty monument was a tribute to the exuberance of an age that had, in some ways, gone mad with pomp and decorative effect. Versailles was intended to be the most splendid of all the splendid palaces and mansions which had been built to

celebrate the reign of the Sun King.

Everything about Versailles suggests either monumental scale or spectacular opulence. Splendour and grandeur were the key themes which governed the work of the Versailles craftsmen. The gardens around the palace, the stonework of the building, the interiors and the furniture, all demonstrated the obsession of the age to tamper with the natural symmetry found in nature. From all over Europe architects, artists, sculptors, carpenters, joiners, upholsterers and a whole battery of stonemasons descended on Versailles to seek commissions from the royal household. Working under the direction of such renowned architects as Bernini, craftsmen turned this former hunting lodge into the most magnificent palace Europe had ever known.

The furniture designed for Versailles was monumental in its classicism and sumptuously ornate in its appearance. No chair or bed or wall hanging was left unembellished. Everything was lacquered or veneered or covered with marquetry inlay. No expense was spared to reflect splendour in every detail of that vast establishment.

American furniture

There can be no stronger contrast to the ostentatious luxury of French furniture than that of American furniture of the 17th century. The earliest settlers had nothing but the simplest furniture, and it was not until the closing decades of the century that American furniture evolved any sophisticated styles. The styles reflected current fashions in the mother-countries, England and the Netherlands. Even less flamboyant than these fashions (which were themselves a sombre scaling down of French exuberance), American furniture of the "William and Mary" style continued well into the early 18th century. This furniture design was distinguished by lightness, simplicity and informal elegance. Maple, pine and walnut were the popular woods in use and these were employed on such utilitarian pieces as the highboy (chest-on-stand), the secretary-desk (a bureau-bookcase, usually with mirrored doors) and a whole range of winged armchairs and gate-leg tables with turned legs and oval tops. One was called the butterfly

Above:
An American sunflower and tulip chest, originating in Connecticut in the late 17th century. Index of American Design.

Left:
Dutch oak *kas* or cupboard, with the panels stained black to resemble ebony. These pieces became popular in the Dutch colonies in America.

Opposite:
American press cupboard, a development of the court cupboard, made in Massachusetts in the late 17th century. Museum of Fine Arts, Boston.

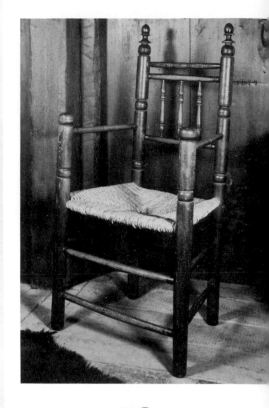

table, because the flaps were shaped like wings; these were first evolved in New England. New York remained a bastion of the Dutch style for almost another 100 years and long continued to prefer the massive type of furniture, such as the *kas*, a cupboard carved and painted with foliage and fruit.

By the end of the 1600s American furniture, in line with English developments, was often manufactured in two separate tiers, with an upper part resting on a stalwart base. This was the method of production of the secretary-desk and the highboy. A great deal of faking goes on with these types of antiques and special note should be made of signs of trimming on the exterior rear surfaces. The outside of the backs should be of the same wood and any differences should be treated extremely sceptically.

Silver

Any serious discussion of the history of English silver must start in 1660, the year of the Restoration of Charles II to the throne. As one consequence of the Puritan Revolution, little silver produced before the middle of the 17th century still survives. What early silver does exist is extremely rare and is usually in private collections, cathedrals or museums.

Among the most typical of mid-17th-century silverware are the two-handled bowls or cups sometimes known as candle cups, which are believed to have been used to hold concoctions of spiced wine and milk to treat fever and other illnesses. These cups, examples of which still turn up for sale occasionally, were styled with either straight sides or bellied bowls, and had two handles because they were often filled with hot food or drinks. Most English examples were produced with a pattern of lions and unicorns, surrounded by foliage. The handles were often large, sometimes several inches across, and were occasionally styled in the form of caryatids. Many of the cups were covered.

A good comparison can be seen in the very luxurious Augsburg cup and cover which is now in the Wallace Collection in London. Made in 1600 of silver and silver-gilt, the cup still reflects the influence of the Renaissance.

In England, the return of the monarchy led to a renewal of interest in silver ceremonial pieces, such as the ceremonial salt made in 1662, now in the possession of the Worshipful Company of Goldsmiths in London. This truly splendid piece, with its great eagles and hounds, was described by Samuel Pepys and given to Catherine of Braganza, the wife of Charles II.

Salvers were in evidence at this time and, as the skills of English silversmiths improved and Huguenot silversmiths began to compete with them, their silver plate decoration enjoyed a reputation for excellence. Indeed, it

Opposite above left:
Brewster-type armchair, made in Massachusetts in about 1650. These were named after an elder of the Massachusetts community. Metropolitan Museum of Art, New York.

Opposite above right:
Carver chair, made in America towards the end of the 17th century. These were named after a governor of the Massachusetts Bay Company, and are less elaborate than Brewster chairs. American Museum, Bath.

Opposite below:
Dutch chair of carved walnut, c.1700. Rijksmuseum, Amsterdam.

Below:
A finely decorated early 17th-century Dutch silver-gilt ewer and basin.

was not long before English silver plate as a whole became the most sought-after of any country.

The Huguenot silversmiths, once they had overcome the jealous antagonism of their English counterparts, brought to the plain style of English silverware the delicacy and subtle humour of the continental Baroque form. A typical example is a porringer on display in the Victoria and Albert Museum, London. A small two-handled cup made in 1668, it is embossed in the Dutch manner with flowers and scrolls.

In 1697 the government, in an effort to prevent silversmiths from melting down coins to extract the metal, introduced the Britannia standard. This obliged silversmiths to produce wrought plate in a new, higher standard silver, which had to be marked with the "figure of a woman commonly called Britannia". The result was a period of quite exceptional work, purely English in character, in heavy high-quality silver. The years of the Britannia standard, which ended in 1720, were among the most productive in the history of silver in England.

Above left:
English standing salt, made in about 1662 and known as the Seymour Salt. It is of silver-gilt and rock crystal. The Worshipful Company of Goldsmiths, London.

Above right:
English silver candle snuffer and sugar caster of the Restoration period.

English silver before 1697 and after 1720 was usually stamped with four marks, including the *lion passant*, the date letter, the sterling standard and the maker's mark. Forgeries have always existed and probably always will; the Victorians practised this on a large scale. Detecting such forgeries is immensely difficult and it is only possible after years of experience in the silver trade.

From about 1680 onwards, there was a surge of interest in silver coffee- and tea-pots, and early in the next century this was stimulated by a blossoming of coffee-houses in the cities. Silver coffee-pots of this period were normally plain, straight-sided and tapering. At the Worshipful Company of Goldsmiths in London can be seen an excellent set of silver tea-pot, kettle and chocolate-pot on matching stands, made in 1719 by Joseph Ward. Though plain in appearance, this set serves to illustrate the English pre-occupation with such subtle qualities as the graceful line and the elegant form which made English silverware so enormously popular abroad.

Well worth seeking from this period are such collector's items as silver sugar casters, mugs (whether covered or open), salts, silver travelling sets, certainly candlesticks (though these are now extremely costly), drinking cups and tankards.

French silver made during the reign of Louis XIV received all the sophisticated attention that could be lavished upon it by that splendid age. Such pieces as have survived come richly decorated or ornately carved and have more in common with the Rococo than the Baroque style. Yet dignity was not always sacrificed to pomp. An

English silver tankard, made in about 1698. Victoria and Albert Museum, London.

example of graceful simplicity is the Avignon inkstand, made in 1670 when Louis XIV was at the height of his prestige. The piece itself is singularly lacking in ornamentation, yet in its own way it reveals the quiet dignity that characterizes the best in French silverware of the period.

One of the better-known examples of French Baroque silverware is the so-called Chatsworth toilet set, pro-duced by Pierre Prévost in 1670. It now belongs to the Duke of Devon-shire and can be seen at Chatsworth House. The set is thought to have been made for Mary, daughter of James II of England. As with all such toiletry services, the central piece of the Chats-worth set is the mirror, but the various accoutrements of the cosmetic arts were also included by Monsieur Prévost – the ewer and basin, a long tray to hold candlesticks and snuffers and a variety of boxes and flasks.

Occasionally a particularly fine French Baroque silver dinner service turns up. One such, at Berkeley Castle, Gloucestershire, had long remained anonymous until it was identified recently. Though made in 1737, the set nevertheless bears all the features of the flamboyant style of high Baroque. The terrines or serving dishes in particular are amply adorned with the foliage motif typical of Baroque silverware.

Examples of minor French silver-ware are often auctioned at salerooms. Such peculiarly French contrivances as silver soap boxes shaped like orbs, highly ornate mirror frames in silver-gilt (more Rococo than Baroque) and interesting chocolate-pots such as that made by Edmé-Paul Leblond of Paris in 1703 are outstanding examples.

Whereas the trend in Europe tended towards the ornate and the flowery, the influence of Quaker Puritanism in New England pushed American silver-ware design in the opposite direction: pieces were required to be plain though of good quality. This fitted in per-fectly with the aspirations of American silversmiths. The earliest of these had been trained in London, but they fled to America to escape the restrictions imposed on them by the guilds. Indeed, they so abhorred these institutions that they founded only free associations of craftsmen and for a long time after the War of Independence they refused to use the sterling mark on their silver.

American silversmiths contributed a new kind of quiet simplicity in silver-ware. During the 17th century they often made use of the Baroque curvi-linear motif, as with the very distinc-tively American porringer, a shallow bowl used for drinking purposes and found in almost every New England home. Two-handled bowls, developed from the Dutch brandy-and-raisin bowl, became immensely popular in New York in the late 1600s, and these were followed by small but com-paratively ornate drinking cups of silver.

American church plate also was im-portant. This often began as domestic plate that was taken regularly to service. A few candleholders survive, though these are now extremely rare. Lastly, it is still possible to find fine examples of American tankards. These, especially in the early 1600s, were rather plain, but they often sported a domed lid of fine design.

Left:
American standing Communion cup of silver; 1700. Museum of Fine Arts, Boston.

Above:
French miniature case of about 1670, decorated with gold and enamel. Victoria and Albert Museum, London.

French porcelain

The first true porcelains, as distinct from glazed pottery, to appear in Europe were imported from Asia by Portuguese and Dutch explorers in the 16th century. The arrival of these strange and beautiful oriental pieces soon aroused the curiosity of collectors of the exotic, and it was not long before the great Italian family of Medici had in their possession some of the finest Chinese porcelains ever known.

So highly did Europe regard Chinese porcelain that an almost obsessional desire sprang up to discover the secrets of the manufacture of these delicate, translucent ceramics, brought from sources throughout the Far East. It was this passion that led to the evolution

of the European porcelain industry.

There were many false starts, as European potters attempted to reproduce the process by which they thought the oriental porcelains were made. All these early attempts were made of kaolin, a material of whose properties the western potters were still entirely ignorant. The improvement of the various pastes used in the glazing of their ceramics then became the main object of the new breed of craftsmen. Not surprisingly, each centre of production kept secret its hard-earned knowledge of new processes and its newly-won skills. The result of these experiments was a wide range of works of art, with each centre producing a style of different type and quality from those of its rivals.

In France by the latter half of the 17th century, the oriental style had established a virtual monopoly. At Mennecy, Rouen and Saint Cloud, guilds of potters were lovingly creating the "porcelain of China" according to the secret processes championed by each centre of manufacture. Several were even granted letters of patent by the French authorities to encourage them to continue their efforts to perfect their porcelain.

A few attempts were made to break this monopoly, but these were extremely costly and very often led to the ruination of those private potters who tried to change from pottery to porcelain. As often as not their fate lay in the hands of the rich – the great families who protected their protégés from

Opposite:
Pair of Chinese vases of the K'ang Hsi period (1662–1722), painted in underglaze blue. Such pieces were highly popular in 17th- and 18th-century Europe. Victoria and Albert Museum, London.

Left:
An English stoneware mug with a silver rim, made in Fulham in about 1680. Hanley Museum and Art Gallery.

Below left:
Chinese porcelain teapot with openwork panels of bamboo design and with a blue glaze. K'ang Hsi period.

Below:
Chinese ivory carving of a dignitary. Late 17th century.

the competition of the monopolist and the attentions of the government.

While most of the early European porcelains were imitations of oriental style, craftsmen also based much of their design on the pottery for which they were justly renowned. The early Rouen porcelain vases, for example, with their distinctive white and blue designs, were essentially based on the pottery produced at Rouen at this time.

Although we cannot be certain, it seems that Rouen was the centre of the first experiments conducted in France to produce the now world-famous soft-paste porcelains. One man stands out as the creator of this astounding innovation – Edmé Poterat. Again, we do not know exactly when he started to manufacture soft-paste porcelain wares, but in 1673 his son, Louis, managed to obtain a licence permitting him to make pottery and porcelain "in the fashion of Holland".

Much of the work completed by the Poterat family is signed with the letter "P" and this should be watched for when searching for examples of his craft. Much Poterat porcelain is still available at reasonable figures, and includes such items as dressing-table pots, Saint Cloud sugar sifters, wine coolers and a whole range of delicate vases.

The early examples were generally finished in the traditional blue and white colours preferred by craftsmen of the time, but a little later more varied use of colours and designs began to filter through to the manufacturing centres at Chantilly, Rouen and Saint Cloud. This was probably a reflection of the general trend towards a more ornate style as typified by the late Baroque period.

Special note should be taken of the works of Pierre Chicaneau (a potter at Saint Cloud), Edmé, Louis and Michel Poterat, and Barthelemy Dorez, who founded a factory at Lille in 1711. Although their works are not always attributable, certain identifiable marks or signs can be found.

In essence, Rouen porcelains were characterized by simple shapes; vases, saucers and cups (generally without handles) usually decorated in blue and white designs. The Saint Cloud work-shop began its porcelain development by imitating the works of the Rouen factory and there may be some difficulty in distinguishing between the two. But the marks of the Saint Cloud factory are well known: each piece has either a small fleur-de-lis or a sun. Look out especially for the mark ^{S}T^C, which refers to Saint Cloud Trou, Trou being the manager of the factory until 1766. Later Saint Cloud pieces revealed the more complicated colours and patterns of foliage and fruit which typified later Baroque porcelains, in imitation of the Chinese originals.

Above:
French soft-paste porcelain vase from Rouen, dating from the end of the 17th century. It has been ascribed to Louis Poterat. Musée National de Céramique, Sèvres.

Opposite:
Dutch vase, made of tin-glaze earthenware and with polychrome decoration. It was made in Delft in about 1700. Victoria and Albert Museum, London.

Left:
One of a set of Merryman plates, decorated in blue and made in about 1690. They were always made in sets of six and inscribed with a line from a rhyme. City of Manchester Art Gallery.

Below:
Delft tulip vase of tin-glazed earthenware and painted blue: c.1700. Such pieces served as inspiration for potters throughout Europe. Collection of Van Oss.

English pottery

During the 17th century English pottery began a period of extraordinary development which was to culminate in the blossoming genius of Josiah Wedgwood in the middle of the 18th century. The work of relatively unknown, early 17th-century potters is now much in vogue. Part of the reason lies in the fact that so much slipware (a technique whereby pipeclay designs are trailed through a pipe on to an earthenware base, and then fired under a lead glaze), delftware or maiolica (both terms used in England to describe earthenware coated with tin glaze and painted in colours before firing) and stoneware (earthenware glazed and fired at a temperature high enough to ensure a non-porous product) has survived from this period, and so much fine pottery too. Nothing has caught the attention of the collector today so favourably as English slipware, produced in the main by a small number of rural craftsmen.

Some continental slipware was being produced at this time but, despite its rather ornate appearance, it never attained the quality of the best English examples. Supreme among the early slipware centres was Wrotham, a village in Kent. Here a constant stream of jugs, posset pots and cups poured forth from the potter's kiln. It all bore the distinctive mark of true slipware: the "trailing" quality of the design

Left:
Dutch narrow-necked jug of the end of the 17th century. This decoration of exotic flowers and birds, which is known as Vogelesdekor, is typical of Dutch work of this period.

Above:
A Delft plate of tin-glazed earthenware. The landscape is painted in blue. Victoria and Albert Museum, London.

Above:
English delftware tankard decorated with bosses, and made in Lambeth in the second half of the 17th century. Temple Newsam House.

Above right:
English slipware or lead-glazed earthenware made by the Wrothman potteries in Kent in 1653. Large beakers of this design are known as tygs. Stoke-on-Trent Museum and Art Gallery.

Right:
English brown stoneware wine bottle of 1680, with decorative motifs applied by stamping. Victoria and Albert Museum, London.

almost seems to have been squeezed on to the clay as if it were being poured from a cake-icing syringe.

Besides Wrotham slipware, there are also some fine examples of the work of the Staffordshire and Derbyshire centres and a great deal of green-glazed Yorkshire ware can still be found by the patient collector. Simple in execution, Staffordshire pieces such as honey pots were produced with striped or dotted designs and a very pleasing sense of proportion.

Pewter

The manufacture of the alloy known as pewter and the making of pewter articles are extremely ancient crafts. Certainly the Chinese were producing all kinds of pewter vessels more than 2000 years ago. The Roman occupation of Britain left behind a quantity of pewter plate which has stood up to the ravages of time remarkably well. At Bath, in particular, several examples of Roman pewter can be viewed in the Pump Room. These date from about AD 200 and they are in fine condition. The Greeks, too, are known to have used this alloy in the manufacture of their pots but all traces have been lost. Pewter was also used extensively in Europe during the Middle Ages.

Pewter had been probably used in England since the 10th century, but few pieces have survived from this period. It is likely that most of the plate, as it became worn and decayed (pewter is a rather soft metal), was either abandoned or melted down. The earliest pewtermakers were held in some contempt and were probably viewed as the poor relations of the goldsmiths and silversmiths.

The sudden spurt of church building from the 10th century onward led to a growing demand for pewter. When new, pewter gleams like silver and was therefore very popular for use in candlesticks in churches and castles; it probably also found a demand among those who could not afford gold or silver. By about 1610 most of the church plate, bowls, flagons and even fonts were being made of pewter, a rare honour for a metal believed to have been the base metal described in the Bible. Indeed, one of the finest examples of workmanship to come down to us from the 17th century is the so-called Netherhampton Flagon,

Below:
An English red slipware dish of about 1700, depicting William III. Victoria and Albert Museum, London.

made in 1634 by the villagers of Netherhampton, perhaps for the cathedral at nearby Salisbury and now in the possession of the South Wiltshire and Blackmore Museum in Salisbury.

Because of its softness pewter is easy to mark, and by the beginning of the 17th century pewter pieces were being "signed" with the mark of the maker. This was called the "touch" and the guild of pewterers kept a register of these marks to make it easier to identify the work of individual craftsmen.

Styles in pewterware changed only slowly, in contrast to the fairly rapid changes in design that occurred with silver. For a long time pewter plates appeared in a crude, flat form. It was only towards the end of the 16th century that the customary depression appeared in pewter plates. In time, too, the edges of the plate rose so that liquids no longer ran over. Since pewter is unaffected by the ravages of vinegar and salt, it was found to be an extremely useful material for storage purposes and has long been used in surgeries and hospitals. Indeed, it was the commonest material for ordinary use in home and shop until late in the 17th century, when it was finally superseded by earthenware and wooden articles which were being increasingly used as tableware.

Dolls, dolls' houses and miniature furniture

Towards the end of the 1600s a craze developed throughout Europe for anything miniature. Whether it was glass, delftware, silver or porcelain, it was eagerly sought, together with the various small items of furniture on which the pieces were placed.

Among the first to take a keen

interest in this form of collecting were the Dutch. They evolved cabinets in which to place their treasury of miniature cups and vases. These cabinets found a place on the wall in the best room of the house. The English evolved a radically different approach to the problem of how best to exhibit their miniatures: they built miniature houses for them. Occasionally they even commissioned architects to design the house, and sometimes stipulated that the design should resemble the family home. In time these became known as dolls' houses, although originally they were known as "baby" houses (doll being a derogatory term at the time for a prostitute).

As often as not these baby houses were graced with extremely ornate façades and rather drab interiors, though the better ones contained a number of rooms, and even halls, stairways and doors. Almost from the beginning these miniature houses were given to children, proof of this being the record of one given by the future Queen Anne in 1691 to her godchild, Ann Sharp. Yet when we think of the quality of the miniatures which furnished these houses, we might wonder

why they were given to children, for many of the first dolls' house miniatures were made in silver. No doubt such lucky children were warned severely to be careful with these "toys".

Dolls' houses could be built to any size and specification, and they could be made to contain a great variety of "toys". The word is used with some caution here because in its original sense it meant any article of small size that could be handled or toyed with, rather than something that was intended as a plaything. Indeed the kind of toys that were imported into England from Holland would probably not have been considered smart enough to grace a room of the 17th-century dolls' house.

There are several places where examples of late 17th-century dolls' houses can be seen. In the Bethnal Green Museum in London there is a particularly fine example of miniature furniture in the form of an oak and walnut writing desk, probably made in 1690 or 1691. In every detail the miniature corresponds perfectly to the full-size furniture of this period, even to the veneering and the moulded top.

Small boxes

Small boxes have been a part of the history of human affairs for thousands of years. They have appeared in an astonishing variety of materials, in all guises and configurations. They have been used to convey tokens of love, esteem and malice. They have been used to transport secret messages of state and even aid an assassination. They have been given by kings in token of valuable service and to secret agents to enable them to commit suicide. Some have been constructed from the crudest materials, others from gold and precious stones. One, believed to have been the toilette casket of Marie Antoinette, fetched £600 at auction in 1961. Today it would fetch far more.

In England, at the beginning of the 1600s, the use of cosmetics was fairly restrained and during the Commonwealth it was virtually outlawed. Thus small boxes for make-up powders, unguents and general creams were commonly sombre and plain. But with the re-establishment of the monarchy and the introduction of the manners and taste of the French court, styles in toilette usage, materials and the boxes they were contained in changed dramatically. So much so that when young ladies married, they expected to receive gifts of toilette sets with at least 20 to 30 pieces.

At this time, too, patchboxes came into fashion. Patches were worn on the cheek, initially to disguise an unsightly spot. Later they appeared as distinct marks of beauty, and many a forehead wore large patches with coach and horse designs. Each patch

Above left:
An English doll of the last years of the seventeenth century, dressed and made up in the latest fashions. Victoria and Albert Museum, London.

Left:
The Nuremburg dolls' house of 1639. Germanisches Nationalmuseum, Nuremburg.

Opposite:
Russian dress ornament of the early 18th century; Baroque jewellery stressed the importance of the setting of the jewels.

or pair of patches was contained in a little patch box. These were generally shallow, but large enough to allow two fingers to pull out the patch. Powder boxes were slightly larger and had enough room for the pad used to dab the powder on to the face. Many tiny boxes were made for the purpose of holding scent bottles, and there were even a number made to be suspended from rings, worn about the waist. These so-called *etui* were used to contain everything from spyglasses to scissors; they were general-purpose boxes for carrying miniature tools of various kinds.

It is thought that snuff-taking started on the Continent, France being the probable country of origin. The Scottish soldiers accompanying James I on his way to the throne of England in 1603 were reported to be carrying with them "sneezing milns" or mulls made from rams' horns. These can still be found in antique shops, and are fitted with small snuff spoons and a hare's foot to dust the snuff from a moustache. Pipe smoking became popular in James I's reign, and tobacco has always required a box to keep it in; some of the tobacco boxes made at the end of the 17th century reached a fine degree of artistry. Many were made with silver or gold trimmings and others were beautifully lacquered and inlaid with mother-of-pearl. Many of the finest snuff and tobacco boxes were made of enamel, solid silver or gold. One which is now highly admired is the Charles I commemoration silver snuffbox, made in 1713, on which part of the inscription reads: "Thee Glorious Martyr, Rebells did destroy, they, God, who was their aim, could not anoy."

Baroque jewellery

By the late Middle Ages jewellers had become fairly adept at mounting precious stones on enamelled metals. This concentration on mounting continued throughout the Renaissance, when chasing and enamelling were considered the prime arts of the jeweller. What counted was not so much the quality of the jewel – however beautiful it might be – but rather the excellence of the setting in which it was placed. Thus pride of place would, for example, be given to a ruby or sapphire

set in enamelled gold. The jewel, it was thought, could only be truly admired when observed within a properly created setting. This idea fitted in perfectly with the general Renaissance preference for balance as conceived on classical lines.

By the beginning of the 17th century, however, the emphasis was gradually changing in favour of the jewel; the intrinsic beauty of the precious stone was coming to be appreciated for its own sake. This was partly due to the important progress which had been made in cutting techniques; it need hardly be said that the more facets that could be cut into a rough diamond, the more beautifully (after polishing) it would capture and reflect the light. By the middle of the century cutters were able to make up to 16 surfaces in precious stones, a fine achievement

considering the crude nature of the tools then available.

This change of emphasis coincided with a reversal of roles of the craftsmen most concerned with the making of jewellery. In essence, the jeweller was becoming more important than the goldsmith when it came to the setting of precious stones. In time enamelled settings went out of fashion, at least where quality gems were concerned. It became important to consider what the effect would be of a kind of setting for the stone; whether the colour of the gem would be enhanced by the colour of its background setting. Soon the term "matching" came to be used. This concern with the stone itself and giving it the correct prominence coincided with the spreading influence of Baroque ideas. The result was a tendency towards a taste for the ornate,

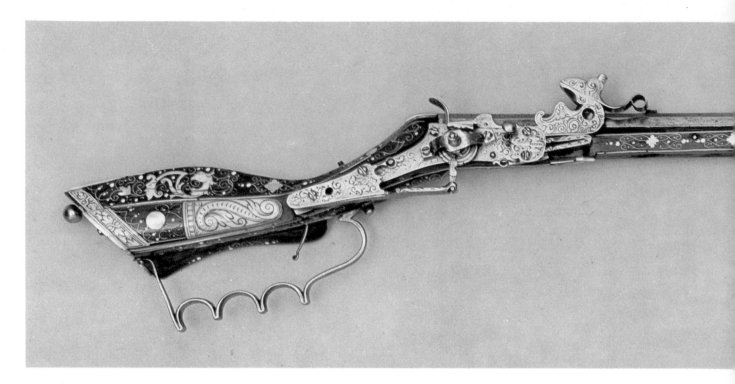

for jewels of a massive size, intricately worked and highly attractive.

Where the Renaissance had made use of figured and arabesque motifs, the Baroque Age took as its theme naturalistic floral patterns. Many craftsmen looked to the botanical gardens founded by Henri IV of France for their inspiration. Hanging pods of gems became popular and the numerous collections of drawings of flowers being produced during the late 17th century provided many a designer with ideas based upon a floral theme.

Scrollwork of diamonds and other precious stones was adopted as a central theme of Baroque jewellery; this is shown very clearly in the royal crown of Denmark. Produced in 1670 by Paul Kurtz for King Christian V, the crown combines balance and lightness. On a base of matt gold two sapphires are set (one of which is the famous Blue Mountain sapphire). The only piece of enamelling to be seen is the orb at the apex of the crown.

While the technique of enamelling tended to decline as the importance given to the gem itself increased, it occasionally reached a level of excellence rarely equalled. Apart from this, the backs of jewels continued to be ornamented in enamelled metals, and miniature cases and watches achieved a pre-eminence which they retained for over a century. Gold and enamel clock and musical boxes were being made as late as 1770, and are still high in demand and price.

In the royal houses of England and France the taste in jewellery was changing rapidly. In England especially styles were becoming predominantly feminine in elegance, and with simple lines. Clasps continued to be massive, with enormous stones. Pearls were extremely popular and were often given a Baroque appearance: they were modelled in such a way as to make them seem "natural", as if they had simply been removed from the shell and were now hanging from a clasp in exactly the untreated quality in which they were found.

As the 17th century matured, jewels grew both in size and magnificence. The great mirror of Great Britain, for example, came into the hands of James I and was bought for the then princely sum of over 600,000 *écus*. There is a jewel in the Natural History Museum of France which once belonged to the Sun King himself: a 132-carat sapphire, possibly one of the largest such gems in the world. Indeed, it was part of Louis XIV's image of himself that he purchased and then offered as gifts all manner of sumptuous jewellery. The Louvre contains another of his jewels, the Hortensia diamond, a gem of more than 20 carats weight. One of the four *parures* owned by Louis has several hundred buttons of diamonds, pearls and coloured stones.

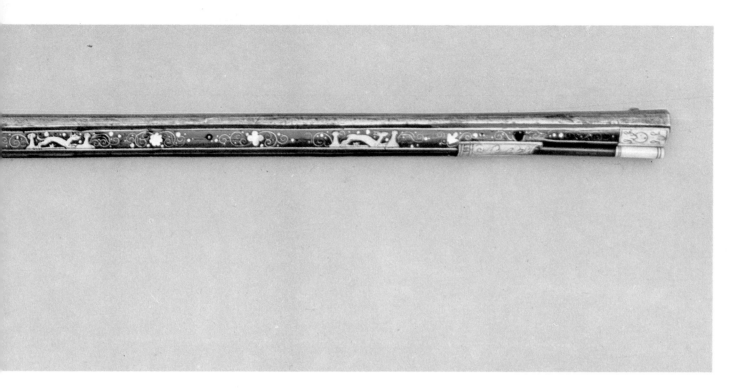

Above:
Sporting wheel-lock gun, made in the late 17th century in the extreme south of Poland. Jagdmuseum, Munich.

Opposite:
Austrian flintlock holster pistol. The barrel is finely marked and has some silver inlay. T. H. Porter.

Below:
A watch of the late 16th or early 17th century. It is encased in a silver skull and housed in a leather case.

Not only women cherished the luxury of wearing sumptuous jewels: men too indulged in the collecting and wearing of expensive gems. Indeed all the courtiers of the Versailles court were obsessive followers of the royal fashion and it is said that the king's ministers changed the settings of their jewels almost every three years.

Extravagantly ornate diamond, sapphire, ruby and pearl jewels, set in gold, silver and enamel were worn in stomachers, brooches, rings, necklaces, pendants and hair ornaments. The more gems, the more exquisite the setting, the more expensive the piece and the more in demand it would be. In fact so popular did Gilles Légaré, the king's goldsmith, become that he was permanently lodged in the Louvre, to enable him to attend closely to the king's directions for new jewels.

The sumptuousness of French jewellery design had its effect on the rest of Europe and there followed a rich variety of imitative pieces which appeared in all the royal houses of the continent. William III of England commissioned a gorgeous pendant of gold and rock crystal in 1690: framed in enamelled gold and decorated with leaf and flower designs, the centre of the pendant holds a tiny miniature of the king. In its exquisite workmanship it represents a magnificent achievement of the Baroque Age.

Glass

For the three centuries which ended with the coming of the Rococo period the art of glassmaking was dominated by Venice. There the Society of the Art of Glass-making set the prime standard for the rest of the world to admire. Indeed, apart from the medieval Waldglas of Germany nothing of comparable quality to Venetian glass was made anywhere before the late 16th century.

The Venetians had long assimilated the best qualities of glassmaking as it had been practised by the Alexandrians, the Byzantines and the Arabs, and by the late Middle Ages the Venetian glassmakers were being jealously re-garded in Italy and throughout Europe for the beauty, clarity and lightness of their crystal, aventurine, enamelled, lace (opaque white) and so-called ice-glass, all of which poured forth in a steady stream from the Venetian factories. It was only with the downfall of the Republic in 1797 that Venetian glass began the decline from which it has never fully recovered.

England, like every other country in northern Europe, imported its best quality glass from Venice, yet a fledgling industry had been established in Britain since the 13th century. Most if not all of England's early glassmaking factories owed their existence to foreigners. In the 1620s the English glass manufacturing monopoly, once held by Verzelini, passed to one Sir Robert Mansell. He reorganized the whole industry, introduced the use of coal as a fuel instead of wood and encouraged much experimentation to find new ways to produce fine-quality glass. In the late 1660s, after the Restoration of the monarchy, a new name in glassmaking history appears, George Ravenscroft, a chemist whose interest in crystal glass (glass of great clarity) led him to discover the merits of powdered lead.

Originally known as flint glass, lead glass had the effect of making the glass pliable when soft, yet heavier and much more brilliant. Ravenscroft was the

Left:
English decanter of about 1680. It is probably the work of George Ravenscroft. Victoria and Albert Museum, London.

Above:
Venetian glass ornamented with a wreath-shaped stem. Victoria and Albert Museum, London.

Left:
Venetian clear glass *biberone* or decanter, with slight blue glass decorations on handle and rim. Victoria and Albert Museum, London.

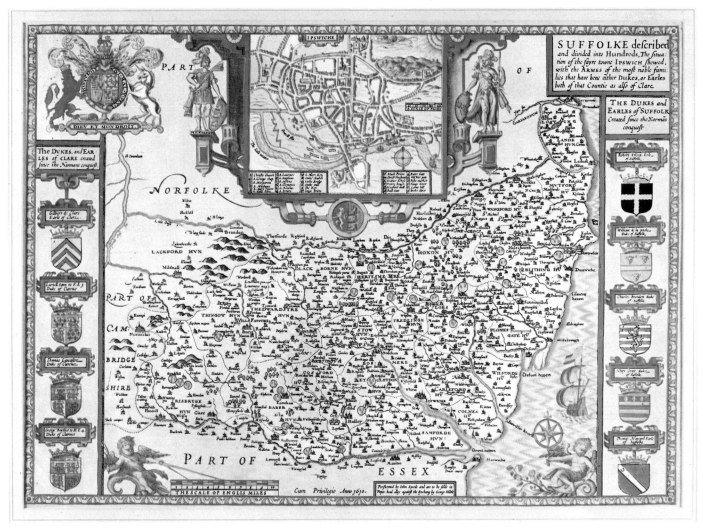

first to manufacture lead glass success-
fully and for this he was allowed to
mark his glass with a raven's head.
After his death in 1681 he was succeeded by Hawley Bishopp, who continued to improve the qualities of lead
glass, and by the end of the century
English glass of lead dominated the
glassmaking industry. In drinking
glasses, especially, English glassmakers
clearly led all others and English drinking glasses of the 17th and 18th centuries were at times miraculous works
of art.

Large numbers of these vessels were
produced in varying qualities and today they are differentiated according
to the style of the stem. From about
1670 or 1680, the so-called first period
drinking glasses appeared. These
evolved with spiralled or moulded
decorations, winged stem and a tapering bowl. This group also includes the
heavy balusters which developed in
goblet or wine glass form. The second
period drinking glass represents the
golden era of English glassmaking –

the arrival of the English glass production of the 18th century.

There is little remarkable about
French glassware of the 17th century.
The few specimens to have survived
appear rather inferior, and it is certainly true that French glassmaking
lagged behind the rest of Europe until
well into the 18th century. The exception, however, lies in the experiments
of Bernard Perrot, whose work in the
area of plate glassmaking has earned
him an important place in the history
of the subject.

By the 17th century, French glassmaking was concentrated at four main
centres, each of which was granted a
patent which took the form of a monopoly. They were the Loire Valley, the
Paris region, Normandy and Brittany.
Two of them were run by Italians and
two by French owners employing
Italians.

It was on the personal recommendation of Cardinal Mazarin that a 30-year
concession was obtained in favour of
the Loire Valley factory. The family

Above:
Map of Suffolk, made by the cartographer
John Speed in 1610.

Opposite above:
Coloured wine bottles of the late 17th and
early 18th centuries.

Opposite below:
A selection of English glasses of the 1680s
and 1690s.

Above:
French *bouquetiers* of clear glass. These were characterized by an uneven brim and a wide mouth, and were supposed to be used for flowers. They remained popular until the early years of the 19th century. Victoria and Albert Museum, London.

which owned this factory was connected with Bernard Perrot, who set up his works at Orleans in 1662. It was here that he discovered a novel method of making mirrors; but soon afterwards the royal commissioners forbade him to continue production and forced him to accept a small pension in return.

The fact that most French glassware came from the hands of Italian craftsmen is an indication of the decline of Venice as the chief glassmaking centre of Europe. Italians wandered all over France and even farther afield and we find records of their enterprise at such widely differing centres as Fontainebleau, Verdun and Marseilles. As early as the beginning of the 1600s Nevers had become famous for the quality of its little glass enamelled figures of men and animals, but the conditions under which the people worked there were so terrible that most of the employees lived extremely short lives. Pendant ear-rings and chains of glass ornaments were credited to Nevers and many members of the nobility owned the wares of Nevers. Among the most interesting pieces surviving from these works are the range of miniatures in glass which can now be seen at the Museum of Cluny.

The first recorded glass workshop in America was opened in 1608 in Virginia, for the production of bottles.

These at first were probably no better in quality than the Waldglas of Europe. The key requirement among the pioneers for glassware was practicality; such things as glass beads were needed as currency for trade with the Indians. It was well known at the time that the Venice glassworks had long been expert at beadwork and it appears in the Virginia Company's records that several of their workmen were brought over from Venice to augment their experience of this work. Little more is heard of the Virginia works after 1621, and in 1625 the well-known Salem factory began production. Bottle- and window-glass production continued there for over 30 years, a considerable mark of success in a country of such recent settlement.

Overall, the impression left of the American glassmaking industry is that it operated in fits and starts until 1739 when the first permanent factory was established, at Salem; before then most of the glass needed by the American colonials was imported.

Clocks and watches
Until about the middle of the 17th century time-keeping was a haphazard affair. The variety of clocks which had come and gone through the previous few centuries mainly kept time by marking the hours: that was the most that could be expected of them. Acsurate time-keeping was in any case hardly required during the Middle Ages. Only the rich could afford this luxury and they invariably looked upon the clock as a quaint trinket.

The pieces themselves were often extremely crude but mechanically complicated, needing frequent repairs and recalibration. When they stopped working it was usually something fairly serious: perhaps the spring would snap, usually carrying off several escapement wheel teeth at the same time. There was also an ever-present risk of dirt seizing up the mechanism.

It was only during the scientific revolution in the 17th century that scholars began to take a more serious interest in horological mechanisms. The revolution caused by the astounding discoveries in astronomy and physics of such scholars as Galileo and Tycho Brahe resulted in part from the great improvements in the basic tools they were using: the telescope and the clock. Time and its measurement became a subject of the greatest interest by the 17th century and in the eyes of scientists the clock was the most excellent expression of this interest. Indeed, it was not long before scientists and clockmakers were closely collaborating to improve the accuracy of the clock.

The result of this merging of science and technology was the pendulum clock, an invention of critical importance at the end of the 16th century. Suddenly a mechanism had arrived which could keep time to within not hours, but minutes and even seconds. An era of low-precision time-keepers had ended and the era of high-precision time instruments had begun.

With the invention of the pendulum also came the need for an improved type of escapement (the means by which control is exercised over the driving force of the clock). Most of the older types of clock worked on the balance-wheel principle and many were actually converted into pendulum clocks. There are many examples of these conversions still around, but care should be taken when considering a purchase. The old crown or escape wheel was usually set horizontally into the clock mechanism. With conversion, these were removed and replaced vertically; this indicates a later or earlier period for the clock than may be suggested by such other details as type of finish or wood used. To make matters even more confusing, several redesigned pendulum clocks can be found with the crown wheel installed horizontally.

The honour of inventing the pendulum clock is generally given to Galileo, although Leonardo da Vinci, whose notebooks contain drawings of what looks like an oscillating pendulum mechanism, must also be given some credit for the idea.

Ideally, the pendulum should swing completely freely of any outside interference, but in practice it comes to rest simply because of air resistance. An impelling force to keep it moving is therefore provided by a heavy weight or spring through the wheels of the clock. The best escapement is the one that allows the pendulum to swing for the greatest period of time, although the verge escapement, the one available at

Above:
English table clock of the 1660s, made by
Samuel Knibb. Worshipful Company of
Clockmakers, Guildhall, London.

Opposite:
Watch made in Geneva in about 1660,
decorated with crystals and enamelling.
British Museum, London.

or other of these mechanisms or a slight
refinement of them.

All the pendulum clocks of the 1650s
and most of the next decade had an
hour hand and a hand, known originally as a second minute hand, to mark
the minutes (this was, rather con-
fusingly, sometimes known as the
second hand). Huygens built a pendulum clock with a hand marking the
seconds, but this was to remain a rarity
for a long time to come.

Basically, the pendulum clock's
time-keeping performance depended
on the length of the pendulum, the
width of the arc through which it
swung and the degree of vibration to
which it reacted. A long pendulum
travelling through a small arc and as
free as possible of outside vibrations
was the best that could be produced at
the time.

Clocks of the 17th century came in a
great variety of types and shapes. There
were table clocks in metal, wood and a
combination of both. With the introduction of the pendulum came a vast
selection of wall clocks and case clocks,
which are found in short, medium-
long and long cases (these last are often
known nowadays as "grandfather
clocks"). This was also the age of the
pediment, turret, lantern and basket
clocks. Their periods ranged from one
hour to thirty hours, and eventually
the eight-day movement came into
common usage. By the end of the century, one-month, three-month and
even one-year period clocks were
coming into fashion, and with them
came increasingly accurate mechanisms, so much so that by this time they
were operating to a one-second accuracy within 24 hours.

A typical English long case clock of
the late 17th century had a walnut
veneer case. Many of these also had an
inlaid marquetry of various woods, the
inlay taking the form of carved fruit,
flowers and foliage. The case itself was
often ornately carved, especially
around the clock face. Intricately
worked columns, with arabesque
spirals and floral patterns were in
evidence.

A number of clocks built at this time
had brass faces, often surmounted with
brass ornamentation. This might appear in the form of colonnades, above
which would be a series of carved

the moment of the pendulum's invention, was possibly the worst imaginable
for this task. The verge escapement involved the use of a whole set of teeth
on a pallet. As soon as the whole pallet
is free of one of the teeth of the crown,
the next pallet engages. This is slow,
cumbersome and extremely complicated.

During the next 100 years a whole
range of modifications were made to
the basic escapement mechanism, two
of the most important being the dead-
beat and the anchor. Most of the clocks
likely to interest collectors contain one

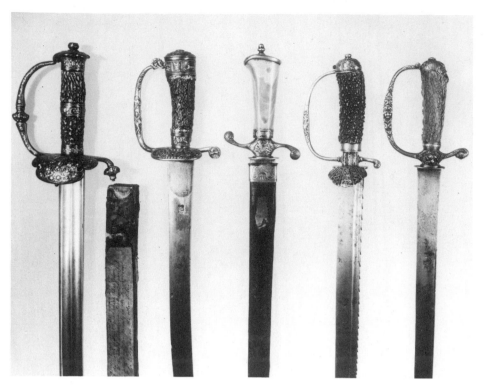

Above:
A selection of 17th-century English swords, designed for hunting.

figures, and capped with a large brass half-sphere.

One rather peculiar clock of this period was an "inclined plane clock". This rested on a sloping wooden ledge and worked by its own weight. As soon as the clock finished its descent, it was lifted off and placed again at the highest point.

The earliest long case clocks came from England and they were made of oak. Later walnut replaced this wood, though for a long time most provincial long cases were of oak. Ebony was used extensively as decoration or veneer for the walnut clocks and several of these have fetched as much as £7,000. Some of the clocks made by Thomas Tompion have gone much higher, one changing hands for no less than £23,000.

Perhaps the most exquisite of all clocks and watches to come down to us from the Baroque Age are those produced by the French craftsmen. For example, there are the very beautiful French ormolu clocks of this period, and of the 18th century. Several of these are ornamented with Sèvres china and have a series of Watteau figures on them, supported by mounts in the form of seated boys.

The French, as with everything else they produced during this luxurious age, expended a great deal of time and effort on perfecting their clocks and watches. Gold, silver, precious jewels and ceramics were used in abundance. Even at the time they were made they commanded high prices.

But the English, too, created some beautiful clocks, although generally these were not so sumptuous in style. There is the renowned bracket clock made in 1685 by Henry Jones, for example. The case is of veneered oak and walnut. The clock itself has a verge escapement and the dial is decorated with cherub spandrels. It even has a calendar aperture.

Metalware
Since the earliest times beaten copper utensils have been made: a long list includes urns, frying pans, kettles and warmers. There is still a great deal of copperware about and when brightly polished it has a charm of its own.

Copperware can often be found side-by-side with brassware and antique shops still hold out the attraction of something fairly valuable turning up now and again in these fields.

Brass has also been produced since time immemorial and has been used in a variety of ways. Horse brasses, firedogs, candlesticks, door-knockers, trays and letter racks can still be found, and they are generally inexpensive when compared with the prices paid for more desirable antiques of the 17th century. Many of the fittings and utensils connected with the fire-place were made of brass and these can still be discovered by the diligent collector. Alewarmers, though less common before the 18th century, are now extremely popular with copper and brass collectors. They often came in the form of asses' heads or slippers.

Perhaps the best hunting-ground still open to the small collector is in kitchen equipment. There is much 17th-century copper, brass and ironware about which can be purchased for as little as a few pounds (though the older it is, the more expensive the article is likely to be). First and foremost to look out for is the large iron or brass (and sometimes copper) cook pots which were used for the cooking of stews and soups. Traditionally known as cauldrons, some of these pots had hooks on them, a reminder of the times when they were hung inside the chimney.

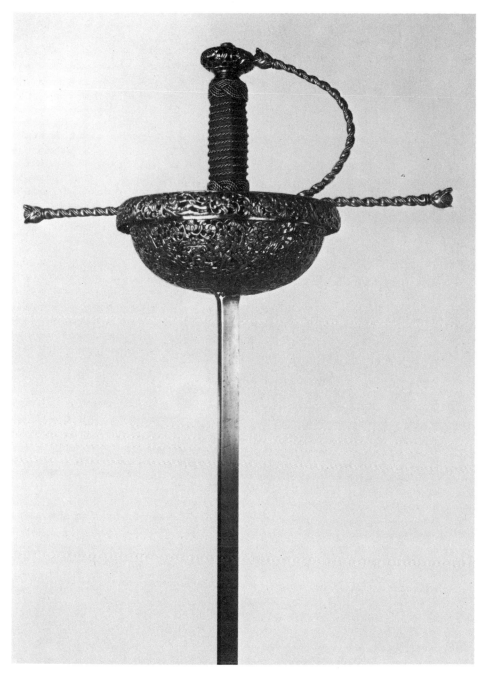

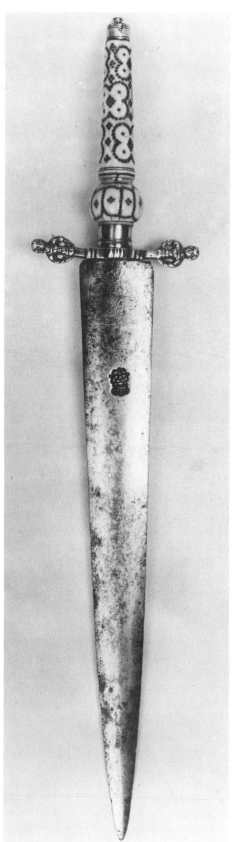

Left:
Italian cup rapier of about 1640; the guard is made of pierced and chiselled steel. Victoria and Albert Museum, London.

Below:
English bayonet dagger made after 1686. Victoria and Albert Museum, London.

It was in the 17th century that basic improvements were made in the method of roasting meats. Until then these had been cooked simply on a spit, which the cook had to keep turning to prevent the meat scorching. In the 17th century a variety of metal jacks came into use. In the larger houses the heat from the fire turned the spit, but most were operated by little treadmills in which a small dog trotted inside a wheel. Several collectors specialize in the acquisition of roasting grid-irons. These were placed on the hot ashes of a recently killed fire and on these was placed the raw meat. Every so often the ashes would be fanned by a bellows.

A vast number of other hearth utensils were coming into use by the beginning of the 17th century, including such implements of cooking as iron and brass trivets to support a cauldron or pot over the fire. In time these grew in size until they came to be termed grates and became fixed additions to the fire-place.

Also extremely common is the great amount of metal mouldware that evolved during the 17th century and onwards. Many thousands of copper cake moulds can still be found in antique shops in and around major cities and towns.

The 18th Century

Introduction

At the beginning of the 18th century
the development of courtly art had
practically ceased. Only in France before 1715, in the last, fading years of the
reign of Louis XIV, did the Baroque
linger on. Versailles, a masterpiece of
theatricality, was the evocation and
embodiment of the power of Louis
XIV. The palace was still not complete
at the beginning of the 18th century,
and his death in 1715 marked the disappearance of the last great performer
of courtly art.

The 18th century witnessed an unprecedented growth in commercial
activities. Trade flourished, industries
grew and banks multiplied. Out of this
commerce emerged the middle classes.
They were both the creators and the
recipients of the new wealth. As the
century progressed so their numbers
multiplied and their importance grew.
Throughout England, France, the Low
Countries and America they flourished.
Not only did they acquire much of the
power and the wealth once reserved for
royal and princely courts but they also
became the artists and the craftsmen,
the writers and journalists. Most signi-
ficantly, they also became the con-
sumers.

The style which emerged at the end
of the 17th century and which was to
flourish during the first half of the next
is known as the Rococo. In many ways
it was the antithesis of the Baroque. It
was not a royal art but one suited to the
aristocracy and the middle classes. It
was not intended to inspire but designed to be lived with. The grand and
heavily marbled interiors of the
Baroque era disappeared and were replaced by more intimate rooms.
Boudoirs, small dining-rooms and re-
poseful drawing-rooms replaced ban-
queting halls, throne rooms and
galleries. The new classes required
houses in which they could live com-
fortably; they did not wish to hold

court. Dark and sombre colours were replaced by lighter ones. The Baroque had been ostentatious, its proportions huge, its effect magnificent. The Rococo by comparison was playful and capricious, diminutive, delicate and nervous. It arose first in France, but was also suited to the needs and tastes of other countries and quickly spread throughout Europe: nor was it long in establishing itself in America. Although for fifty years it was happily accepted outside its country of origin, it never reached those heights of ornamention which are the hallmark of the French Rococo.

By 1750 the Rococo was on the wane. In its place appeared a more refined and classical style. Though suited to the middle classes, the Rococo had been initially an aristocratic style; in its purest form it had reflected the tastes of people dedicated to pleasure.

It has always been associated with the name of Madame de Pompadour, the mistress of Louis XV, and in its wildest form it suggests to us an image of a society haunted by the unreasonableness of its own desires. Across the Channel from France lay a society more rational, more moderate and more disciplined. The break with the Rococo was in a way a reflection of a new morality. For the English, the ostentation of the Baroque and the frivolity of the Rococo was misplaced. Those styles, the dreams of kings, lay in the past, made bereft by the strictures of commerce. Under the auspices of the architect and designer Robert Adam a new classical style emerged. The essential characteristic of this style, known as the Neoclassical, was its simplicity. Its forms were clear and uncomplicated, uncluttered by superfluous ornament. In reaction to the

Above:
A pair of walnut chairs, made in the early 18th century. Arms of this shape are called shepherd's crooks.

Above:
English walnut armchair of the early 18th century.

Above right:
English folding card-table with cabriole legs and a walnut veneer, of about 1720.

Rococo it was consciously restrained and eminently suitable for a society dedicated to work and order. Though the style originated in England it spread, like the Rococo, throughout Europe and left its mark in America. With the crisis of puritanism caused by the French Revolution, the Neoclassical style found its most sympathetic patron; it reached its purest form in France in the early 19th century.

The 18th century, dominated by these two distinct styles, presents an attractive prospect for the antique collector: attractive both aesthetically and practically. The middle class, which became in that century the upholders of taste and fashion, constituted a huge number of patrons. Artists, architects and craftsmen no longer had to rally round a single royal patron or a small clique of aristocrats. There was a large and prosperous population which wanted houses, furniture, paintings and ornaments. It was numerous enough to guarantee a large sale of articles. This means that for the collector there are more antiques of the 18th

century than of previous centuries. More furniture survives and there is an abundancy of silver, glass and porcelain. They are easier to come by and they are cheaper than for earlier centuries. The wide range of antiques is another attraction. The 17th century had filled its interiors with chairs, tables, beds and consoles; the 18th century, however, witnessed a flood of new items. This is particularly true in the field of furniture; writing-tables, book-rests, dressing-tables, tables for playing backgammon, tables for playing cards and chess, occasional tables, stools, desks, screens and much more. Clocks and watches, once regarded as complex and inessential, became important pieces of equipment for the household and the private person.

The 18th century may not offer the collector the scope of the next, but it does offer him far more than the preceding ones. Of course many of the antiques are expensive. These must be left for the museums or the very rich. There is much, however, that any collector can buy and call his own.

English furniture

The 18th century is often considered the finest period of English cabinet-making and certainly the techniques and designs were copied throughout Europe and America. In the second half of the century, chairs of the Chippendale style could be found as far afield as Philadelphia, Lisbon and Venice, and by the end of the century the styles of Hepplewhite and Sheraton had spread farther still. Indeed, the demand for furniture made cabinet-making a prosperous business. This is reflected in the sizes of the establishments: records show that these shops employed journeymen, chairmakers and cabinetmakers, upholsterers, carvers and smiths. By the middle of the century designers and draftsmen had been added to the pay-rolls.

The first style of 18th-century English furniture is referred to as "Queen Anne". It is also sometimes known as the Age of Walnut. This was the most commonly used wood and was particularly suitable for veneering. Oak, which had been so popular during the previous century, almost disappeared. It was still used for dining tables, however, probably because it was better able to withstand heat. A characteristic feature of the Queen Anne style was the graceful curve; the straight lines of the William and Mary style were abandoned. The complex carving of the later decades was barely in evidence during this period, and the style, though well-proportioned, was simple and relied for its decoration on the exquisite patterning of the walnut wood itself.

A distinctive feature which was introduced during the Queen Anne period was the cabriole leg. The name is taken from a French ballet term and the leg resembles the foot, calf and knee of a ballet dancer. It was usually terminated with a club or a claw-and-ball foot, while the knee was often carved with an acanthus leaf or shell; both popular motifs during the period. It was essentially a pleasing design, but it had the added advantage of being able to support a prodigious weight. Chairs were thus able to abandon the stretchers of earlier eras. The graceful curve of the leg was reflected in the hooped back, and a central splat replaced the cane-work of earlier chair backs. The central

splat itself was carved to fit the shape of the human back and further comfort was afforded by a cushion dropped into the seat. The earlier practice of heavily stuffing the entire seat was abandoned. The cabriole was introduced into practically every piece of furniture which required a leg; tables, chairs, chests and the stands for cabinets.

The early Georgian style which followed did not eclipse the Queen Anne style: in many ways it was a continuation of it. In 1720, however, there was an occurrence that was to have a profound effect on the development of English cabinetmaking. In 1709 there had been a severe winter in France which had led to an acute shortage of walnut. In 1720 the French finally banned its export. The English, who had been reliant on French supplies, were now forced to turn elsewhere. Walnut was available from Virginia

English tallboy or chest-on-chest with walnut veneer; 1740.

Above:
Early 18th-century English mahogany settee in the style of William Kent. It was made in about 1735. Temple Newsam House.

Left:
English carved mahogany bookcase, made in about 1735.

Opposite:
English walnut chest of drawers, made in about 1725, with a sliding panel above the top drawer.

after an Act of Parliament was passed in 1721 which stopped the tax on imported woods. American wood became cheaper and immediately more accessible. Furthermore, if walnut had to be imported from America there was no reason why mahogany too should not be shipped from the West Indies, where it grew in plentiful supplies. This had been impractical when woods had been readily available from Europe. Mahogany is hard and durable and ideally suited to intricate carving; it was not long before it became the primary species used by cabinetmakers. The immediate impact, however, was negligible. In 1721 mahogany imports to England amounted to a mere £276. In 1750, however, £30,000 was spent on this wood and in 1800 the total had reached £80,000. The most commonly used, and the only species with a reddish tinge, was that imported from Honduras, but mahogany was also imported from Jamaica and Cuba.

Perhaps the best known designer of the 1730s was William Kent. Mention must be made of him not so much because of his furniture designs themselves but because he designed furniture in relation to the proportions and the decoration of his interiors. He was the designer of both the house and its

contents. This system was later adopted by Robert Adam. Kent's furniture was intended for the large Palladian houses which he designed. The furniture was heavy, without an inkling of Rococo, excessively carved and gilded, and ponderous to the extent that it could live only in the grand settings for which it was designed.

His style was not that of his contemporary cabinetmakers. They carried on in a manner that remained essentially loyal to the Queen Anne style. The main differences were the elaboration of ornament and the acquisition of more solid proportions. The first change was caused largely by the introduction of mahogany. Because of its plain and austere grain this wood was not ideal for veneers, and so decoration was achieved primarily through carving. A feature of larger early Georgian furniture was its architectural character. Pediments, pilasters and capitals were employed in the decorations and were derived from the styles of architecture. This was the period, after all, when every young Englishman made the Grand Tour and returned home with the avowed intention of contriving some Italianate paradise on his gentler and greener lands.

After 1735 French influence was more apparent and the delicate Rococo forms became predominant. French motifs such as the *cabochon* (a domed oval design taken from jewellery) and leaf and ribbon appeared. The solid splats on the backs of chairs were pierced; tracery, scrolls and strapwork

were introduced. By 1750 half the furniture being produced in England was constructed of mahogany and the French Rococo was winning popularity. The stage was set for the most triumphant period of English cabinet-making.

The Rococo was transformed into a distinctly English style by Thomas Chippendale. He was born in Otley, Yorkshire, in 1718, the son of a joiner and the grandson of a carpenter. In 1748 he moved to London and in 1753 he set up his cabinetmaker's shop in St Martin's Lane. In 1754 he published a pattern book, *The Gentleman and Cabinet-Maker's Director*, a catalogue of the latest furniture fashions, illustrated with 160 plates. It was reprinted in 1755 and again in 1762, and became the textbook on which many other cabinetmakers based their designs.

Though the inspiration was certainly Chippendale's, the drawings were executed, and one suspects some of them actually designed, by two commercial artists, Matthias Lock and H. Copland. With the *Director* Chippendale became a legend, even in his own time. Only a few pieces of furniture are known actually to have come from his workshop, and his reputation has obscured the skill of many of his contemporaries. Most notable among these were William Vile and John Cobb, both of whom were patronized by the Crown. Such an opportunity never fell into the hands of Chippendale. He was by no means the greatest craftsman of his day but he surpassed others in the art of self-

advertisement. His name is now used to describe the furniture styles of the mid-18th century.

The style set out in the *Director* was the English transposition of the French Rococo. Together with this were some designs of Gothic and Chinese origin – Chippendale was sharp enough to exploit passing fancies–and these blended sweetly with the predominant Rococo style.

For the most part the Chippendale chair abandoned the cabriole leg. Straight legs and stretchers returned. The backs were given a pierced and interlaced central splat which often incorporated carved scrollwork. The uprights, on either side of the splat, curved gently up and out and were often joined at the top by a "Cupid's Bow". Though this style owed much to the Rococo, it could not easily have been created without the steely mahogany, the hardness of which facilitated such intricate carving. Upholstered chairs, on the other hand, were copied largely from the French and were adorned with cabriole legs, carved scrollwork and arm supports. That French taste played such a significant part in English furniture design at this time can be judged by the fact that Chippendale actually imported French chair frames and completed them in his own shop.

It would be mistaken to imagine that all Chippendale's furniture designs were for carved mahogany. Some he finished with lacquering, gilding or painting. It seems that he considered

Above:
Designs for "Ribband back chairs" from Thomas Chippendale's book *The Gentleman and Cabinet-Maker's Director* (1754).

Right:
English mahogany chair, after Chippendale and made in about 1760.

Opposite left:
English carved mahogany wall fitting, intended to support a candle or lamp, and made in about 1740. Lady Lever Art Gallery.

Opposite right:
English mahogany writing desk of about 1759, showing the typical cupboard located in the kneehole.

gilding suitable for the drawing-room, mahogany for the dining-room and the library, and lacquering for the bedroom. Further decoration appeared at about this time with the revival of marquetry, also heavily influenced by French taste. Particularly popular were floral designs worked in such exotic woods as satinwood.

Before passing on to the next stage in English cabinetmaking, mention should be made of other cabinetmakers and their pattern books. Chippendale's *Director* caused an epidemic of them. In 1759 Ince and Mahew published *The*

Universal System of Household Furniture, and in 1765 Robert Manwaring produced his rather more specialized book, *The Cabinet and Chair Maker's Real Friend and Companion*. These were only two of many.

In 1773 a much more significant and influential work was published. It was entitled *Works in Architecture* and was a series of folio engravings by Robert and James Adam. It included, as well as architectural drawings, many illustrations of furniture and was to play a crucial role in the spread of their style through England and Europe. In 1754

Robert Adam had studied the newly discovered ruins at Herculaneum near Naples and he was later to derive many of his decorative motifs from ancient Greece and Rome. In his interior designs he planned his rooms down to the last detail. Carpets matched ceiling decorations and furniture, fireplaces and fabrics were all carefully integrated. Fine examples of his work can be seen in Kenwood House and Osterley Park, both near London. His designs, however, were enormously expensive and far beyond the means of the middle classes. None the less,

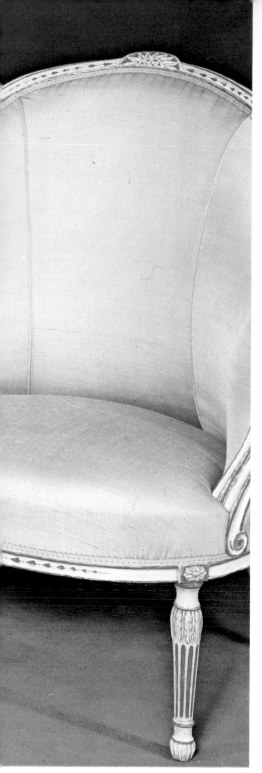

Left:
A pair of chairs designed by Robert Adam in the late 1770s, influenced by the Louis XVI style.

Above:
English chair designed by Robert Adam in about 1760, and incorporating Gothic motifs. Alnwick Castle, Northumberland.

Below:
Bedroom at Nostell Priory, Yorkshire. The Chinese wallpaper was hung by Thomas Chippendale in 1769.

though his work may not have been copied in detail, its influence was huge.

His style was the basis of the Neo-classical movement and it led to the abandonment of the Rococo. It was an essentially rectilinear style; clean straight lines and perfect proportions replaced the sweeping curves and asymmetrical designs of the previous decades. The furniture was light in form and the delicacy of some pieces gave them a distinctly fragile appearance. Though mahogany was still the most commonly used wood there was a greater influx of lighter toned woods,

was now almost totally replaced by veneering. Much of the late 18th-century cabinet-work owes its beauty to the exquisite selections and arrangements of different veneers.

The impact of Robert Adam's classicism can be grasped by looking at *The Cabinet Maker and Upholsterer's Guide*, published in 1788. The designer involved was George Hepplewhite. He died in 1786 and the book was published by his widow, Alice. No style other than the classical appears in it. This particular brand of Adam's style had emerged in about 1775 and lasted for some years after Hepplewhite's death. To refer to it as his style, however, is in a sense misleading for he made little attempt to be original. At the beginning of the *Guide* we find the words, "We designedly followed the latest or most prevailing fashion". So with Hepplewhite as with Chippendale the name is expressive of a prevailing style rather than of the furniture actually made in his shop.

Hepplewhite remained loyal to the Adam style; indeed it is known that Adam commissioned furniture from Hepplewhite knowing well that it would blend with his own designs. Hepplewhite's real achievement was to make Adam's Neoclassical style available to a wider public. Although he simplified the other's designs, he retained the straight and tapered legs; he employed the heart and shield shape in the backs of his chairs, and classical motifs for ornamentation. Perhaps his only original contribution lay in his introduction of the Prince of Wales' feathers as a decorative motif. His distinctly elegant and delicate style, however, was as prey to the fickleness of fashion as earlier ones.

By 1790 the style of Hepplewhite was already on the decline. Its father style, Neoclassicism, was entering another stage. In furniture, the leading light of the last decade of the 18th century was Thomas Sheraton. Though he had been a journeyman cabinetmaker in his early years, he had spent most of his life as a drawing teacher and gathered his knowledge of furniture through numerous visits to the shops. Between 1791 and 1794 he published, in four parts, *The Cabinet-Maker and Upholsterer's Drawing-Book*. As with his predecessors, his name is used to

notably satinwood and harewood. Adam's delight in satinwood must have been instrumental in its almost universal adoption by cabinetmakers. Its colour varies from pale yellow to a dark orange and it is ideally suited to veneering. It was often used in conjunction with other exotic woods: tulipwood, kingwood, ebony and rosewood, to mention just a few. As a result, carving, which was the chief ingredient of Chippendale furniture

Above:
English candlestand, carved and decorated with gilt, of about 1760.

Above right:
The saloon at Nostell Priory, Yorkshire, designed by Robert Adam in 1772.

designate a general style. He was not, after all, even a cabinetmaker and the furniture which bears his name was constructed by his contemporary cabinetmakers. Throughout the British Isles his book had some 700 subscribers and, as with earlier pattern books, it also made its way to America.

His style abandoned many of the curved lines which Hepplewhite had used and created an even greater emphasis on straight lines. In chair designs he returned to the square back and placed stress on all the vertical elements.

This he often achieved through the use of reeding and fluting. If Adam's and Hepplewhite's designs look fragile, Sheraton's furniture seems too insubstantial to bear even the lightest of loads.

Sheraton's style covered the last decade of the 18th century. The French Revolution and the chaotic sequence of styles which came in its wake forms the story of the following chapter.

French furniture
The French styles of the 18th century

Opposite:
Late 18th-century English sideboard in the style of Hepplewhite.

Left:
English Pembroke table made in the manner of Adam in about 1790. Pembroke tables were usually round or oval, with two hinged leaves.

Below left:
English side-table designed by Robert Adam in 1779. Drummonds Branch, Royal Bank of Scotland.

take their names, not from the cabinet-makers, but from the reigning kings or government bodies. The development of furniture during this period can be divided into four phases: the Régence, Louis XV, Louis XVI, and the Directoire. The Régence, as an institution, began in 1715 on the death of Louis XIV. In that year Philippe d'Orleans was appointed Regent and he retained that position until the majority of Louis XV in 1723.

The furniture style which is classified as Régence cannot be pinpointed so specifically. In many ways it was a transitional style. Spanning the years 1700 to 1720, it bridged the gap between the Baroque and the Rococo. While it incorporated some of the characteristics of the previous period, it also introduced many of the features which were to become the hallmarks of the following style – the Rococo. A typical example is the cabriole leg. During the reign of Louis XIV it had made a shy appearance, but during the Régence it became obligatory. The massive, sombre furniture associated with the Baroque began to acquire the

gracefulness and suppleness that we now connect with the Rococo. Curves gently modified the older rectilinear forms, and ornamentation multiplied. Classical and mythological ornament was discarded in favour of more natural forms. The shell motif was elaborated; flowers and garlands were employed while bronze figures appeared on the tops of the cabriole legs of bureaux and tables.

A central figure of the Régence was Charles Cressent. He was the foremost cabinetmaker of his day and was in addition a sculptor and a bronze worker. His art reached its peak in the production of commodes; these pieces of furniture were a speciality of the period and usually consisted of wooden chests mounted on sculptured bronze legs. Not only did Cressent construct the cabinetwork but he designed and built the bronze mounts. He discarded ebony, a wood which had been particularly popular at the end of the 17th century, and replaced it with lighter woods. These were better suited to veneering and more sympathetic to his dazzling bronzework. The most popular woods during this period were amaranth and rosewood. Both contained purplish tinges and varied from light to darker tones. With the introduction of these woods cabinetwork became more colourful, a relief after the sombre days of black ebony. Lightness of colour and lightness of design, which were to become the characteristic traits of the Rococo, thus established themselves during the Régence.

The reign of Louis XV may have been politically disastrous for France but it witnessed the finest years of French cabinetmaking. During those years the craft reached its highest standard of perfection. In 1760 Jean-François Oeben was commissioned to make the *Bureau du Roi*, which was completed nine years later, after his death, by his pupil Jean-Henri Riesener. In the arts of veneering, marquetry and bronze work this bureau must rank as one of the finest pieces of craftsmanship of all time.

By its date of completion, however, the Rococo had passed its zenith and was giving way to the demands of the classical world. The style associated with the reign of Louis XV reached its finest moment in the years between 1740 and 1760. In terms of grace and elegance, lightness and charm, it could not have been bettered. All the designs for furniture were characterized by complex mixtures of curves, the profusion of ornament and asymmetrical patterns; surfaces were remorselessly covered with floral marquetry, mirrors and porcelain plaques, and marble, onyx and alabaster were used on the tops of commodes and tables. Lacquering came into vogue and a large quantity of woodwork was actually sent to the Orient to be decorated. As this fashion for lacquering grew, so French craftsmen took up the trade; most notable of these were the Martin brothers. Applied metal ornament was also prolific and it is not surprising to learn that the cabinetmakers Juste-Aurèle Meissonier and Jacques Caffieri were both trained as metal workers before they turned to woodwork. Meissonier wrote a book on the subject of metal ornament, entitled *Le Livre d'Ornements*.

A reaction against such a profusion

of ornament and curves was inevitable. As in England, it appeared in the form of Neoclassicism. The reign of Louis XVI (1774–92) is associated with the classical revival but it must be noted that the style, referred to as *à la Greque* or *à l'antique*, made its appearance as early as 1760.

It was in ornamentation, paradoxically, that the classical influence first made itself felt. Greco-Roman motifs began to mingle with French floral decorations; fluting, pilasters, capitals, Greek palm leaves, symmetrical wreaths and garlands. After these were introduced there came a change in the actual contours of the furniture. The traditions of classical architecture found their way into 18th-century furniture. This desire for structures and supports to be evident could only mean the demise of the Rococo. Its glorious curves and the abundance of ornament all too easily disguised the structural integrity of the furniture.

When the transition was complete, rectilinear forms had taken control. The only remaining curves were to be found in the controlled forms of the circle and oval. Gone forever were the sinuous curves of the preceding decades. When Louis XVI ascended the throne the new style had taken firm control and it was to remain predominant until the Revolution in 1789.

The cabinetmaker's search for beauty now lay in the perfection of proportions. The harmonious division of the parts, the use of symmetry and the severity of the outlines were the hallmarks of the Louis XVI style. Mahogany was the most widely used wood but instead of being sumptuously carved, plain panels with delicate borders were often the only concession to decoration.

The finest craftsman of this period was undoubtedly Jean-Henri Riesener. Though it was he who completed that masterpiece of the Rococo, the *Bureau du Roi*, he later assimilated the new style and became its greatest exponent. Other important *ébénistes*, or cabinetmakers, were Martin Carlin, Nicolas Petit, René Dubois and David Roentgen. We know more about the work of these specific craftsmen than we do of their English contemporaries, since the strong guild system obliged them to stamp their names on their work. This legislation ensured a high standard of workmanship, for those pieces that did not pass the standards set by the guilds were confiscated and sold for the benefit of the guild.

The period of the Revolution, between 1789 and 1795, was chaotic for furniture producers, as for so many others. The Directoire, the government which lent its name to the prevailing furniture style, lasted from 1795 to 1799. Like the Régence, the Directoire was a transitional style, which bridged the gap between the Louis XVI and the Empire styles.

Much of the furniture of the period was designed in the tradition of the previous style but what marked it apart was the added angularity and severity. Also apparent was the intensified interest in the Antique. No longer content to recreate the spirit of ancient Greece and Rome, the cabinetmakers actually made faithful copies of the ancient originals. Tables, couches, marble thrones, vases and smaller ornaments were scrupulously studied and copied.

Opposite:
English oval breakfast table. A variety of small tables became popular towards the end of the 18th century.

During this short period much of the ornamentation consisted simply of symbols of the Revolution. The Phrygian cap, the tricolour cockade of the Republic, clasped hands symbolizing fraternity, and other symbols all appeared on furniture and fabrics. For a short period furniture acquired a remarkable clarity of design and a purity of line which was to disappear with the advent of the Empire style at the beginning of the next century.

American furniture

The majority of settlers in America in the early part of the 18th century were English. Although some came from France, Germany and the Low Countries, the sheer numbers of English ensured that their culture overrode all others. For this reason the colonies inherited English styles in architecture, furniture and the decorative arts. Very little furniture was actually imported; the expense of such a practice was prohibitive. Craftsmen brought their native traditions to the new country and it is interesting to note that colonial newspapers carried the advertisements of newly arrived cabinetmakers, conversant in the latest European fashions. Many pattern books arrived in America shortly after their publication in England. Most notable among these was Chippendale's *Gentleman and Cabinet-Maker's Director*, which appeared there in 1762.

With the accumulation of wealth up and down the eastern seaboard there was an accompanying desire to acquire elegant furniture. It seems that the puritan outlook of the original settlers was capable of modification. The furniture styles that resulted can be divided into approximately the same categories as the English: William and Mary, Queen Anne, and Chippendale before the Revolution, and Hepplewhite and Sheraton after the Federal government was established in 1789. The Declaration of Independence in 1776 and the subsequent upheavals had brought much of the fashionable cabinet-making to a halt and it is not surprising that the Adam style almost passed

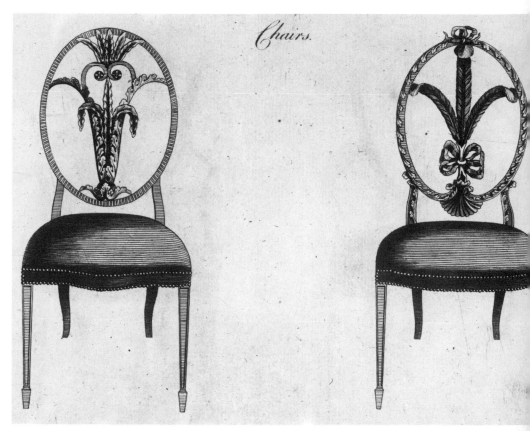

Chairs.

Top:
Designs for oval-backed chairs, engraved by George Hepplewhite.

Above:
Designs for drawing-room chairs, engraved by Thomas Sheraton.

Left:
English mahogany sideboard, in the style of Sheraton, c.1790.

Below:
English mahogany dining table of about 1800, with pillar-and-claw style legs.

Opposite:
French commode in the Rococo manner of the Louis XV period. Wallace Collection, London.

America by. When normal relations between England and the United States were resumed, some 15 years later, the Hepplewhite style was in favour in England and the Americans made an abrupt change from the Chippendale to the prevailing English fashion. It remained in vogue until 1800. Even despite the arrival of the classical style, Chippendale designs retained some hold in the United States until the end of the century.

Bearing in mind that the American cabinetmakers kept close to the English styles there is little point in making a survey of the general development of American furniture. The essential characteristics have already been outlined. There were, however, developments that did not correspond to those in England and these we shall mention.

Two chairs introduced into America at the beginning of the 18th century were the tall slat-back chair and the banister chair. Both had made their appearance in England at the end of the Jacobean era. The first was designed as an armchair or a sidechair and consisted of turned uprights which were joined by perhaps four, five, or six horizontal splats. It had usually a rush seat and was most commonly made of maple. The banister chair differed only in the back. The two side uprights were joined at top and bottom by turned rails and these were connected by turned, vertical banisters (the term banister was a corruption of the English word baluster). The development of open-back chairs otherwise followed closely upon English patterns. The Queen Anne style was loyally retained until the 1760s, when the Chippendale style came into vogue. From then on there were few deviations from the English evolution.

A contribution from settlers other than the English was in the form of the kas. It originated in Holland and the word comes from the Dutch word kast which literally means large cupboard. Although not a beautiful piece of furniture it was none the less useful. It provided a large storage space but at the same time was easily dismantled and moved. Its attraction, however, lay in its panel paintings. The fronts and often the sides were painted with fruits, flowers and birds, often in trompe l'oeil style. It became a standard piece of American furniture and was produced throughout the 18th and 19th centuries.

A very distinctive piece of American furniture of this period was the highboy. It was introduced in about 1700 and retained its popularity throughout the century. This was a chest of drawers mounted on a stand which was itself often fitted with drawers. The top section usually consisted of a row of two or three small drawers over three

or four long ones. The lower section had only two rows of drawers, which were variously arranged. The stand itself was supported on cabriole legs while the top was terminated with a broken pediment.

By the middle of the century Philadelphia had become the undisputed centre of cabinetmaking. The town was prosperous and expanding rapidly – by the time of the Revolution it had a population of some 35,000 – and it was there that the finest examples of American cabinetwork were made. The term "Philadelphia style highboy" is given to those highboys made there between 1760 and 1775. The predominant feature was the broken pediment consisting of scrolled swans' necks. On the base was a richly carved recessed shell and the supporting cabriole legs were festooned with acanthus leaves. The most notable cabinetmaker in Philadelphia during the period was Thomas Affleck. Born in Scotland, he arrived in America in 1763 and became the leading designer of the Chippendale style there. Though he was banished from Philadelphia for his royalist sympathies, he was able to

return in 1783 and continued his business on Second Street.

Fine furniture was not restricted to Philadelphia. Highboys were also made in Newport and, although their decoration was more restrained and their cabriole legs slimmer, they achieved as high a standard of craftsmanship as their counterparts from Philadelphia. In Newport two cabinetmakers, John Goddard and John Townsend, developed another distinctive piece of American furniture, the block-front. In this design, applied to chests of drawers, desks and dressing-tables, the front of each drawer was cut in such a way that the ends of the drawers were raised while the centre was depressed. The block-front was usually cut from a single piece of mahogany and apart from the special feature itself the furniture followed prevailing styles. Practically all of these articles were made in New England, and the finest came from the workshop of Goddard and Townsend. Another major feature on them was the shell motif. Their carving corresponded with the contours of the furniture so that the shells on the ends were

Above:
English workbox on a stand, after Sheraton. Temple Newsam House.

Right:
French secretaire, finely inlaid and in the style of Louis XV. Private collection.

Opposite:
English desk and bookcase of 1795, after Sheraton. Victoria and Albert Museum, London.

raised while the central one was depressed.

A further peculiarity of the Chippendale period was the *bombé* or kettle-shaped base. This design appeared on chests of drawers and secretaries and was a development which occurred only in Boston. It is associated particularly with the workshop of John Cogswell. As with Newport and Philadelphia, Boston was an important trading centre but even so it is surprising that before the Revolution its population of 14,000 was able to support no fewer than 150 cabinetmakers, chairmakers and carvers.

The pre-eminent cabinetmaker in Boston at the end of the century was Duncan Phyfe. His early furniture was closely modelled on that of Hepplewhite and Sheraton but he soon succumbed to the influence of the French Directoire and Empire styles and his work really belongs to the following century.

Provincial furniture

The furniture which has been described so far was made for the fashionable classes. It originated in London, Paris and the larger American cities and even in its own day was expensive. Today the finest pieces are either in museums or arrive on the markets with price tags which place them beyond the buying power of most antique collectors. A set of six Chippendale dining-chairs or a Queen Anne walnut bureau can cost as much as an expensive car. Nevertheless, a collector who is interested in the 18th century should not lose heart. Reasonably priced furniture does exist; it simply is not the best. To begin with, the collector should confine himself to the smaller pieces; stools, corner cupboards, dining-chairs, upholstered chairs, dressing tables, small tripod tables and games tables. That is by no means an inconsiderable or restrictive list. He will also find it less expensive to confine himself to provincial furniture. The works of country craftsmen and provincial cabinetworkers are considerably cheaper than the more fashionable works which were produced by Chippendale or Riesener.

A familiarity with the best furniture and a knowledge of its development is essential. As a start, it is good to aim at

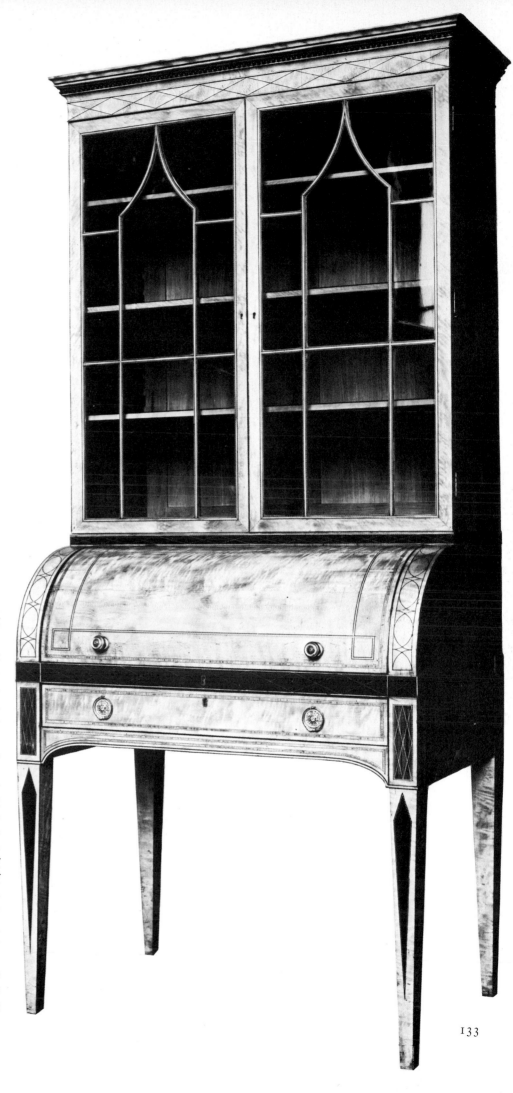

the best, as it is from there that many of the features of more modest furniture were derived. A working knowledge of the main-stream developments gives the collector a guide-line and a better ability to scrutinize the humbler pieces which come his way. Before looking more closely at provincial furniture there is a general point which must be mentioned. The furniture which was made in the capital cities and larger towns can be dated quite easily because it was made to conform to the latest fashions and was constructed with the latest refinements in skill. Furniture made in the country, however, can be much more difficult to date. Fashions in style radiated slowly from the cities and many of the skills of the local craftsmen were handed down from one generation to another. It is therefore possible, and even likely, that a provincial chest which appears to be Jacobean is in fact of the 18th century. For many pieces of furniture the systems of construction and the decorative styles remained unchanged from one century to another. In the same way it is possible that a piece which has all the features of the 18th century is of the following century. Provincial craftsmen were often quite as slow in discarding a style as they were in adopting a new one.

Most books on English antiques deal almost exclusively with the first-rate furniture designed for the rich and constructed in London. Some make a small concession to country furniture by making brief mention of it. This betrays a rather simplistic view of the development of furniture, and is certainly misleading for the small collector who cannot afford the finer pieces. Outside London in the 18th century

Above:
Comb-back Windsor chair, probably made in Pennsylvania.

Left:
French *chiffonier*, made in the Louis XV style in about 1763; attributed to either Oeben or Riesener. Louvre, Paris.

Opposite:
An upholstered wing chair with cabriole legs, made in America in the early 18th century.

136

there were two strands of development. One followed closely upon the London styles and was comparable in both looks and construction. This style can be seen clearly, for instance, in the chairs which were made for the Assembly Rooms in York by local craftsmen. In deeper rural areas, however, London fashions were not so readily adopted. Country craftsmen made brave attempts to emulate the walnut and mahogany styles and such features as cabriole legs, though somewhat wanting in poise and balance, became regular features in much oak furniture. When the classical style was introduced they did not fail to take account of the change and many introduced tapering legs, fluting and beading. In very isolated areas of the country, though, little or no impact was made and there Jacobean or even earlier styles survived throughout the century.

A fundamental difference between country furniture and fashionable town furniture lay in the different woods which were used. Outside London only a very few cabinetmakers adopted walnut and mahogany. Nearly all country craftsmen remained faithful to oak. Not only was oak indigenous and consequently cheaper to transport, but it

was also sturdier than walnut and many other exotic woods. Its major disadvantage was that it was not easy to carve. Hard and brittle, it was not sympathetic to the prevailing curvilinear style. Other local woods were used for this, particularly elm and beech, and also yew and fruitwoods. Further characteristics of the country furniture which set it apart from the mainstream developments were the use of the traditional peg construction instead of dovetailing, the employment of turning rather than carving, rush and plank seats and the widespread use of painting for decoration.

The most famous piece of country furniture to develop completely independently of the London cabinetmakers was the Windsor chair. It came into being at the end of the 17th century and it is not known how it acquired its name. Windsor chairs were made of various local woods. Elm was usually used in the construction of the seat and beech for the legs, stretchers and upright spindles. Ash or yew were better suited to the bent members. The earliest type was the comb-back; this took its name from the horizontal toprail into which the vertical spindles were inserted. After 1750 the hoop-

Above:
Louis XV commode, with typical asymmetrical Rococo ormolu scrolls for decoration.

Opposite above:
French settee, stamped with the name of Jean Nadal and made in about 1760. Rijksmuseum, Amsterdam.

Opposite below:
French *duchesse brise*: an armchair which could be used as a sofa. It was made in about 1760. Musée Nissim de Camondo, Paris.

Right:
American block-fronted tallboy or chest-on-chest, made in about 1755, in Newport, Rhode Island. H. F. duPont Winterthur Museum, Delaware.

Opposite above:
French bed of the early 1790s, made of steel and bronze gilt. Musée Nissim de Camondo, Paris.

Opposite below:
Worktable made for Marie-Antionette by Riesener in about 1788. Musée Nissim de Camondo, Paris.

back came into common use; here the spindles were often replaced by pierced back-splats, the chair's one concession to Chippendale. Decoration was otherwise limited to turning and the simple carving of the arm supports. The Windsor chair appeared in America in the early part of the 18th century and gained immense popularity there.

Aspiring collectors of country furniture of this period should be warned that quite as many reproductions of these pieces exist as of the more fashionable wares. Partly as a result of the Arts and Crafts movement in the 19th century, an enormous quantity of cottage-style furniture was mass-produced at that time and in the early decades of the 20th century. The pieces have swamped both homes and antique shops and the collector should buy warily.

The French styles described earlier were even more of the metropolis than the corresponding English ones. The four main periods relate almost exclusively to Parisian furniture, most of which is simply too expensive for the small collector. French country furniture is usually referred to as provincial and the degree to which it was influenced by the Paris fashions depended on the proximity of a certain province to the capital and its degree of affluence.

The Louis XIV style was not adopted beyond the courts. Its sumptuousness was quite unsuited to country needs. The Rococo of Louis XV was, as we have seen, far more adaptable and was consequently adopted to differing degrees by all classes in all the provinces. Its popularity in some areas was so great that it lasted well into the 19th century. Naturally, it did not acquire

all the brilliance of Parisian cabinet-work but it nevertheless adopted the characteristic Rococo curves and the asymmetrical mouldings and ornament. When the Louis XVI style prevailed in Paris the country cabinet-workers continued in the Rococo traditions and made very few concessions to the classical idiom. Some classical ornament appeared while the curves were a little modified. It was only in the larger towns close to Paris that the classical style really took a firm root.

Most provincial French furniture was sturdily built and simple in both general form and decoration. Its comparative simplicity does not, however, detract from its essential good quality and great beauty. Most was made of local woods; oak, elm, beech, walnut and fruitwood. The availability of particular woods differed from province to province and contributed to regional differences in style. Oak, for instance, was plentiful in Normandy while walnut trees were more prolific in central and southern France. Mahogany was used only rarely and there was little use made of veneering and marquetry; solid wood was preferred. In the 18th century the range of furniture grew more extensive as new wealth created new demands and cabinet-making flourished. A bed, a stool, a table and a cupboard were no longer sufficient, as they had been in the previous century. Commodes, tall-clock cases, occasional tables and even secretaires became common articles in French provincial households.

Based though it was upon the Rococo, this furniture nevertheless acquired regional characteristics. These were dependent on climate, native traditions and plain economics. Beds, for instance, were more or less covered-in according to climate. Those made in Provence, in the south, were quite open. Others, designed to keep their occupants warm in the cold winters of northern or mountainous areas, were entirely enclosed, a room within a room. The development of regional characteristics is a vast subject and beyond the scope of this book. French provincial furniture offers a rich field for the collector because of its diversity and its sheer quantity. It is a large subject and requires wide study.

Above:
Dutch bureau bookcase, made in about
1720. It is veneered with walnut, amboyna
and thuya. Rijksmuseum, Amsterdam.

Right:
American ladder-back chair of maple,
made in about 1710. H. F. duPont
Winterthur Museum, Delaware.

Opposite:
American secretaire, constructed in
walnut and made in Philadelphia in 1707.
Colonial Williamsburg.

Just as cabinetmaking flourished in the provinces in England and France, so in America too furniture was made outside of the major cities. For the colonies, the early 18th century was a period of rapid development and increasing prosperity. Large towns such as Portsmouth, Salem and New York grew up quickly while smaller settlements developed into towns. New settlements themselves sprang up along the eastern seaboard while at the same time colonists began to move inland towards the west. As trade developed and industries grew so luxuries multiplied, and there can have been few settlements without their own cabinetmakers, however humble.

Country furniture made in America during this period may be divided into two types. There was that based quite closely on the styles of the principal cabinetmakers in the main centres and another type which was made by craftsmen who did not properly assimilate the mainstream styles, except in the most superficial manner. The first type was made in the larger communities such as East Windsor, Connecticut. There, Eliphalet Chapin, who had worked in Philadelphia for three years, made furniture which closely resembled the work of the Philadelphia cabinetmakers themselves. The essential difference lay in its greater simplicity. He and other cabinetmakers of his calibre produced pieces of equally fine proportion but they used less elaborate ornamentation. A cabriole leg, which in Philadelphia would have been decorated with acanthus leaves, was often left plain.

The more primitive type of furniture was made by humbler craftsmen who did not have the benefit of training in the larger towns. New motifs were happily mixed with more traditional decoration and methods of construction. They might, for instance, introduce the pierced back-splat of Chippendale origin and at the same time retain the turned legs of the William and Mary era. The mixture of styles is almost their most distinctive feature. As a general rule, provincial furniture was painted. This was done because the grain of the wood was of such poor quality that it could not be used as part of the decoration. There is not quite the abundance of 18th-century oak

Above:
Mahogany lowboy, probably the work of William Savery of Philadelphia.

Opposite above:
Dutch walnut side-table of about 1700. The "apron" below the drawer was later popular in America.

Opposite below:
A New England slat-back rocking chair of about 1750. It is painted to resemble walnut.

furniture in America as in England. Although it was very popular at the beginning of the century, it was slowly replaced by lighter woods. Most popular were maple, walnut, pine and fruitwood. Even sycamore was recognized as adaptable to the more curvilinear styles of the 18th century.

Recognizing reproductions and fakes

The greatest danger for the collector of 18th-century furniture lies in the huge quantity of reproductions which were made in the 19th century and during the present one. While the Victorians were making their own furniture they were also busily copying the designs of Chippendale, Hepplewhite and Sheraton. It is therefore crucial that the collector should familiarize himself with

some of the methods of construction of the 18th-century craftsman, and also with the manner in which old wood ages. He should also keep his eye open for pieces of furniture which have been added to or are a combination of two or more pieces.

Patination, the process by which wood changes colour through the accumulation of dust and dirt in the grain, is the crucial sign of age and genuineness. Through wear and polishing, the dirt works deep into the grain and causes the surface to darken. Patination occurs mostly where the wood is exposed to wear. Dark patches are thus visible around handles, on chair arms and on the undersides of tables and other flat surfaces. At the same time, parts of the furniture become bleached by exposure to light. The variegated

Above:
Boston chair, made in maple during the first half of the 18th century. The style derives originally from China. Connecticut Historical Society.

Left:
American armchair of the early 18th century. It is of ebonized pine, maple and oak, and is unusually ornate. Henry Ford Museum, Dearborn, Michigan.

Opposite:
A mid-18th-century American interior in the Palladian style, at Gunston Hall, Virginia, built in 1755.

surface which thus results simply defies imitation and cannot be faked. Patination is not something that the collector can easily learn to recognize and he should study carefully the genuine articles of the period which can be seen in museums and the shops of the more reputable dealers. Only in this way will he come to recognize the scars caused by two hundred years of wear and tear. He should also learn to recognize the different tone of different aged wood. With age, mahogany changes from red to dark brown while walnut acquires an increasingly golden hue. Oak turns to a dark colour which is almost black. The collector who can recognize the subtleties of 18th-century wood is unlikely to fall for the later copies.

Even with this knowledge the collector can still be fooled, for there is a large amount of reproduction furni-ture that has been constructed of old wood. The collector must be able to recognize the signs which give this type of furniture away. All 18th-century pieces of cabinetwork were constructed of one piece of timber (except where veneer was employed) and any inconsistencies in the grain or the colour should arouse suspicion in the collector. He should also look for nailholes where none should be and for signs of wear in places where the piece is unlikely to have been handled. The furniture should also be checked to make sure that the wood is of con-sistent thickness throughout. If the doors or the fronts of the drawers are of different thicknesses, there can be little doubt that the piece is a marriage of two or more original pieces of furniture.

When the collector has satisfied him-self that the wood is genuinely old and that the piece has not been constructed of different articles of furniture, he must then look at the specific details. No alternative exists other than to set out a rather tedious list. First, close scrutiny of any beading should be made. The 18th-century craftsman carved the beading out of one piece of wood so that the grain is consistent all the way through. The 19th-century craftsman glued on separate beads while the modern faker may make separate beads out of plaster of Paris. All carving should rise above the sur-face of the rest of the timber and appear very bold; no 18th-century carver ever economized with wood. Later carving is flatter and sometimes even counter-sunk. In and around old carving there will be conspicuous signs of patination.

Veneers and inlays may often give a piece of furniture away. Eighteenth-century veneers are relatively thick, often an eighth of an inch (3 mm), while later veneers are thinner. Through shrinkage, 18th-century inlays will have been forced up in places, so that a very even surface is usually the sign of a later work. Also, by now, the solid tops of 18th-century circular tables will have shrunk across the grain, so that the measurement of the diameters, across and with the grain, should manifest different widths.

Legs should be checked to make sure that there are no bandages of veneer. These will have been put on to hide any joins and only in the later pieces of Sheraton should the veneered bandage be expected. Legs were always made of one piece of wood and thus the grain should run in a straight line from top to bottom. Legs resembling crabs' claws, which appear on pieces of pedestal furniture, were an invention of the 19th century and never appear on 18th-century cabinetwork.

Drawers are often a good test of genuineness. No 18th-century drawer was ever made completely to fill the distance between the back and the front of the chest or desk; an inch or two was always left to allow the circulation of air. Until about 1770 the grain of the bottom-boards ran from back to front and these were constructed in two or three pieces and are often likely to be cracked. They were always nailed to the sides, not screwed. The sides of drawers were always constructed of oak and made to extend below the bottom-boards so as to function as runners. Runners which have been glued, or which are actually part of the bottom-boards, are certainly a sign that the piece is not of the 18th century. As a general rule, the drawers, due to shrinkage, tend to fit badly. Always check the dovetails of a drawer. Those which have been cut by a modern machine will have pins and tails which are of the same size. In 18th-century dovetailing the pins were much smaller than the tails and were also cut at a more acute angle.

A door on an item of furniture may also give a collector a clue to its age. Single doors were always made to open to the right. Handles and locks were on the left-hand side. Where two doors met, a thin moulding was screwed on to the right-hand door. This was to allow for shrinkage and it

covers the gap which appears between all doors. Mouldings of the following century are thicker and much wider, and the collector should familiarize himself with the differences. The hinges on a door may also prove a give-away; only on corner cupboards should the hinges be visible. On all other pieces of furniture the hinges lie concealed. Doors up until about 1720 were fixed with pin-hinges. After about 1750 the doors of top sections of 18th-century pieces of furniture were attached with three hinges. When fitting shelves the 18th-century cabinetmaker always fitted them into grooves cut in each side of the cabinet. He never rested them on pegs or other additional supports. When constructing the back of

a chair the craftsman never allowed the top rail to extend outwards beyond the sides; this did not happen until the 19th century.

Genuineness can also be ascertained by scrutiny of locks, handles and other metal attachments. No 18th-century lock was stamped with the name of the maker or with a patent number. Any hint of filing is a sign that these might have been rubbed off. Although old lock cases were made of brass, the bolts and levers were made of steel and were always square or oblong. The keys which were made to fit these locks were also made of steel and had circular, bow-shaped handles which were usually thin and refined. The escutcheons or key-hole covers on each piece

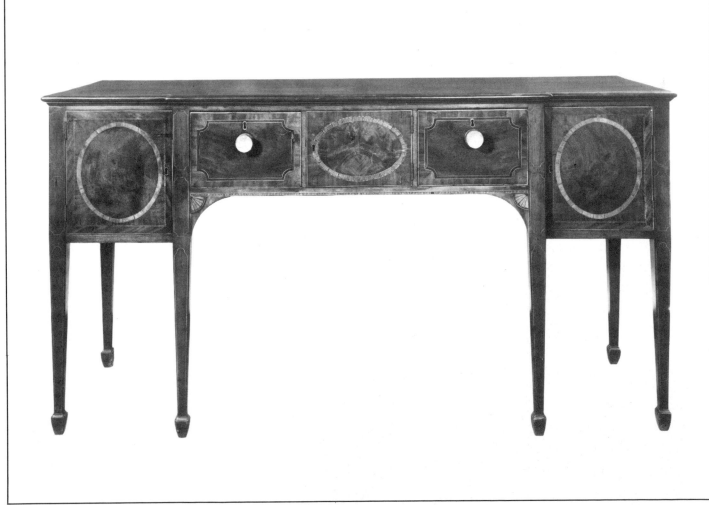

of furniture should always be of one size and design. Genuine 18th-century escutcheons were rounded at the bottom while in the following century they were squared off. They were always positioned in the middle of a drawer, not at the sides, and if they are not perfectly in line the piece will have been renovated or newly built.

All brass details should be looked at carefully. Brass of the 18th century had a higher proportion of copper than present-day brass, and acquires a green colour which modern brass cannot. As with patination so with brass: the collector must familiarize himself with its texture and colour. Before about 1760 castors had wheels made of strips of leather and a hub which fitted up and into the leg. The bucket-castor, a castor into which the leg was fitted, was introduced at about the same time, 1760, as the brass wheel.

Although the collector is unlikely to be able to remove a screw from a piece of furniture he should none the less know that 18th-century screws were not pointed. The first pointed screw was exhibited at the Great Exhibition in London in 1851 and they did not come into common use for a few years after that. It should also be noted that the heads of screws, due to the humidity in the air, rust. Eighteenth-century screw heads will by now have stained the wood around them.

Finally, the collector should note any glass or marble which is incorporated into the furniture. As a general rule the 18th century used coloured marbles, green, pink or mottled. White was not introduced until the following century. Glass which has been in a door for some 200 years will have warped and the collector should keep his eye open for a slight outward curve. He should also know that in 18th-century pieces the panes of glass were separated by bars. Cheaper and more modern furniture may have bars laid across one sheet of glass. A quick look at the back of the doors will resolve this matter.

Opposite below:
American sideboard in the Hepplewhite style and made of mahogany in about 1790. Baltimore Museum of Art, Maryland.

Opposite above:
American mahogany sofa, made in Salem in about 1795. Museum of Fine Arts, Boston.

Left:
Mahogany bookcase made in Charleston, South Carolina in about 1790. Yale University.

Silver

Collecting silver dated earlier than the 18th century would be an expensive pastime indeed. Prior to the middle of the 17th century only a limited amount of silverware was produced and what now remains is mostly owned by museums or royal households. Silver of the 18th century, however, is much more abundant and it was in England that the greatest quantity was produced. We could therefore do no better than begin our survey with English silver. The most important factor affecting the production of English silver at the beginning of the 18th century was the massive influx of

Huguenot silversmiths from France into the country. After the Revocation of the Edict of Nantes in 1685 the Protestant Huguenots were forced to flee from the persecution of Louis XIV. Three years later the Glorious Revolution brought a Dutch sovereign to the English throne, and the accession of William and Mary, both Protestants, turned England into a refuge for the Huguenots. Indeed, William's court architect and designer, Daniel Marot, was himself a Huguenot who had fled to Holland in 1685.

The influence of this minority was substantial. When they came to England they brought with them their

Above:
English tea-caddy inlaid with satinwood, c.1785. Victoria and Albert Museum, London.

Opposite above:
Gold ewer and basin, made in 1701 by Pierre Platel. Chatsworth House, Derbyshire.

Opposite below:
The Louis XIV toilet service of 1685; such heavily ornamented work was common in early 18th-century England. Chatsworth House, Derbyshire.

interpretation of the monumental Baroque style of Louis XIV and by 1700 the English style of silverware, so long influenced by the richness of Dutch designs, had been superseded. It is perhaps ironic that after the arrival of the Dutch Protestant king the predominant style should switch from Dutch to French, especially at a time when England and France were at war.

However, the change did not occur without a struggle on the part of the London silversmiths. They despatched petitions to their guild, the Company of Goldsmiths, in an attempt to hinder the Huguenot craftsmen, whom they considered to be threatening their own livelihoods. The flood gates had been opened, however. After 1689 the flow steadily increased and was further encouraged by an annual government grant of £15,000 which was set aside for the relief of the immigrants.

English silver of the first two decades of the 18th century was thus dominated by two distinct styles: the French and the native English. By 1725 each had

Two early 18th-century silver cups; that on the left was made by Jacob Mazdas, on the right by Paul Crespin. Hermitage Museum, Leningrad.

assimilated some of the characteristics of the other and the two styles began to merge into one. The most noticeable feature of the Huguenot style was its classical sculptural decoration. The floral ornaments of the Restoration period were slowly discarded and replaced by classical motifs such as caryatid handles and acanthus leaves. By 1700 Restoration decoration had practically disappeared and was only to be found on a very few pieces, such as wall-sconces (candle-brackets) which were particularly suited to heavily embossed ornament. One Dutch feature which was retained was the embossing of some surfaces with parallel flutes. Sometimes these covered the entire surface but more often they were employed over only part of the vessel. The lavish ornament of the Dutch period was replaced by more restrained decorations which never obscured the function of the article.

Although the English silversmiths also abandoned many of the Restoration forms and motifs they did not accept the classical ornamentation imported by the Huguenots. Beside this foreign style existed one which, it is often claimed, emerged first in England. This claim, however, should be accepted rather warily for the same style appeared in other European countries, notably Germany and the Low Countries, at the same time. It was based on such simplicity and plainness that articles were designed to be totally free of any ornamentation. In addition to this, every piece, whether a salver or a candlestick, plate or bowl, was based on the elementary shape of the rectangle, octagon or hexagon. If the function of a particular article denied the use of these shapes, then a mount was made which could incorporate them. English silversmiths thus relied for effect upon proportion and the reflection of light on plain, unmarked surfaces. Ornament had no place in these designs. This style is usually referred to as Queen Anne but it outlived her reign by many years and if it must be given a label then Early Georgian would be more appropriate.

Although these two distinct styles lived side by side it should be noted that both Huguenots and English silversmiths sometimes practised each other's styles. The Huguenot, probably at the request of his patron, was often prepared to simplify his ornamentation. An example of this practice can be found in the work of Paul de Lamerie. Right up to his death in 1751 he produced a few relatively undecorated articles, while at the same time the English brothers, George and Francis Garthorne, adopted the more complex decorative style of the French.

It was inevitable that these two styles should merge; by 1725 this had come to pass, although the characteristics of the Huguenot style predominated.

During this decade, the new style, the Rococo, crossed the Channel from France and by 1725 had made its influence felt in both the work of the English and the Huguenot silversmiths. They avoided the excesses of their French counterparts but nevertheless assimilated the essence of the style. The new designs incorporated such movement and nervousness, such flowing lines and foliated decoration, such complex curves and multi-planed surfaces that the spectator is unable to focus on any one detail. This was the essence of Rococo silver design. The most influential figure during the early development of the style was Hubert-François Gravelot. He arrived in England from France in 1732 and established a drawing school in St Martin's Lane, London, at which silver-smiths studied. He brought with him a knowledge of French Rococo design which he passed on to his pupils. Soon afterwards books of designs were published but it would be unfair to suggest that the silversmiths, like the cabinet-makers of the period, relied heavily on design books. Their work was, on the whole, more inspired and more individual.

By the end of the 1720s the styles that had dominated the first decades of the century were spent. It is interesting to note that de Lamerie, who was to become the leading light of all the Rococo silversmiths, made a centrepiece in the manner of his early French style as late as 1733. Nevertheless, this was an anomaly because by that date he was the outstanding Rococo craftsman in a group which numbered such names as Paul Crespin, Charles Kändler, David Willaume and Simon Pantin. The style which they employed lasted from the 1720s until the 1760s, when it was

Three silver baluster casters made by Paul de Lamerie in 1738 in the high Rococo style.

Above:
English silver gilt wine service, in the Adam style of 1780.

Opposite:
An English silver tea caddy of 1766, with *chinoiserie* decoration. Victoria and Albert Museum, London.

eclipsed by the classicism of Robert Adam. It can be divided into approximately three phases. The first spans the years between about 1725 and 1740 when it was considerably restrained in comparison with what was to follow; flat-chasing was extensively used and asymmetrical decoration made only a casual appearance. During the following decade silversmiths began fully to exploit the forms and decoration of the Rococo. After 1740 great use was made of cast-decoration, and pieces of silverware began to acquire reliefs which depicted animals and pastoral scenes. Flowers, shells and festoons appeared while handles were often modelled as dolphins or birds. Even without these details the shapes of the articles would have been complex. Often the curves and the undulations were far more exaggerated than the function of the piece warranted. By 1750, though, this

form of the Rococo was on the point of decline. Perhaps it is not mere coincidence that in 1751 Paul de Lamerie died. Cast-decoration was used less extensively and greater stress was laid upon flat-chasing and engraving. It should also be noted that silversmiths did not fail to exploit the prevailing fashions for Gothic and Chinese motifs, which often appeared in pierced decoration.

During the early 1760s classical forms and decorations were being introduced and by 1770 the Rococo style had practically died out. It has already been pointed out that the Neoclassical style was very much the invention of Robert Adam single-handed, and in his comprehensive designs for houses and their interior details silver was not forgotten. Whether Adam had any working arrangements with silversmiths is not known, but it is certain

An English silver hallmark. The first mark indicates the maker – in this case J. Tibbits; the second is the silver standard; the third denotes the assay office – Sheffield – and the fourth indicates the year, 1775.

that many of them worked from his designs. Some very likely received commissions from Adam. His designs did not come from Greco-Roman silver but from bronze articles, mainly vases, which were then being discovered at Pompeii and Herculaneum. The most adaptable form which he was to employ was the urn shape, and this he applied to all hollow-ware. Objects to which this shape could not be applied required original designs; these Adam devised with alacrity. He based his designs on plain reflecting surfaces against which he could set off carefully chosen classical motifs. As with the furniture of the period, simplicity and clarity were all.

The simplicity of his designs was ideally suited to the new methods of mass-production which were then revolutionizing the manufacture of silverware. During the last decades of the 18th century, Birmingham and Sheffield emerged as important centres of silver production and the new methods of production that they employed suddenly made silverware available to a large sector of the population which had hitherto been unable to afford it. This was made possible by the invention of silver plate. Superficially it was indistinguishable from solid silver, but it was considerably cheaper. In 1743 Thomas Boulsover had discovered a method by which silver and copper could be fused together. Furthermore, this plated metal could be rolled and hammered without the coating of silver being lost. The implications of this invention were not fully realized until the 1760s when a certain Matthew Boulton, in his factory in Soho, Birmingham, began its mass-production. Mass-production was not, of course, the dirty word which it is now and Boulton determined to make his articles as perfect and as plentiful as possible. Indeed Boulton is known to have supplied the Royal Household with silver plate; a fine recommendation of its quality.

The mass-production of silver plate required further inventions along the production line to enable it to be swiftly and economically rendered into saleable objects. An early such invention was the fly-punch. This could pierce the plated metal without breaking the silver coating away and leaving the copper exposed, as the old method of simply cutting the silver with a fret saw could not be used on plate. Shortly afterwards came the invention of the swage block; this facilitated the production of large quantities of silver ribbon, which could then be cut and applied to appropriate articles. Another invention was that of die stamping. This enabled manufacturers to produce thousands of small component parts, say of candlesticks, which then might be sold to independent craftsmen throughout the country and assembled by them. One more invention was the drawbench, consisting of tapered holes through which metal was pulled and transformed into thin silver wire of a consistent thickness and texture for use in the production of cake baskets and other items.

Although Neoclassical silver plate of poor quality does exist, some of it is quite as pleasing aesthetically as the solid silverware made by individual craftsmen. Silver plate is not to be scorned by the small collector but if he does aspire to pieces of higher quality then he will be able to find much that

was made by craftsmen in competition with the manufacturers from Birmingham and Sheffield. Notable London silversmiths of the period were Hester Bateman, James Young, John Scholfield, Paul Storr, Andrew Fogelberg and Robert Sharp. All their work had elegance, proportion and balance in common. Delicate classical motifs – acanthus leaves, palm leaves, small medallions – were carefully incorporated and the resulting effect was so satisfactory that it lasted into the 19th century and was copied as far afield as Russia and southern Italy.

French silver

The story of French silver of the period is a rather sadder one. In the last years of the 17th century French silverware suffered from a veritable holocaust of destruction. It is estimated that some hundred thousand articles were melted down by Louis XIV to help pay for his attempt to subjugate the rest of Europe. It is, therefore, not surprising that, however diligently the collector may

English silver teapot, made by Hester Bateman in about 1783. Private collection.

search, he will find very little silver-ware of the period. The situation failed to improve at the beginning of the new century. The ruling of 1688 which had imposed restrictions on silver manu-facture and led to the destruction of so much, placed the craft of the silver-smith in a state of suspended animation until about 1720. On top of this was the fact that after the Revocation of the Edict of Nantes in 1685 France lost some of her finest silversmiths. How-ever, even if the Huguenots had re-mained in France and practised their craft, much of it would anyway have been destroyed, melted down to pay for an enormous army at war. As it was, the Huguenots found a refuge in England where they could continue to work.

Despite the standstill, a number of silversmiths emerged who, in the next decades, became remarkable exponents of the Rococo style. Jacques Ballin, Thomas Germain and Nicolas Besnier were perhaps the most outstanding. Under their skilful leadership the

monumental Baroque style dis-appeared and was replaced by one that was light and exquisite. As in England, the silversmiths were based in the capi-tal; the best craftsmen were drawn there by the lure of court patronage and a rich bourgeoisie. The style reached its zenith in the late 1730s and early 1740s and the articles that were produced might almost be considered to have been decorated to excess. Decoration was not thought of as an addition or an attachment, but an in-trinsic part of the piece. In fact, it com-pletely took over. The function of the article, so apparent in English silver of the period, disappeared under a cascade of foliated decoration. Entwining leaves twisted and curled around them-selves, cartouches grew into wildly asymmetrical *rocaille* forms, and cherubs, struggled against enveloping foliage. Throughout most of the reign of Louis XV these wild and splendid forms held sway.

In the following reign these forms were disciplined and the French silver-

Above:
Silver teapot, chocolate pot and kettle, made in England by Josiah Ward in 1719. The Worshipful Company of Goldsmiths, London.

Opposite above:
Early 18th-century English silver of plain, geometrical design.

Opposite below:
Early Georgian silver sauceboats, made by Edward Pocock.

smiths adopted a Neoclassical style that was the direct counterpart of the English manner. The same urn-shaped vessels began to predominate, while medallions and carefully controlled classical foliage replaced the wilful madness which had been the Rococo. The designs of Robert Adam were copied and provided the ideas for the principal features of French silverware. During the 1770s there was little to distinguish between the work of the London and Paris silversmiths. The one relic from the Rococo in France was the skill and detail that was lavished upon the smaller pieces such as snuff-boxes and bonbonnières or sweet boxes. With the Revolution of 1789 the art of the French silversmith came to an abrupt end; not until the end of the century was there any sort of revival. In 1797, a new system of hallmarking was introduced; it was to form the foundation of the modern system in France.

American silver

The collector who wishes to invest in American silver should bear in mind that, unlike the practice in European countries, there were no controls to guarantee the purity of the alloy. Nevertheless, subsequent tests suggest that the American silversmith used alloys that were very much up to European standards. Furthermore, there was no system of hallmarking and American silver is seldom marked. When it was, only the name or initials of the maker were included.

The first known silversmiths to practise in America were John Hull and Robert Sanderson, both of Boston. They were mainly active at the end of the 17th century but are mentioned here because it was they who trained the first generation of 18th-century craftsmen. The most gifted of these was John Coney. Shunning ostentation and elaborate decoration, he produced pieces that were simple and bold and clearly influenced by the undecorated English style of the Early Georgian period. Other important silversmiths in Boston who worked in a similar manner were Jeremiah Dummer, John Edwards and Edward Winslow. It was these four who represented the most important focus for silver production at the beginning of the 18th century.

Farther north, in New York, was another band of silversmiths. Unlike the settlers in Boston, the population of New York was made up primarily of Dutchmen and it is not surprising that they adopted the decorative style of their 17th-century forefathers. The essential characteristic of New York silverware was its elaborate ornamentation. The most renowned silversmith of the period, though, was Bartholomew Le Roux, a Huguenot. He died in 1713, but his son, Charles, continued in his father's craft and was later to become the town's official silversmith. Others were nearly all of Dutch origin, as is testified by such names as Jacobus van der Spiegel, Gerrit Onckalbag and Jacob Boelen.

During the third and fourth decades of the century the Boston and New York styles came closer together and although the latter still retained its interest in bold decoration there was, nevertheless, a greater interest in simple form and design. As in Europe, the middle of the century was swept up by the Rococo and it was during this period that America's most renowned silversmith came to the fore. Paul

Opposite:
American sugar bowl of about 1700, made by John Coney.

Right:
English silver mustard pot of 1747, made by Edward Wakelin. Ashmolean Museum, Oxford.

Below:
Italian silver travelling dinner service, made in the mid-18th century for Cardinal York. Reproduced by gracious permission of Her Majesty the Queen.

Revere the Younger was the son of a Huguenot who had settled in Boston in 1715. The father had been apprenticed to John Coney and was responsible for the training of his son. Paul, born in 1734, received his first commission at the age of 24. He is especially remembered now for *The Sons of Liberty Bowl* which he made in 1768. He was active until his death in 1818 but he did not confine his pursuits to the production of silverware. He established a copper-rolling mill and even manufactured false teeth and spectacle frames.

The most notable Rococo silversmiths in New York were Myer Myers and Daniel Fueter. They, like their contemporaries in Boston, were heavily influenced by the delicate, asymmetrical forms imported from Europe. In the second half of the century other towns became important centres of production of silver, notably Philadelphia. The pre-eminent craftsmen there were Philip Hulbaert, Richard Humphreys and Edmund Milne. As affluence spread, so more towns were able to indulge in the craft and by the time of the Revolution both Newport and Salem could boast of skilful silversmiths.

After the Revolution came the Neoclassical style. In Boston Paul Revere continued to dominate his contemporaries; indeed, his finest pieces were made in the Neoclassical manner. But Boston was now no longer the leading centre for the production of silver: Philadelphia could boast Joseph Richardson Jnr., while in New York Daniel van Voorhis and Gerrit Schank,

Above:
Silver sauceboats made by Paul Revere in about 1785.

Opposite above:
English coffee pot and mug made in Sheffield plate about 1765.

Opposite below:
A set of saltspoons made by Paul Revere. Metropolitan Museum of Art, New York.

Simeon Bayley and William G. Forbes produced silverware quite as fine as that made in Boston. The Neoclassical style dominated the last years of the century and even spilled over into the next. It was not until the second decade of the 19th century that the style eventually gave way to the fashionable opulence of the Empire style.

One of the attractions of silver, for the collector, is that much of it is marked and therefore easily identified. However, the collector should still be wary. Many dictionaries and books of hallmarks exist but the collector who put all his faith in these would be foolish. Forged hallmarks have not been unknown while not an inconsiderable amount of silver simply failed to get marked at all. Unmarked silver was once rather frowned upon but in recent years it has commanded higher prices on the market than before.

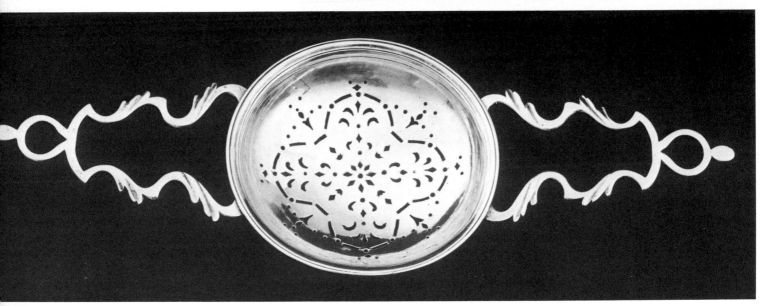

Added to these problems is the fact that American silver is not marked with any regularity. This may seem a depressing prospect to the collector who thought that hallmarks were a fullproof sign of authenticity. Hallmarks are a guide but the collector needs to be armed with further knowledge. First, he must become familiar with the prevailing styles and then come to recognize patination. Recognition of the latter is of vital importance. A piece of silver that has just left the factory is easily spotted by its bright and glittering finish. For the collector of antique silver such pieces are of no interest. With the passing of time,

however, silver acquires a remarkable mellowness. The collector who is able to spot this patination may pick up a piece of 18th-century silver which is unmarked and has been ignored by dealers and other collectors. Once a decision has been made to collect silver of this period, it might be a good idea to purchase, from a reputable dealer, a small piece of 18th-century silverware which can be carried in the pocket and used to compare with patina on pieces found in markets and antique shops. Investing in silver requires the same amount of knowledge as is needed in the collection of furniture.

Above:
A punch-strainer, made in Boston, Massachusetts, in about 1765 by Samuel Minott. American Museum, Bath.

Top:
Three American porringers of the mid-18th century; these were used for soup, hot alcoholic drinks and so on. American Museum, Bath.

164

Glass

At the close of the 17th century glass was being produced throughout Europe at a quite unprecedented rate, but nowhere as fast as in England. There also, due to the revolutionary techniques of George Ravenscroft in the 1670s, some of the finest 18th-century glass was made. The abundance of glass that has come down to us from that period is due mainly to his discovery of lead glass. Soda glass, which was made before this discovery, contained a high level of alkali and consequently suffered from tiny interior cracks. These eventually resulted in the disintegration of the material. It almost goes without saying that very little glass which is dated before the 18th century now remains. It is from the period following the invention of lead glass that most collections are made.

Before discussing the form and decoration of English glassware some mention must be made of the development of the metal itself. Early lead glass had a distinctive greenish tint. This was eradicated at the beginning of the 18th century but was replaced by a blackish, and sometimes bluish, tint. This can be found in glass made until about 1730, when a colourless and brilliant glass was developed. This clear and brilliant glass was ideally suited to engraving and air twists and by the middle of the century was the most commonly used, although tinted and coloured glass was still manufactured. In Bristol after 1750, dark blue and opaque white glass was made while in the north of England a paler blue glass was produced. In the second half of the century Birmingham became well known for its deep red glass. On the whole, though, coloured glass was not popular and most collectable glass of the period is clear.

One of the main delights of 18th-century English glassware is to be found in the wide variety of drinking glasses, which were subjected to many changes in both form and decoration throughout the century. At the beginning of the period the predominant style of the drinking glass was one of remarkable simplicity and balance, perfectly in tune with the plainness and elegance associated with the Queen Anne period in other fields. The name of this early glass, "baluster", describes the stem; it was derived from an architectural term applied to a short pillar, slim at one end and bulging at the other. The bowl was funnel-shaped and its base often incorporated a "tear", a small air bubble. The stem was decorated with knops or swellings and the foot was folded under. The glass itself was thick and heavy. The shape and the proportions of the English wine glass remained fairly constant throughout the century. The changes in style affected the stem, and it is this which gives away the age of the glass. Many different knops were employed; acorn knops, band knops and mushroom knops, to mention only a few. Other forms of decoration, as we shall see, were also developed.

In about 1715 the baluster stem gave way to the moulded, or Silesian, stem. The earliest stems of this type had four

Above:
English wine glass of 1730, with a so-called Silesian stem. London Museum.

Left:
English glass candlestick with a hollow baluster stem; early 18th century.

distinguishing feature was their engraved decoration. Newcastle must have developed a thriving trade with Holland for it was there that all the engraving was carried out. Some must have been returned to England but most inevitably found its way on to the Dutch market.

In the same decade English glassmakers incorporated the air twist into their stems. The only other country that indulged in this form of decoration was Norway, where the success was due mainly to the large number of English craftsmen who worked there. An air twist was simply an extension of the tear. As the glass was drawn out to form the stem so it was twisted, and this forced the tear into a spiral. This style of decoration became increasingly popular in the 1740s, especially as the Glass Excise Act of 1745 imposed taxes on the materials used in the manufacture of glass. Nowhere else in Europe was this form of decoration employed so extensively and with such brilliance. As the decade progressed, the air twists multiplied and grew in complexity.

In the following decade the glassmakers began to make opaque twist stems. Their success and popularity was immediate. The opaque spiral was created by embedding strips of white enamel in the glass. It was then heated, twisted, and drawn out into long strips. These were then cut to the appropriate length to form the stems. The sophistication of some of the designs was remarkable. The white enamel canes could be embedded into the glass and arranged in an almost infinite number of ways. To add to the complexity, they could be combined with air twists and coloured enamel. These variegated forms of opaque twisting made their appearance during the 1750s and remained in vogue for the next 20 years.

In 1777 a second Glass Excise act doubled the existing tax on glass while three years later Ireland was granted free trade. These two apparently unrelated incidents effected the instant and almost complete withdrawal of the glass industry from England to Ireland. There, in the last two decades of the century, glass cutting came into vogue. Although it had been practised on the Continent throughout the century, the taxes in England had made it prohibitively expensive: to manufacture glass

Above:
Staffordshire vase made in opaque glass and given a chinoiserie decoration. Late 18th century.

Opposite:
English decanters of the late 18th century. Barrie and Jenkins, London.

angular sides. It was not long, however, before six and even eight sides appeared. In this stem, the heavy or bulging end was always at the top so that the slender end tapered off into the foot. Newcastle, or light balusters as they are sometimes known, made their appearance in the 1730s. Compared with other glasses of the period their bowls were large and their employment of tears complex. But their most

out of taxable materials and then hack much of it off was not economical. In Irish cut glass the basic form of the drinking glass was retained. The funnel-or the bell-shaped bowl was most commonly used though knopping was now reduced to a minimum. The cutting, or faceting as it was more usually known, was limited to the stem. In more elaborate glasses it sometimes appeared on the bowls and the feet as well. The most common type of faceting was the hollow diamond, a term perfectly descriptive of the effect. Another type was flat-fluting. Usually six to eight flutes were employed and these covered the length of the stem and then travelled on to the foot. The glass which was used was thicker than that of previous decades and the faceting was deep. Engraving was quite often added to these cut glass articles and usually appeared in the form of Neoclassical

festoons, vines, hops and barley and political emblems, particularly in support of the Jacobite cause.

We have covered the development of the mainstream styles in wine glasses but nothing has been said of the cheaper and undecorated glasses. These form the biggest class of English wine glasses and are usually referred to as drawn trumpets. Unlike the better glasses they were not made of three separate components—bowl, stem and foot—but two. The bowl was drawn out of the stem and the foot added to that. They were made throughout the century, and what makes them attractive to the collector is their relative abundance and cheapness.

Stress has been laid on wine glasses mainly because they represent the finest achievements of the English glassmakers in the 18th century, and also because they fall within the price

Above:
English wine glasses of 1725, decorated with diamond engraving and Jacobite slogans. Victoria and Albert Museum, London.

Opposite:
English Newcastle goblet, wheel-engraved in Holland; c.1740. Pilkington Museum of Glass.

168

range of the small collector. But it would be incorrect to imagine that no other glass work was made. Throughout the century craftsmen turned out decanters, candlesticks, salad bowls, sweetmeat glasses and even teapots in glass. The picture would be further distorted if no mention were made of early 18th-century glass cutting. In the 1740s cutting was applied to the rims of sweetmeat glasses and ten years later decanters, dessert dishes and salad bowls underwent even more extensive treatment. Indeed, the cut decanters of the second half of the century went a long way to exploit the brilliance of English lead glass in a manner which was not equalled in other articles.

A considerable quantity of English glass, particularly that which was made in Ireland in the last decades of the century, was exported to America. From 1780 until well into the 19th century, Irish glass was exported in ever increasing quantities, and as a result genuine American glass of this date is rare. The first American manufactory had been established by Caspar Wistar in Salem County, south New Jersey, in 1739. The predominant feature of this glass was its colour; either amber, blue, green or turquoise. It was also finely proportioned. However, need called for beakers and sturdy goblets, and at the beginning of the century there was little call for delicate and expensive glass. The most renowned name in American glass manufacture during the 18th century was William Henry Stiegel. He began to experiment in the production of glass in the early 1760s and by the end of the decade had established two glass workshops. Sadly, their life was short. Within ten years both had closed down and Stiegel himself was a ruined man. The most distinctive Stiegel glass was of a rich blue or amethyst colour and sometimes incorporated engraving. By the end of the century glass manufacture was a thriving industry in most of the eastern states. No figure comparable with Stiegel emerges, however. American 18th-century glass is rare and is eagerly sought after; the prices which the collector has to pay are high.

On the Continent glass was in greater demand and, although there is not enough room here to discuss its development through the century, there

Above:
Two free-blown tumblers made by Stiegel in Pennsylvania in the 1770s. The decoration is enamelled. Corning Museum of Glass.

Opposite:
American sugar bowl made in New Jersey in the last quarter of the 18th century. Corning Museum of Glass.

are high points of creation which should be mentioned. One of the major contributions to glass production in this period came from Bohemia. The cutting and engraving of glass had been revived at the end of the 16th century, but in the 18th century was to be given a decisive boost by the introduction of water power to drive the cutters' lathes. Deep cutting and high relief were now widely used. To accommodate these forms of decoration thicker glass was required and the articles produced in Bohemia were considerably thicker than the English glass of the period.

Some of the best engraved glass was made in the early part of the century in Silesia. The short, four-sided stem, known as the Silesian stem, was introduced in about 1700. It soon spread to Bohemia, Bavaria and Prussia and, as we have seen, made its appearance in England during the second decade of the century. By the middle of the cen-

tury the German glassmakers were employing both the deep cutting and the high relief in the creation of Rococo decoration. Scrolls and garlands were common and were often employed in conjunction with engraved pastoral scenes. In the latter part of the century the enamel twist made its appearance, but unlike the English glassmakers who showed a preference for white, the Germans were partial to mixed colour twists. The glass industries in Silesia and Bohemia suffered, however, from competition from England, and fell into decline during the last decades of the century. Not until well into the 19th century were they revived.

The other high mark of 18th-century European glass appeared in the Netherlands, although the Dutch were not primarily manufacturers of glass so much as decorators of articles which they imported, mostly from England. Their speciality was diamond stippling, which is thought to have been used

Left:
Late 18th-century Venetian glass basket with applied decoration. Museo Vetrario, Murano.

Below:
English salver and jelly glasses of the early 18th century. Victoria and Albert Museum, London.

Opposite:
Early 18th-century English octagonal decanter. Victoria and Albert Museum, London.

first by a Frans Greenwood, who was of English ancestry and lived in Dordrecht. The technique involved the application of thousands of tiny dots to the surface of the glass by means of a diamond point fitted to a hammer. The beauty of this form of decoration was enhanced by the brilliance of the English lead glass, the softness of which was particularly suited to the stippling technique. Greenwood's designs included flowers, fruit, portraits and figures. The stippled parts picked out the forms while the clear glass defined the shadows and the background.

A number of Dutch engravers employed the technique of stippling, the most notable of whom was David Wolff. He was active in the second half of the century and his subjects ranged from putti wallowing in clouds, to formal portraits and commemorative decoration. His versatility and obvious artistic ability are often cited to support the suggestion that he might have been trained as a painter. Even if this were not so, he and other glass engravers must have had considerable knowledge of contemporary art, for much of their subject matter was based on prints, some of which have now been traced.

Wheel engraving, using a small metal wheel and an abrasive, was also employed in the Netherlands, and to a very high standard. Foremost among the exponents of this technique was Jacob Sang, a contemporary of Wolff. His range of subjects was wide and included portraits, commemorative designs, decorative scroll-work and coats of arms. At the time of his mature work the Dutch were beginning to produce lead glass but its quality was inferior to the English product and the Dutch engravers continued to use the imported wares.

All manner of antiques are faked or reproduced and glass is no exception. Over recent years the quantity and quality of these has improved and the collector needs to have some means of identifying the genuine article. The first thing which he might do is look for the pontil mark on the base, where the glass was attached to an iron rod during manufacture. In the 18th century these marks were never removed (except from cruet bottles, when it was done to ensure that the bottle rested firmly on its silver base and did not

scratch the surface; on the base of articles which were partially raised this was not necessary). The collector should remember that on the intentional fake this pontil mark will have been left on. The test is none the less useful for detecting reproduction Georgian glass.

Familiarity with the weight of glass is important. On the whole, lead glass is heavier than the cheaper soda glass,

but even this test can prove unreliable. Sometimes soda glass is carefully thickened and an inexperienced collector might mistake it for genuine lead glass. Scrutiny of the tints of the glass should be made. Although some soda glass was quite as brilliant as today's much of it contained impurities which caused a delicate tinge. A faker can incorporate these impurities into his forgeries.

When a collector has established that an article is made of genuine lead glass, examination should be made of the form and the workmanship of the piece. This can only be done when the collector is intimately familiar with 18th-century glass. Although the faker can reproduce lead glass he is quite likely to make mistakes in the proportions, the thickness and the joints of the various components. The collector should also familiarize himself with the finish on 18th-century glass. Generally speaking, modern reproductions have a finish which is either too fine or too crude. The middle way of the 18th-century craftsman is seldom achieved.

Finally, mention should be made of modern moulded glass. Reproductions of cut glass are often made in press moulds. The collector can take heart in the fact that only the very best are likely to deceive. In 18th-century cut glass the lines between the surfaces are very sharp and well defined. On moulded glass they are blunter and the collector should be able to spot the difference easily.

A great deal of 18th-century style glass was manufactured in the 19th century and the recent growing popularity of glass collecting has been accompanied by the production of intentional fakes. Only a thorough knowledge of the genuine article will enable the collector to detect the fraudulent wares.

Porcelain

Innovations in manufacturing in the 18th century were not restricted to silver and glass. In the sphere of ceramics, innovations at the beginning of the century led to fundamental changes both in the refinement of production and the availability of particular wares to a wider public. The discovery was porcelain. Porcelain had been made in China from as early as the 7th century AD. In Europe, however, the secret had remained elusive and those who admired the pure whiteness and hardness of porcelain were obliged to import it, at great expense, from the Orient. The high cost of porcelain, combined with an extravagant addiction to its beauty, drove Augustus the Strong, Elector of Saxony and King of Poland, to search for a means of manufacturing it for himself. Researches were begun in 1697 by a Saxon nobleman, Ehrenfried Walther von Tschirnhausen. Unhappily, he was not rewarded with success. In 1704 he met a young alchemist, Johann Friedrich Böttger, who was at the time engaged in the somewhat

more dubious business of trying to manufacture gold out of base metals. The two joined forces but after a year of experimentation had still not managed to produce the precious white porcelain. Augustus, a man of little patience and short temper, had the young Böttger incarcerated but the shortsightedness of this action must soon have dawned on the Elector because he released the alchemist in 1708 and returned him to his laboratory. The experience proved beneficial, for in that year Böttger managed to produce the first specimens of white porcelain. These he manufactured from Kolditz clay. In 1710 a factory, specifically established for the production of porcelain, was built at Meissen, a small town 12 miles distant from Dresden.

Before going further, some explanation is needed concerning the two distinct types of porcelain and the way in which they were manufactured. The two classes of porcelain are known as hard-paste and soft-paste. The first, considered true porcelain, was made from the natural materials of china clay and china stone and then covered with a glaze. Soft-paste porcelain predates Böttger's discovery and was an inferior material which incorporated, with the clay, the artificial ingredients used in

Above:
A selection of Meissen porcelain of varying ground colours, made between 1725 and 1735.

Opposite:
Red stoneware teapot made at Meissen in 1710, with the mongram of Augustus, Elector of Saxony. The Wark Collection, Jacksonville, Florida.

the production of glass. Hard-paste, discovered by Böttger in Germany and used there extensively, was also employed in Vienna; in England it was made in Plymouth and Bristol. At the beginning of the century soft-paste was more prevalent, being made in Rouen, Saint Cloud, and Sèvres in France, and at Chelsea, Worcester, Derby and other English factories. In 1770 Sèvres began to use hard-paste and by the end of the century little soft-paste was made

anywhere in Europe. Knowledge of the processes involved in the production of hard-paste was eagerly sought but it was difficult to come by. The discoveries at Meissen were jealously guarded but it is nevertheless surprising that almost one hundred years elapsed before the methods were adopted throughout England and the Continent.

It is not possible to divide the study of porcelain simply into countries in the same way as has been done with

furniture and the decorative arts. The styles of porcelain decoration were remarkably similar in each country and thus it requires more than a quick glance to ascertain from which corner of Europe a particular piece might come. The best means of classification would be to look at the output of the main centres and build up some idea as to which factories produced the finest wares. Much of the output of Meissen is now very expensive and quite out of reach of the small collector. From other centres, however, articles were produced which do not now command such exorbitant prices.

Nevertheless, a glance at 18th-century porcelain must begin at the Meissen factory. Before Böttger discovered the white porcelain he developed a hard, close-grained, red stoneware which could be engraved, cut, and then polished like a stone. Primitive enamels were sometimes employed in the decoration, although more commonly craftsmen relied upon moulded ornament. The colour varied according to the firing and ranged from red, or reddish brown, to a blackish colour (the latter was caused by over-firing). A considerable amount of this stoneware was produced and manufacture continued for some years after the introduction of white porcelain.

In style, Böttger's porcelain vessels were similar to those made of the red stoneware. Nor was his ware absolutely pure white. It had a very slight brownish tinge while the glaze which he applied was thick and often imperfect. Moulded ornament was applied and sometimes highlighted with enamel colours. Sadly, Böttger's years at Meissen, riddled with intrigues and plagued by desertions, came to an end

Above left:
Porcelain vase from the Meissen factory, of about 1730. Victoria and Albert Museum, London.

Left:
Dutch dolls' house, with a display of fine miniature porcelain. Gemeentemuseum, The Hague.

Below:
Porcelain vulture from Meissen, modelled by J. J. Kändler in 1734. The Antique Porcelain Company, London.

Below right:
Porcelain figure made at Niderviller, in Lorraine, in about 1770. Victoria and Albert Museum, London.

in 1719 when, after a period of heavy drinking, he died at the age of 36. His replacement was Johann Gregor Höroldt, who became chief painter at Meissen in 1720 after he had spent a year in Vienna, where he had learned much about the techniques of enamelling. He introduced new colours to the Meissen factory, which were particularly notable for the faultless surface which they acquired during firing. It was he who developed a distinct style of oriental decoration. Not only did he introduce Chinese and Japanese motifs but he also developed a kind of pseudo-Chinese style in which spidery figures were placed into bogus Chinese landscapes. The term *chinoiserie* is applied to these evocations of Chinese art.

Shortly after his arrival at Meissen, Höroldt introduced landscapes and harbour scenes into his decorative formats. The tradition was continued by Christian Friedrich Höroldt, who became an enameller in 1725. It is thought that these two decorators may have been cousins. This period was also notable for the development of new colours; the underglaze blue which was such an essential part of Chinese porcelain, was introduced in 1725. Other colours – yellow, deep green and purple – also made a notable appearance.

Perhaps the most important landmark in Meissen's history was the arrival, in 1731, of Johann Joachim Kändler. He turned his attention to the modelling of small figures and is often considered to have been the finest exponent of this art. His output was astonishing and if he was not the greatest modeller he was at least the most prolific. His subjects were numerous and included groups of lovers and figures of gallants and their ladies. He depicted people from the Court and at the other end of the social scale portrayed artisans and craftsmen. Animals and birds, allegorical figures and the *Commedia dell' Arte* were further inspiration. It was Kändler, too, who introduced the Rococo to the Meissen factory. Some of the tableware was modelled to such an extent that little or no room remained for painted decoration. Enamelling was simply used to highlight the modelled ornament. Not even the plate, an article renowned for the plainness of its surface, escaped the moulded ornament.

Until the 1760s Meissen led Europe both in the production of porcelain and in its decoration. Brief mention must be made of the prevailing styles of decoration. *Chinoiseries* retained their popularity. A common motif was the formal oriental flower. In 1740, how-

ever, it was abandoned and replaced by naturalistically painted European flowers. Shortly afterwards shadows and insects sometimes found their way on to articles. At about the same time the pastoral scenes of Watteau and Lancret were introduced, while in the following decade the decorators turned to the mythological subjects of Boucher. Moulded decoration first appeared in the form of basket work, but as the century progressed the influence of the asymmetrical Rococo was increasingly felt. Moulded flowers were added, while scrolls appeared on handles and on spouts.

With the advent of the Neoclassical style, the factory at Meissen lost its position as the leading porcelain works in Europe. Höroldt retired in 1765; Kändler died ten years later. It was the end of an era. Nevertheless, the factory persisted. An Academy of Painting, intended to improve the quality of the draughtsmanship of the decorators, was established in Dresden. Asymmetrical moulding disappeared, handles and spouts lost their scrolls and the entire output became locked into a vice of severity and angularity. Classical festoons became the most typical painted ornament. Meissen, however, had now become an imitator of a style; one which had already reached its

zenith in the factory at Sèvres, in France. The last two decades of the century did not, however, see the exclusive use of Neoclassical motifs. Strongly naturalistic decoration continued to be used, particularly in the form of topographical landscapes and miniature portraits.

The Seven Years War (1756–63) and the subsequent intervention of Frederick the Great in the factory's affairs was partly responsible for the decline in the influence of Meissen. For a short time, before the rise of Sèvres, Berlin reigned as Europe's leading factory. The first factory there, established in 1752, closed suddenly in 1757 after Frederick withdrew his patronage. Articles which were made there are, not surprisingly, scarce. Their most characteristic feature is their plain, unpainted finish.

A second factory at Berlin was founded in 1761 and was more successful. In 1763 it was purchased by Frederick and his indulgent love of porcelain ensured its survival. During the 1760s it is estimated that some 3,000 articles were produced each day. Decoration followed the precedents laid down at Meissen. Painters and modellers were imported from there and they continued to paint the characteristic *chinoiseries*, landscapes and naturalistic

Above:
Three examples of Wedgwood's jasper-ware, made at his factory Etruria in 1785–90. Josiah Wedgwood and Sons Ltd.

Opposite:
Two examples of the tiger and bamboo pattern. The bowl on the left was made in Japan in about 1700, and the Chelsea version on the right in about 1755.

flowers. The foremost modeller, Friedrich Elias Meyer, had been employed at Meissen and the work that he carried out at Berlin was similar to Kändler's. His particularly small heads represent his only attempt at originality. He died in 1785 and was succeeded by Johann Geary Müller. By this date, however, the influence of Berlin had waned, its position usurped by Sèvres.

Before turning to Sèvres we should look at Vienna, the first hard-paste factory to be established after Meissen. It was founded by Claudius Innocentius du Pacquier, a man of Dutch descent. His first successful attempt to manufacture porcelain was in 1719, after he had enticed Christoph Konrad Hünger and Samuel Stolzel from Meissen. In 1718 du Pacquier was granted a patent for the production of porcelain throughout the Imperial territories of Charles VI. This privilege lasted until 1744 when du Pacquier, overcome by

financial problems, was forced to relinquish his factory to the state.

The articles produced in his factory did not receive a factory mark, although some can be identified by the initials of individual craftsmen. The decoration employed by the Vienna craftsmen had its own distinct style. In comparison with Meissen, its artistry was not so assured. The colours were softer and the forms more linear. Furthermore, greater respect was shown for the white porcelain itself. The subjects which they depicted were inevitably closely allied to those of Meissen. Formal oriental flowers and *chinoiseries* recurred. Landscapes and heraldry also made their appearance in Viennese work.

The moulded decoration was capricious and wayward. Handles bulged and turned for no apparent reason while some others found themselves metamorphosed into panthers. This

A table centre-piece, made of creamware in Leeds in 1780. D. Towner Collection.

the Rococo style. Artists conversant with the prevailing fashions were lured from Meissen, and the factory, for so long plagued with financial problems, began to see its fortunes improve. During the 1750s the factory was considerably enlarged and its influence steadily grew.

Colours and designs showed the considerable influence of Meissen. The pastoral scenes of Watteau and Lancret were copied and Rococo decoration extensively employed. The foremost painter of landscapes was Philipp Emanuel Schindler. It may seem strange that the decorations of the various factories were so stereotyped but the huge demand for porcelain killed competition and the need for originality. Furthermore, many of the craftsmen travelled from factory to factory and passed on the styles and techniques which they had learnt at other factories.

Independent figures, which had been somewhat ignored by du Pacquier, now began to receive more attention. This was not achieved without the help of recruits from Meissen. Vienna's principal modeller, active between 1747 and his death in 1784, was Johann Josef Niedermeyer. Like Kändler at Meissen, he depicted both society figures and peasants, artisans and beggars. Unlike Berlin figures, they were not direct copies of Kändler's work. The colours were somewhat softer and the details more carefully painted.

Soon, however, the factory was again beset by financial problems. In 1784 it was put up for sale but received no offers. The problem was resolved when a certain Konrad von Sorgenthal undertook to manage it. It was during his years of control that the factory reached its highest point of prosperity and the works which were produced then are now the most well-known and the most highly acclaimed. The Neoclassical style ousted the Rococo and the articles which emerged were characterized by classical simplicity of form – straight lines and simple curves – set off against richly coloured and meticulously executed decoration. All the well-used Neoclassical motifs were employed and were played off against copies of paintings by Angelica Kauffman and the wall paintings of Pompeii and Herculaneum. The fine wares

motif was certainly peculiar to Vienna. Much of this fanciful moulding was indeed an early form of Rococo. Gilding was little used and decoration was sometimes limited to formal, painted surrounds. Vienna produced few figures and these were all based closely upon Meissen models. Indeed, some were even cast from Meissen originals.

The change of régime in 1744 saw the introduction of a factory mark, the Austrian shield, and the assimilation of made in Vienna during this period achieved a sumptuousness equalled only by Sèvres. The principal modeller, Anton Grassi, who succeeded Niedermeyer in 1784, produced some fine biscuit (unglazed white) figures at the end of the century. Sorgenthal died in 1805 and the factory fell into a state of decline.

There is not space to survey all the German and Austrian centres. Nevertheless, mention must be made of some of the other prominent factories. The three most important, from the collector's point of view, are Nyphenburg, near Munich, then in Bavaria; Frankenthal, in the Palatinate and Furstenburg, in Brunswick. In addition, a considerable amount of white porcelain was decorated by independent painters. They bought wares from the factories and added their own decorations. The standard of their work was high and it is interesting to note that those whose work was better than that of the factories often had their supplies of white porcelain stopped.

In France the finest porcelain was produced at Sèvres. Its roots went back to the Vincennes factory, which was founded in about 1738 by Gilles and Robert Dubois, brothers whose characters and technical abilities were both cause for suspicion. The history of the Vincennes–Sèvres factory cannot be covered in terms of individual decorators and modellers. The factory was a state institution, administered by civil servants and financiers, and the style which emerged allowed no room for the peculiarities of individual artists. The history of the factory is long and complex and need not be given in detail. The first factory, after some years of unsatisfactory production and financial instability, was awarded, in 1753, a Royal Warrant which gave it certain exclusive rights. Three years

Soft-paste porcelain figure mounted on ormolu; made in Vincennes in about 1749. Louvre, Paris.

later the factory was transferred from Vincennes to Sèvres and in 1759 was purchased outright by Louis XV.

It produced both hard-paste and soft-paste porcelain, although the former was not manufactured until after 1770. During the remaining decades of the century both the types were made. The production of soft-paste was discontinued in 1804. It is the soft-paste porcelain, made before 1770, which is the more valuable. Connoisseurs, however, agree that the finest wares were made between 1757 and 1790.

Essentially the decoration, like that used in the German factories, consisted of *chinoiseries*, naturalistic flowers and, later, Neoclassical motifs. Nevertheless, there were developments at Sèvres which were both original and influential. The painters at Sèvres were practically the first to depict exotic birds. This practice was later adopted by English factories, particularly Chelsea and Worcester. The quality of painting at Sèvres was high and among other subjects to be depicted were animals, figures and portraits, landscapes and miniatures. Gilding was popular and so were ormolu mounts.

A decorative scheme characteristic of the Sèvres factory was the combined use of coloured grounds with uncoloured panels. The latter were surrounded by gilding, and used for the depiction of various subjects, such as landscapes, which were popular although outmoded later in the century and replaced by flower paintings.

In France, as in Germany and Austria, porcelain figures were made. At Sèvres these were usually made in biscuit, a process that left the figure unglazed.

Opposite:
"The Goatherd", a hard-paste porcelain figure made in Bristol in 1755.

Above right:
Porcelain figures of Harlequin and Columbine, made at Chelsea in about 1760. Antique Porcelain Company.

Right:
English soft-paste porcelain "ship-bowl" made at Liverpool in about 1756. Victoria and Albert Museum, London.

Left:
French porcelain wine-cooler made at Sèvres in about 1753. The National Trust, Waddesdon Manor.

Below:
Porcelain cup and saucer from Sèvres, dating about 1790. Victoria and Albert Museum, London.

The attraction of this process was that it left the contours of the figure sharp and crisp. Glaze, on the other hand, often obscured the delicate modelling of these small figures. The first were made shortly after 1750 and continued to be made throughout the century. Figures made at Sèvres were seldom marked with the usual sign, but instead received the modeller's initials. The most notable modeller associated with the factory was Pierre-Etiènne Falconet. He supplied models from as early a date as 1754 but later took control of the whole modelling department. The quality of the figures was rather different from that of the German and Austrian ones. The practice, adopted at Sèvres, of employing sculptors to design and produce the models resulted in a tendency for the porcelain figures to resemble miniature bronze or marble statues. That unique feeling for porcelain modelling was lost.

Before turning from Sèvres it must be pointed out that vast quantities of fakes and reproductions have been produced. Marked pieces were manufactured at Tournai in Belgium and then sold to Parisian craftsmen, who decorated them in the Sèvres tradition. In England, Minton's produced fine reproductions while John Rose & Co. of Coalport went so far as to specialize in replacements made to order. It is possible, therefore, and even likely, that what is said to be a Sèvres service will contain an article which was manufactured many miles from the French factory.

Other important centres of French 18th-century porcelain manufacture were Rouen, Saint Cloud, Chantilly and Mennecy.

All English porcelain, with the exception of pieces produced in Plymouth and Bristol, was of the soft-paste variety. Production of soft-paste began in earnest in the 1750s, although considerable amounts had been made in the preceding decade. The factory which came to the fore and dominated all others was at Chelsea, London. Between 1750 and 1770 it was managed by a Soho silversmith, Nicholas Sprimont. The factory was then bought by William Duesbury and amalgamated with his factory in Derby.

Between 1750 and its closure in 1784, the factory employed two distinct types of paste. The first was produced until 1759 and articles of this period are considered to be the finest in terms of decoration. In 1759 a lighter and more translucent paste was introduced and had the practical advantages of being easier to model and fire.

Throughout the century the influences of Meissen and Sèvres was strongly felt. The *chinoiseries*, flowers, and Neoclassical motifs made their inevitable appearance. Early Chelsea specimens were undecorated and left white but painted decoration and gilding soon acquired greater importance. After 1750 figures were made and these, of all the factory's wares, are now the most sought-after and command the highest prices. The range of subjects was enormous and included figures from the *Commedia dell'Arte*; depictions of artisans, fishermen and beggars; political figures such as the Earl of Chatham and the Duke of Cumberland; mythological figures, animals and birds. In 1784 the factory was closed and Duesbury, the new proprietor, had workmen and moulds transferred to his factory in Derby. The

Above:
French soft-paste porcelain ice bucket, made in St Cloud in about 1715. Musée National Adrien-Dubouché, Limoges, France.

Below:
A Chinese porcelain flask of the early
18th century, with *famille rose* decoration
applied over the glaze.

Opposite:
Porcelain figure of a shepherdess made in
Bow in about 1765. Private collection.

Above:
Porcelain tea-service from Limoges, France; c.1780. Musée National Adrien-Dubouché, Limoges, France.

Left:
English porcelain jug made at Caughley in about 1780. Such jugs were intended for a wide market. Victoria and Albert Museum, London.

Opposite:
English soft-paste porringer made at Bow in about 1755.

forgeries and fakes number tens of thousands, so great has been the popularity of the Chelsea wares. The collector, with a little experience, will have no trouble in identifying these. Nearly all are made of hard-paste and the collector who can distinguish between the two pastes will be able to spot a reproduction with ease. Some soft-paste reproductions do exist but they are rarer than the genuine article and need hardly concern the small collector.

Downstream of the Chelsea works was situated the Bow porcelain factory. Its early history is obscure. It was founded by Thomas Frye, an Irish painter, and Edward Heylyn, and a patent was taken out in 1744 for the production of porcelain. Not until 1748, however, was good quality soft-paste porcelain produced. Few pieces remain from this decade and it was not until the 1750s that the finest pieces were made. Cups and mugs, ink-wells, bowls and figures were the most common articles. In 1754 transfer-printing was introduced and was later to be used at Worcester and other English porcelain factories, notably Liverpool, although it did not become widespread until the 19th century. The technique of transfer-printing involved the application of a print, taken from a

copper plate, to the surface of the porcelain. This could be done either before or after glazing. Figures made at Bow during this decade imitated the wares from Chelsea but were not so well modelled and were usually left unpainted.

Wares produced in the 1760s were more complex and were richly enamelled in bright and brilliant colours. The figure modelling retained its primitive qualities and did not aspire to great artistry. Indeed, the productions of Bow were not intended for royal patrons or the aristocracy but for the merchant classes, and their relative primitiveness seems better suited to this clientèle than the sophisticated imitations of Meissen which were being produced at Chelsea. In 1775 this factory, like Chelsea, was purchased by Duesbury and had its tools, moulds and workmen transferred to Derby.

In 1756 William Duesbury had established the first porcelain factory in Derby. Aspirations must have been high and in that year it was advertised as the "second Dresden". Articles made prior to 1770 were unmarked and made of a light-weight and somewhat glassy porcelain. They were decorated in pale enamels and closely based on Chelsea designs. Although the finest pieces

were the figures, tableware was also produced. After the acquisition of the Chelsea factory articles from both works were marked with an anchor and the letter "D". The period after 1770 is known as Chelsea–Derby, as much of the porcelain that was manufactured in Derby was sent to Chelsea to be decorated. The influence of Sèvres during this period was considerable. Richer decoration was employed while the biscuit technique was introduced in the manufacture of figures. In 1784 the factory mark acquired a crown and the term "Crown Derby" is used to describe wares made after this date. Duesbury died in 1784 and his son assumed the business. Early types of both form and decoration continued to be used alongside the more fashionable Neoclassical style.

Before terminating this brief survey of the porcelain factories, mention must be made of one of the best and longest-lived: the Worcester factory. It was founded in 1751 and until 1783 employed a soft-paste which was thinner and more durable than most of the other types being used around the country. The first period of the factory's development is known by the name of one of its founders, Wall. This period lasted until 1783. Few figures

Above:
Staffordshire mug made in about 1755, with a salt glaze finish. Fitzwilliam Museum, Cambridge.

Opposite:
Creamware dish from the Wedgwood factory, c.1764. D. Towner Collection.

were made, as the factory preferred to specialize in tableware. *Chinoiseries*, transfer-prints, birds and flowers were the most common form of decoration. The articles tended to be simple in design, the stress being laid on utility rather than ornament. In 1783 the factory was bought by Thomas Flight. The style which followed, which is known by his name, lasted until the end of the century and was characterized by a whiter grade of porcelain and a more severe style, based on Neoclassicism.

In the field of porcelain the question of genuineness is a complex one. The factory mark system is unreliable and can only be trusted if everything else about a piece seems to be genuine. The collector, by comparing the two different articles, can soon come to recognize the difference between hard-paste and soft-paste. But this will only mark the beginning of a long period of learning. The same forms of decoration were used throughout England and the Continent and, to the beginner, a piece made in Meissen may look the same as a piece from Chelsea. Furthermore, the collector will have to deal with vast quantities of 19th-century fakes and reproductions. As has been already pointed out, some of these are easier to detect than others. The collector of 18th-century porcelain will need a patient temperament and the repeated help of a reputable dealer. Although porcelain represents the greatest achievement of the 18th-century potter, there is one other development about which the collector should know. Those who could not afford porcelain were dependent on a cheaper product: earthenware. In the 17th century this was beautifully manufactured in Delft, Holland. The influence of that centre waned with the discovery of porcelain at the beginning of the 18th century, but earthenware was to receive a vital boost in England. At the Wedgwood pottery in Staffordshire, founded in 1759 by Josiah Wedgwood, a style in earthenware manufacture was developed which made the factory the most influential English ceramics centre, far outstripping the importance of any of the English porcelain factories. Its influence spread as far afield as Russia and America. Wedgwood's enormous success was due to his development of cream-coloured earthenware – renamed Queen's ware after the works received royal patronage – jaspar ware and the black basaltes ware. He undercut the prices of the porcelain and tin-glazed earthenware factories

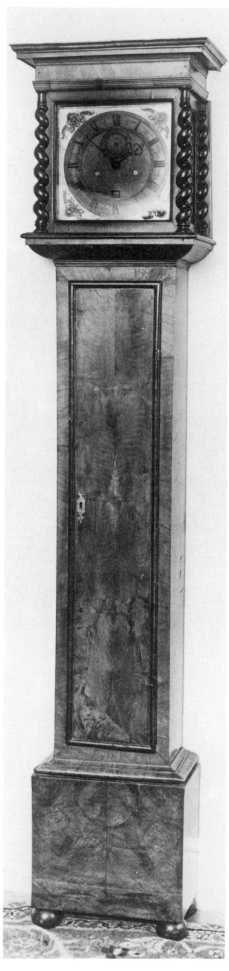

and, employing Neoclassical forms and decoration, produced wares which would be available to all classes of society. Classical relief decorations in white were set off against pale blue, green, and yellow grounds. The forms of the pieces were culled direct from antiquity and were ideally suited to the Neoclassical styles in furnishing and interior decoration.

Clocks and watches

By the beginning of the 18th century both the pendulum and spring-driven clock had reached states of development whereby they were efficient and well matched to their needs. During the 18th century there were no fundamental changes in their mechanisms.

In the broadest terms the development of clocks in England is relatively straightforward. The lantern clock was a product of the 16th and 17th centuries and few were made after 1700. By 1725 their production had ceased altogether. The lantern clock did, however, have one important development: the thirty-hour clock. This term is rather confusing as the lantern clock itself was also of one-day duration, but the term is applied to a long case clock, small and plain, encased in oak and manufactured principally in the country. It required winding every day. After 1700 the thirty-hour clock became one of the most popular timepieces to be constructed in the English provinces. It was an accurate timekeeper but was nevertheless seldom fitted with a minute hand. It seems remarkable that this should be true for so many of the thirty-hour clocks made in the latter part of the century, but in fact the construction of single-handed clocks continued well into the 19th century. These clocks were short, often less than 6 ft 6 in (2 metres), and were designed to fit into cottages and small houses. Normally they were given square dials. The flat-topped hood was

Far left:
Early 18th-century long case clock by Thomas Tompion. Its most unusual feature is its hood, which slides up. National Trust, Britain.

Left:
American long case clock of the late 18th century, made of mahogany. Its decoration shows Neoclassical influence. Victoria and Albert Museum, London.

predominant throughout the century and the only noticeable change in the casing was in the width. As the century progressed, the case broadened, and thin clocks of the early part of the century often show marks where the pendulum has swung and hit the sides. The decoration of the dials and spandrels was often quite up to the standard of London-made eight-day clocks, while the proportions and construction of the oak cases was of fine quality. Thirty-hour long case clocks, once unwanted, are still relatively cheap and therefore attractive items for the small collector.

The finest English clock of the 18th century was the eight-day long case clock. Considerably taller than the thirty-hour clock – sometimes over 8 ft (2.4 metres) – the eight-day clock was made principally in London. It was an expensive item of furniture and provincial clockmakers could not rely on selling as many as their London competitors. A step-by-step guide to the development of the eight-day clock is beyond the scope of this book but there is room to point out some of the major innovations and stylistic characteristics. At the end of the 17th century the break-arch dial (surmounted by a broken wooden arch) made its first appearance and by 1720 the old-fashioned square dial had all but disappeared. Shortly afterwards, the bracket clock also discarded its square dial in favour of the break-arch. One of the advantages of the innovation was that it enlarged the face of the clock, thereby retaining the proportions of the whole. The case had grown considerably at the end of the 17th century and the square dial was beginning to seem rather small. On the other hand, the clockmaker was now confronted with the problem of how to fill the space of the arch. It was resolved in a number of ways. Many designers used the space to display the phases of the moon, the indicators being connected to the workings of the clock. The most popular decorations came in the form of small moving figures. The subjects depicted were numerous: painted figures played shuttlecock, ships pitched and rolled against an angry, painted sea, Father Time reaped his harvest. Less expensive clocks received more mundane decorations,

Gilt clock-case in Rococo style, made by Charles Cressent in about 1725. Musée des Arts Decoratifs.

sometimes consisting of nothing more than a small engraved silver medallion. More practical clockmakers positioned a strike controller there – a lever which enabled the owner to stop and restart the strike mechanism. Often the arch carried the seconds indicator.

The decoration of the spandrels developed in a fairly well ordered sequence. Until the second decade of the century cherubs, depicted in low relief, were especially popular. The middle decades, between 1720 and 1760, witnessed the development of Rococo foliage, while the last years were dominated by classical arabesques and interlaced strapwork. All these decorations were ·executed in low relief but the practice began to fall off towards the end of the century. With the introduction of manufactured iron dials, which could not be gilded or enamelled, relief decoration was replaced by painted ornamentation.

English clockmakers laid less stress upon the cases than they did upon the dials and the mechanics of the object. Consequently, 18th-century English clock cases were comparatively plain. At the beginning of the period the most popular wood was oak. Walnut was also used but due to its shortage, already discussed, it was rarely used after 1740. Mahogany made its major contribution after 1750 and many cases, made just prior to this date, were japanned. The practice died out with the advent of mahogany. Towards 1800 marquetry was introduced.

The predominant feature of the English eight-day clock was its hood. The flat-topped hood of the 17th century was dispensed with and replaced with an architecturally detailed canopy. An architrave, frieze and cornice was supported by pillars, sometimes freestanding, and on top of all these rose domes and pediments. Gilding was often incorporated, although the trunk of the case was usually plain. Occasionally it carried pillars which resembled the ones above.

A popular and more portable instrument was the bracket clock. As with the long case clocks, stress was placed on function and the designs for cases remained comparatively plain. As the century progressed and growing affluence enabled households to own more than one clock, so the need for clocks

Opposite:
English longcase clock made by Thomas Tompion. The olivewood is inlaid with medallions of ebony and satinwood. British Museum.

Below:
Bracket clock of about 1750, with a round rather than the more usual square dial.

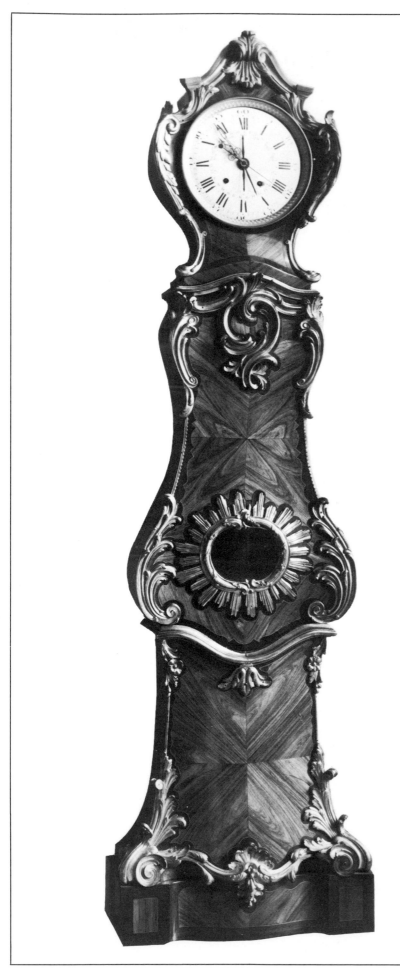

to be easily portable lessened. As a result there was a tendency for them to grow in size. Early in the century the break-arch dial was introduced and this had the immediate effect of increasing the height. Ebony veneer was a particularly popular form of decoration for the cases and gilded ornament played an ever increasing role. Towards the end of the century these characteristics began to disappear and mahogany cases came into fashion. The arched dial led to the introduction of the bell-shaped top and this motif lasted throughout the century. In the 1770s circular, brass-framed windows were introduced and liberated the bracket clock from its rectangular shape. Despite this new-found freedom, English bracket clocks still retained their simple and functional aspect.

This was never the case in France. French clockmakers were primarily concerned with decorative appearance and the art of time-keeping was somewhat sacrificed to this end. The fanciful appearance of many French clocks is remarkable. Clock dials were mounted on the backs of bronze elephants; some were supported by cherubs who themselves were kept aloft on billowing clouds, others were carried on the shoulders of Father Time. Porcelain clock cases were made at Sèvres and others imported from Meissen. Ormolu was especially popular and was employed with a notable lack of restraint, while *bombé*-shaped cases were a noticeable feature of long case clocks.

The art of clockmaking in America did not start in earnest until the middle of the century, when Boston and Philadelphia rapidly emerged as the leading centres. Many early American clocks contained English mechanisms and the cases were similar to English designs. One original American contribution was the banjo clock, so-called because it resembled an inverted banjo. It was invented, however, during the closing

Left:
A French clock with a rosewood case; its Rococo decoration is typical of the Louis XV period. Louvre, Paris.

Opposite:
French clock of Louis XV's reign. Victoria and Albert Museum, London.

Above:
Five 18th-century watchcases, in horn, leather and tortoise-shell inlaid with silver. Private collection.

Opposite:
A musical table clock made in London in about 1767. Many of these clocks were exported.

Left:
French mantle-clock of the 18th century, with typical statuary derived from Michelangelo. Wallace Collection, London.

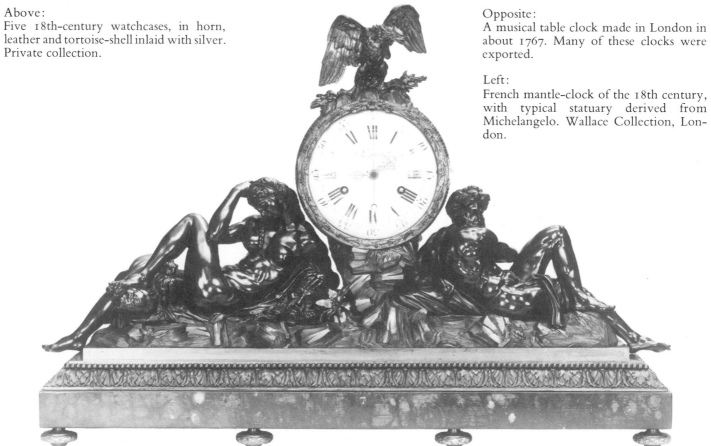

American clock of about 1800. Clocks of this design are known as banjo clocks. Museum of Fine Arts, Boston.

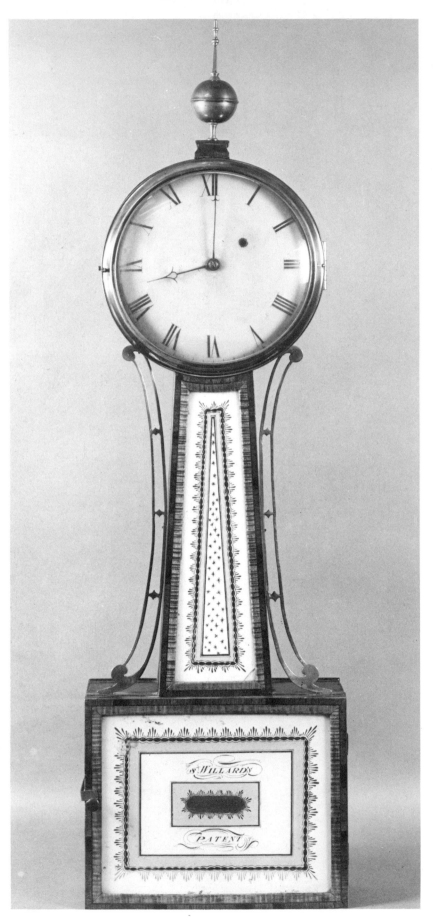

years of the century and is generally regarded as a 19th-century product. The bracket clock was seldom made in the colonies and thus the long case clock predominated. Cases were made by the finest cabinetmakers, notably John Townsend of Newport, to incorporate imported English mechanisms.

Toys

The 18th century witnessed a growing regard by adults for the needs of children. They were no longer simply regarded as miniature adults but were seen as creatures whose tastes were fundamentally different from those of their elders. One of the results of this change in attitude was the appearance of a profusion of toys. Children, no longer expected to behave as parodies of their parents and elders, were at last allowed to indulge and enjoy themselves.

The most significant item of the 18th-century toymaker's craft was the dolls' house, and the miniature constructions incorporated the prevailing fashions in architecture. Indeed, some dolls' houses made in England were designed by Robert Adam, while Thomas Chippendale, as an apprentice, was commissioned to make dolls' house furniture. These small constructions enjoyed the same vogue in Europe as they did in England. In France, dolls' houses appeared in the form of single rooms. Simple in design as these were, they were nevertheless elaborately decorated in that ornate style typical of French interior decoration in the 18th century. In America, dolls' houses only appeared in the second half of the century and those which are dated earlier were usually imported. In contrast to the French designs, the colonial dolls' house was plain and undecorated and somewhat reflected the domestic architecture of colonial America.

Miniature furniture was also made and, as we have seen, cabinetmakers turned their attention to this craft. Much furniture was made in Germany, especially at Nuremberg, and was usually made of wood, bone or paper. Smaller articles, such as glasses and chandeliers, were also manufactured.

Dolls of the 18th century were not the sophisticated creatures that appeared in the following century.

Left:
A pair of acrobat dolls, made in England in about 1800. Bethnal Green Museum, London.

Below:
English dolls' house of about 1740. Museum of London.

Wooden limbs were crudely attached to the body by shafts which passed through holes driven through the torso. Glass eyes were rare and the facial features and expressions were painted on. Although the construction of the body remained the same throughout the century, clothes became more elaborate and by the end of the century they perfectly reflected the latest fashions.

Other toy figures appeared in the form of tin soldiers. In Germany, partly as a reflection of growing military might, the manufacture of tin soldiers reached an unprecedented level. Flat figures, which could stand up with the aid of a stand, began to be produced in Nuremberg in 1775 and it was not long before the industry had spread throughout the country. By 1790 there were as many as eight foundries turning out toy soldiers in the town of Furth. Not until the 19th century were toy soldiers produced in any real quantity in other European countries.

Another plaything which appeared in the 18th century was the moving, clockwork toy. As early as the first decade of the century dolls were made with ingenious clockwork mechanisms. In the years which followed, craftsmen emerged who became celebrities solely through their mechanical inventions. In 1773 a certain Henri Louis Jacquet-Droz designed and built a figure which was able to draw the likeness of Queen Marie Antoinette, while another, made by Henri Maillardet, had the extraordinary ability to write short rhymes, both in French and in English. Mechanical toys of the 18th century are numerous and are an attractive prospect for the collector.

Many other toys were made. The Noah's Ark was particularly popular in the colonies, while paper and cardboard puppets were plentiful everywhere. Cardboard dolls on to which clothes could be attached were, like the Ark, popular in America. Nor was cardboard employed for dolls alone. Furniture and even model ships and carriages were wrought from the material. Because of their delicacy few remain and are rare collector's items.

Below left:
English dolls' house of the early 18th century, painted to resemble bricks. It was intended as a practical plaything.

Opposite:
A toy stage coach, made in about 1790.

Below:
A late 18th-century doll made of porcelain and wood, showing the crude joints of dolls of this period.

The 19th Century

Introduction

The 19th century witnessed a complete transformation in the life-style of Western man. The population of Britain, for example, more than doubled during the century and the remorseless drift of workers from the land to the expanding industrial cities irreversibly changed the social structure. In 1800 men relied on sail power to cross the oceans; 100 years later they sailed in massive iron warships. Other forms of transport changed likewise. The horse and the carriage, the established modes of land transport in 1800, were superseded by the railway train in the 1840s; by the end of the century the internal combustion engine would make its appearance and shortly afterwards the aeroplane. The bicycle, unknown in 1800, was being mass-produced by the 1870s. By 1890 messages would no longer be sent by hand, but might be posted, telephoned or telegraphed. Improved methods of printing, the establishment of libraries and of an educational system, limited in its scope but for the first time available to almost all, began the process of eliminating illiteracy. Moreover, once people could read they could be influenced by publicity and an entirely new method of selling was inaugurated, an innovation that would profoundly influence the production of furniture and much else besides.

It was the accumulation of wealth during the 19th century, however, that most influenced the production of antiques. The period of the Regency, which in mood and styles may be said to end in 1830, was one of self-assurance. The rich had inherited their money, they were used to things of beauty in their homes and had acquired from their parents and grandparents an instinctive appreciation of elegant furniture and decoration. It was, in fact, an age unmatched in history for its elegance. All that was soon rapidly to

change. For the first time a large middle class emerged (the middle class of Tudor times and even of the 18th century had consisted of relatively few families by comparison), a class which in the space of a decade or two acquired wealth, often enormous wealth. Below this class came a section known at the time as the lower middle class, infinitely less well off but nevertheless able to employ a servant or possibly two, and furnish their homes in the

prevailing fashions. To meet this growing demand furniture was mass-produced. This furniture was offered for sale in shops, with the purchaser viewing the exhibits and then choosing what he most liked, and so in effect the commercial manufacturer of the product became the arbiter of taste – more often than not a person wholly unqualified to act in this capacity.

English design between 1830 and 1880, like almost every aspect of

Above:
A selection of Victorian lockets, representing various members of a single family.

Opposite:
Two parian-ware figures of 1846. Godder Reference Collection, Worthing.

English society of that age, led the world. It reflected the mid-Victorians' hope that the machine, that modern Prometheus, would be the bearer of prosperity, the engine of civilization. The mechanized cotton industry had forced open England's ports to the world's food. Bread became cheaper. By mid-century everyone knew that the English common people were better fed and better clothed than their European brethren. By mid-century also the conviction had grown that England, so long accustomed to look across the Channel in praise of other people's art, was able to produce goods, "objects of *vertu*" as that age called its curios and ornamental pieces, as ingenious and artful in decoration and as cheaply as any other nation, including even the French.

Industrial inventions had opened the way to new methods – stamping, moulding, pressing, cutting, shaping –

which were to transform English design and bring "art" into every household. Mass production was able, at last, to make high art part of everyday popular culture. The hallmark of that art was ornament. John Ruskin, the revered sage of the Victorian middle class, was no worshipper of the machine but he shared the Victorians' faith in the gospel of work. He exalted Gothic ornateness above Neoclassical simplicity, partly because the long labour which Gothic carving required attested to the craftsman's love for his work. "Work" was a catchword of the times; so was its handmaiden, "utility". To what better purpose could art be put than to adorn the products of the workshop of the world? It was one of the discoveries, or rediscoveries, of the mid-Victorian age that utilitarian objects could also be works of art. However trivial an household object might be, its value would be enhanced by

Above:
English papier-mâché tray and boxes.
Private collection.

Opposite above:
A selection of Regency copper cooking
moulds, from the Royal Pavilion in
Brighton.

Opposite below:
Two English vases made in the last years
of the 19th century by the de Morgan
workshop, decorated by Fred Passenger.
Private collection.

lavish decoration. There were markets
to be captured and ambitious manufacturers listened to the advice of those
people who instructed them that useful objects fetched higher prices if they
were also beautiful, and "beautiful"
came more and more to mean "ornamental". The Industrial Revolution
was to join together in one common
civilizing enterprise, art, science and
machinery. Elegance was to be married
to abundance, intricate decoration to
strength. Art was no longer to be the
preserve of the aristocratic connoisseur,
nor the rare child of the isolated
Romantic genius. Art was to be the
common possession of the ordinary
people of an enlightened, progressive
and powerful nation.

Iron came into its own. The iron-
founders who pioneered the use of cast
iron in civil engineering were also the

leaders of taste and fashion in domestic
design. Improved methods of casting
opened the way to the ornamental use
of iron in richly embellished, but inexpensive, chairs, tables, umbrella
stands and garden sculptures. Yet how
were cast iron objects to be kept light
in weight if they were laden with ornament? The solution was simple: the
use of open, reticulated motifs such as
serpents, scrolls, leaves, branches and
vines. Thanks to the early pre-eminence
of iron, the prevailing motif of mid-
Victorian design·became the sumptuous curve, exploited as it had not
been exploited·since the days of the
Baroque.

It was a feature of Victorian design
that one·material was deliberately
transformed to make it look like another. However fretfully Ruskin might
fulminate against the dishonesty of the

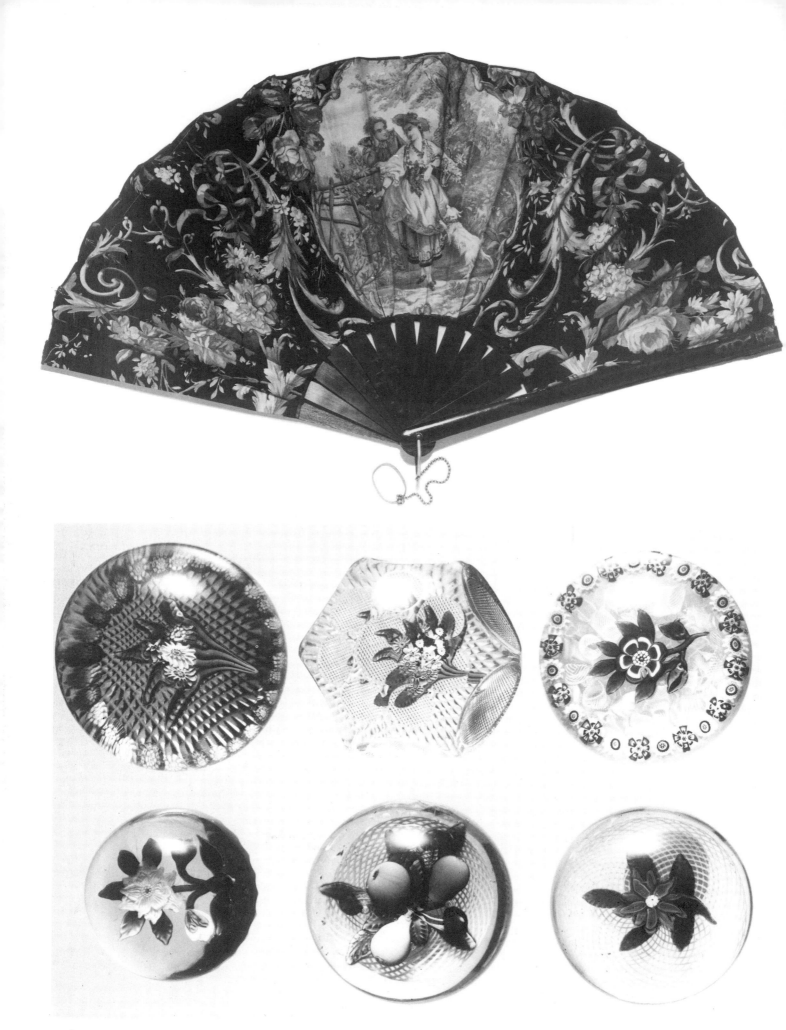

Right:
A Chinese mirror frame of the early 19th century, made of carved boxwood.

Opposite above:
A printed cotton fan from mid-Victorian England; lace fans were also highly popular at this time.

Opposite below:
A selection of 19th-century French glass paperweights.

practice, the transformation of materials exactly suited the Victorian taste for innovation and "science". The Great Exhibition of 1851 was crowded with materials masking themselves as marble, wood, stained-glass. Even "imitation ormolu" (even though ormolu itself is a brass imitation of gold) was boldly displayed. Imitation was not offered apologetically as an economic saving, although it certainly was that, but proudly proclaimed as a triumph of ingenuity – the art of alchemy brought to perfection by modern technology. Nor were transformation and imitation the end of the matter. There were also new methods of mass production. Watt's sculpture machines, though not entirely new, were able to reproduce original works in any size; so was Cheverton's carving machine. The Victorians did not blush at the mass production of art. They looked upon it, not as a symptom of degeneracy, but as an example of progress.

Another example was the electroplating process, discovered in the late 1830s, capable of applying metal ornament in intricate detail to a wide variety of surfaces. By means of a galvanic battery cell, a fine film of gold, silver or copper could be laid on objects, even natural ones. Hence the abundance of flowers and insects plated so thinly that every stamen, every hair of the original was retained. The purists railed against the corruption of nature; the masses prided themselves on their cleverness and filled their houses with delightfully curious productions.

People who took such pleasure in mass production, in imitations, in ornament for ornament's sake were, not surprisingly, careless of stylistic purity. They saw no incongruity, no offence against aesthetic canons, in randomly mixing the Gothic with the Greek, the Roman with the Egyptian. It is no accident that the age has no convenient label, like "Art Nouveau" or "Art Deco", to describe it, since no single word or phrase could encompass the multiplicity of styles so natural to an age of invention and innovation. The Victorians were exuberant in the pleasure which they derived from variety. The eclecticism of their taste has earned them the condemnation of later generations. The collector who sneers at the "tastelessness" of Victorian design, however, may find that it is nevertheless satisfying to recapture the Victorians' sense of fun and their spirit of energy.

The triviality and the materialism of the time brought its natural reaction. In 1848 a group of painters and poets, notably D. G. Rossetti, William Holman Hunt and John Millais, formed themselves into what came to be called the Pre-Raphaelite Brotherhood. Their

Above:
English picture incorporating skeleton leaves, seaweed and flowers; such pieces were often made privately in mid-century.

Below:
Sewing table made in Salem in about 1800.

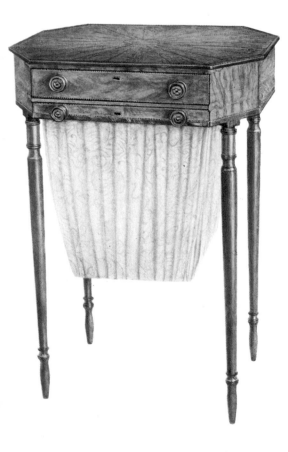

aim was to turn art away from the growing materialism of industrialized England and, using the literary imagery and symbolism of the medieval world, return to the values and inspirations of the time of Raphael and his 15th-century predecessors. This was to have a significant impact on the world of antiques, for from it sprang William Morris's Arts and Crafts movement in the late 19th century. Morris, inspired by the Gothic Revival, sought to re-vivify the decorative arts by restoring the task of production to craftsmen. Machinery was eschewed and the methods known to the Middle Ages and the Renaissance were reintroduced. This revival found both supporters and critics, but it had a number of important side-effects, such as a renewed interest in the Indian folk art of North America and also the advent of Art Nouveau, after 1895. Thus, a history of 19th-century antiques must tell not only of industrialized mass-production but also of the harking back to times past, their values and methods.

English furniture

In 1815, with the final defeat of Napo-leon, a changed world of easier and faster communication emerged. Ideas and influences were exchanged more rapidly and terms to describe periods become blurred. In England, the term "Regency" takes furniture into the 1830s. In fact it encompasses the last years of George III's reign (the Prince of Wales acted as Regent from 1812) and continues even after the Prince's own death in 1830, but it is a conveni-ent word to describe the last period of antique production before the advent of mass-produced pieces in the reign of Queen Victoria.

Furniture of the Regency period was usually veneered, either in mahogany, rosewood or satinwood. Other woods, such as the amboyna wood of the West Indies, were also imported. New types of furniture were developed. The davenport, a small writing desk with drawers, appeared for the first time, although it was not to reach its greatest popularity until the reign of Queen Victoria. Another innovation was the so-called sofa table, which had drawers and flaps for extension and was de-signed for use when ladies entertained their friends to tea. Looking-glasses had for long been pieces in drawing-rooms, but it is at this time that the tall cheval glass, which reflected the whole figure, was introduced.

Much furniture, inspired by the Gothic romantic novels of the time, seem grotesque to modern generations, but such pieces, gross in size and often embellished with animal legs and sphinxes, must not detract from the true and lasting impression of Regency furniture; simple lines, good propor-tions and considerable elegance. The day-bed, with its curve-over end, often

with *chinoiserie* decoration, typifies the leisurely style of Regency life.

Mention must be made of the Prince Regent himself. "The First Gentleman of Europe", although a spendthrift and debauchee, was a man of the greatest culture, and his influence on the age in which he lived was paramount. His London residence, Carlton House, was decorated and furnished by Henry Holland with many fine pieces of French furniture. Carlton House was later unhappily destroyed but the Prince Regent's summer residence, the Brighton Pavilion, remains. It has been described as the greatest example of *chinoiserie* in the Western world and,

although in part damaged by fire, it is essential viewing for the collector.

The Regency style went out of favour for a number of reasons. Styles themselves evolve and few manufacturers can refrain from making what they deem to be improvements. In this particular case, however, there was an additional and novel cause for a change in fashion. In the 1840s there was a Victorian religious revival which had an impact in many fields, not least in that of furniture. Art and architecture, furniture and decoration, should all, it was felt, reflect a moral purpose. To the Victorians, the Regency period had been one of flippancy and irreverence,

American serpentine chest of drawers in the Federal style, c.1815. H. F. duPont Winterthur Museum, Delaware.

Above:
Sofa in the English Empire style, decorated with chinoiserie and gilt; c.1815.

Left:
A Sheraton-style chair of about 1805, made of mahogany.

and Prince Albert abandoned the Royal Pavilion as a mark of his disapproval. True craftsmanship would gradually be restored and by the end of the century furniture would again reflect the search for comfort and a means of displaying wealth. It should be noted in passing, however, that the advent of machinery did not, as is often supposed, affect furniture production much before the 1870s. Equipment for cutting veneers was employed early in the century, it is true, but its full impact was not felt until later in Victoria's reign.

Designs until about 1850 were characterized by revivals of earlier styles and various combinations of them. In the 20 years following the death of George IV (the Prince Regent) in 1830, an astonishing range of styles followed each other in rapid succession – Greek and Egyptian, Rococo, Elizabethan and, ultimately, the Gothic Revival. With so many styles simultaneously in favour, styles became related to the function of individual rooms. Thus, while the Greek style, with the ostensibly masculine connotations of its decorative images, was considered suitable for halls and dining-rooms, Rococo was accepted as permissible for ladies' boudoirs. Rococo was in fact to last until the middle of the century, and a considerable quantity of it was exhibited at the Crystal Palace Great Exhibition of 1851. None, however,

was displayed at the exhibition of 1862, which indicates that its fall from favour was abrupt. Perhaps Rococo's greatest contribution to Victorian furniture was the balloon-backed chair. The Elizabethan revival was in large measure inspired by the historical novels of Sir Walter Scott, who furnished his home in Scotland with 16th- and 17th-century pieces. The same idea was employed at some of the great houses, notably Hardwick Hall in Derbyshire, and was also aped by the newly-rich middle-class. The outstanding rival to the Elizabethan style in furniture was that of Gothic, but much of this was marred by commercial designers whose pieces were often characterized by Gothic ornament only. The most distinguished exception to this was the architect A. W. N. Pugin, for he stuck rigidly to simple Gothic designs. His most important work was the new Houses of Parliament (1837–43), where he designed every detail of the interior, and produced a Gothic masterpiece.

Regency sofa table in pale mahogany.

The Great Exhibition of 1851 marks the decisive point in English 19th-century furniture production. The variety of styles exhibited was so extensive that it compellingly revealed the dangers inherent in eclecticism: ornament was seen to have been emphasized at the expense of utility and, even worse, much of the ornamentation was inappropriate and, as often as not, conflicting. The search for novelty for its own sake was the principal cause of the disharmony, as the artist Richard Redgrave noted when he wrote in his *Supplementary Report on the Exhibition of 1851,* "The hunger after novelty is quite insatiable. . . . Ours is certainly a chaotic period." The English exhibits at Paris in 1855 showed a considerable improvement, but this was in large measure the consequence of immigrant French craftsmen.

The middle years of the century saw the emergence not only of new forms of furniture but also new materials. Davenports (so named after a Captain Davenport, for whom the first was made) were already known, but it is at this time that they began to be produced in great numbers. Canterburies (stands in which to keep sheet music) were introduced, as were chiffoniers (a combination of chest and sideboard), hardly a middle-class home being without them. Two of the most characteristic pieces of the time were sideboards, which were extremely heavy, and large but usually simply designed wardrobes. The woods employed were in general mahogany or walnut. Significant, too, was the popularity of upholstered furniture, illustrating the prevailing desire for comfort. Victorian drawing-rooms would have an abundance of such pieces, including love seats, ottomans, sofas and elaborately decorated footstools. Velvet was the most popular material for this purpose and these pieces of furniture

Opposite above:
English sofa table in the Regency style, made in 1810. Royal Pavilion, Brighton.

Opposite below:
English carved mahogany side table, designed by Philip Hardwick in about 1834. Goldsmith's Hall London.

Below:
Baltimore ladies' desk of mahogany, with inlays of satinwood and holly.

were often deeply buttoned. Drapery and fringes were also favoured and would remain so for many years. Marble furniture also came into fashion and was used for inlaid table tops and ornaments.

Two materials must be mentioned, neither of which was new but which were now employed for the first time for furniture. Cast iron was used in the production of all manner of furniture, usually made in the prevailing styles of the time. It was used extensively in garden furniture and in public parks and buildings, especially for seats and benches. It was durable, would tolerate hard wear and did not rot or warp from inclement weather or discolour from sunlight. The most notable other item of furniture then extensively made in metal was the iron, or more usually brass, bedstead. It would appear that this was adopted for reasons of hygiene and brass bedsteads were to remain popular until well into the 20th century. They went out of favour abruptly during the inter-war years, and until the 1960s they could be bought for a modest sum. Today, however, with a resurgence of interest in all things Victorian, they command high prices. However, they are likely to make a sound investment. Since brass is a hard substance, any bedstead made of this metal is likely still to be in good condition; its value will inevitably rise and in the meantime the collector can, after all, have it for his personal use, since these bedsteads were generally well made, are often pleasing in appearance and were designed to be comfortable.

The second substance newly used in the production of furniture was papier mâché. It is believed to have been invented in Persia and had been used in Europe in the 18th century for decorative work, but now it came into high favour. Music canterburies, chairs and even small tables were made of this material. It was soon realized that papier mâché was essentially impractical for such pieces but it for long remained popular for smaller items such as workboxes and especially for trays. Many of these smaller pieces are still to be found in shops and on stalls but, because of the vulnerability of the material, there are few in perfect condition. They are still offered at a reasonable price, however, and collectors seeking an attractive, inexpensive area in which to make a collection, and one which would not occupy much space, would do worse than to specialize in papier mâché.

We have noted that machinery came into general use in the production of furniture in the 1870s. Not all machines, however, necessarily meant poor-quality furniture. Some, such as machine saws, did no more than cut labour costs and reduce the time needed to make a piece. However, the carving

Right:
A French design of about 1840 for a love-seat. Bibliothèque Nationale.

Opposite:
English Gothic Revival cabinet of 1858. It was designed by William Burgos. Victoria and Albert Museum, London.

Below:
An early 19th-century English walnut davenport, showing its typical drawers up one side. Victoria and Albert Museum, London.

machines and the veneer-peeling machine did have a harmful effect on furniture of the time. Neither was in itself injurious, but, despite its heavy overtones of Christian morality, the period was largely geared to profit and expansion, and the less scrupulous manufacturers could use the veneer machine not for decorative work, as was intended, but to diguise shoddy workmanship. Similarly, the mechanical carving device was often employed to duplicate elaborate hand-carving. Under these circumstances it is perhaps surprising that so much furniture of the period is of a high standard.

Even so, a great deal of mid- and late Victorian furniture seems aesthetically uncertain. We have seen how the earlier years of the century were dominated by revivals in styles and how different styles might be found in different rooms of the same house. This naturally affected only the rich, for they had large houses and these were commonly divided into areas of male and female domination. With the middle-class, however, the situation was otherwise, for their homes were too small to be divided in this way. The furniture they bought was therefore a matter of personal taste. What seems to have marred much of the furniture of the time is that they did not exercise this taste; they bought their furniture,

not so much because it was pleasing to them or thought suitable for their particular home, but because it was considered seemly and proper, as if it fulfilled some moral code ordained by their betters. With responsibility in selection thus abrogated, a sense of muddle in middle-class homes supersedes the relative order of the earlier revival styles. The company set up by William Morris in the 1880s worked against this trend but, while its furniture was often superb, it was in the main producing individual pieces. Some similar firms developed commercial production but they could hardly compete with the inferior pieces now being mass-produced. Genuine pieces by Morris's associates, such as Philip Webb and George Jacob are today both rare and expensive. Like much else, however, they repay study in museums so that the collector can see for himself the striking contrast between this and the other forms of Victorian furniture which are so readily available in shops.

As with the furniture of other times, that of the Victorians reflects the mentality and spirit of the age. It was a time of ever-growing wealth and of supreme self-confidence, a time of invention and enterprise, but it was also a time of social respectability and total acceptance of prevailing conventions. The furniture of the period reflects all these

Previous page:
The Princes' Chamber at the Houses of Parliament, Westminster; a fine example of English Gothic Revival.

Left:
An American settee of the early 19th century, made in Maryland. Baltimore Museum of Art.

Opposite:
A selection of French designs for furniture in the Empire style of 1812.

Below:
The Yellow Drawing Room at Fontainebleau, designed in the French Empire style for the Empress Josephine in the early years of the 19th century.

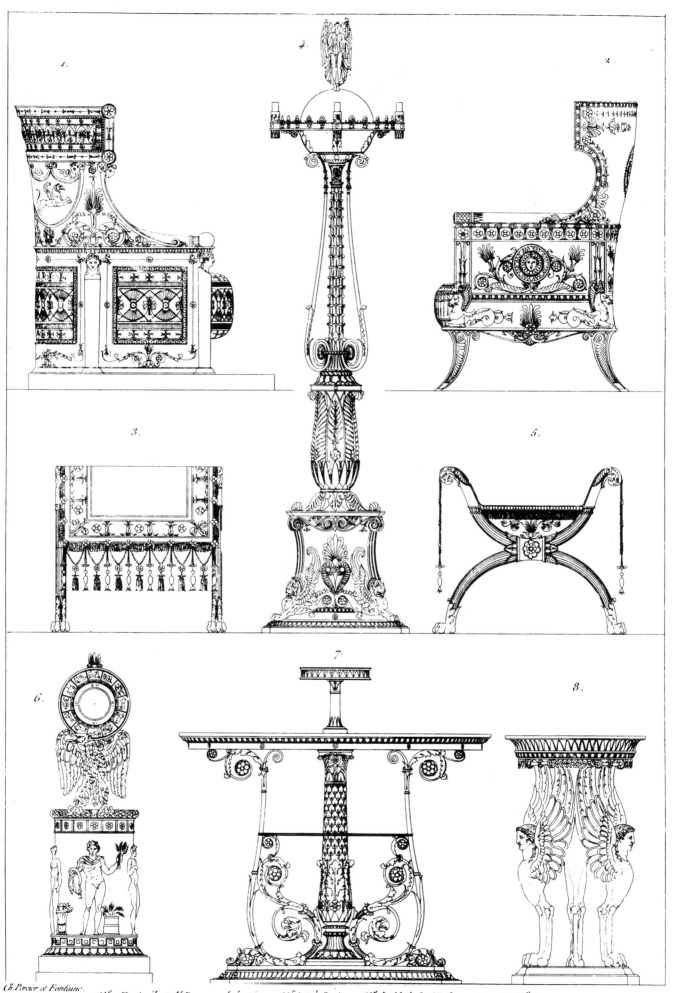

Ch. Percier et Fontaine.

N.º 1. Fauteuil apelé Bergere éxécuté pour M.ᵈᵉ D. à Paris.

N.º 2. Fauteuil éxécuté pour M.ʳ L. à Paris.

N.º 3. Tabouret en X éxécuté à Paris et placé à S.C.

N.º 4. Candelabre éxécuté à Paris pour M.ʳ B.

N.º 5. Côté du Tabouret en X N.º 3.

N.º 6. Petite Pendule éxécuté pour M. W.

N.º 7. Table éxécutée à Paris pour M.ʳ B.

N.º 8. Table éxécutée à Paris pour M.ᵐᵉ de G.

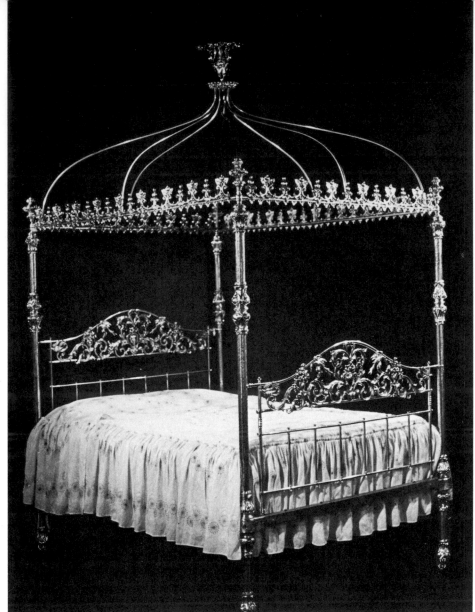

Right:
A mid-Victorian brass bed and canopy.
Most examples are less elaborate than this
one.

Below:
Two Victorian upholstered chairs. Left,
a so-called nursing chair; right, a walnut
settee.

various facets. It is heavy, soundly made and reliable: it cannot in any way offend even the most puritanical and, even though the items are themselves more numerous and diverse than in previous generations, all Victorian homes had a look of sameness about them, since, just as the company chairman, the gentleman of leisure and even in some cases the artist, all dressed alike, so they all furnished their homes alike. It would have been thought improper, even scandalous, to have any piece of furniture which did not have the stamp of moral approbation about it.

Despite Morris and his friends, the century witnessed the change from craftsmanship to mass-production, now a seemingly irreversible process. By the end of the century the East End of London, and similar areas in other cities, was established as a centre for the new furniture trade. The pieces they produced were poorly designed, unattractive in appearance, ill-made and designed for but a short life. It was a trend which would continue into the next century.

European furniture

European furniture followed much the same trends as did the English and need not be dealt with at length. Under Napoleon, France became perhaps the most brilliant centre of European furniture production and its most influential. This was in essence a consequence of political factors, since Napoleon sought to publicize himself, not least in art, and provided generous patronage. Moreover, his military campaigns extended to almost every part of Europe save England and the "Empire" style was thus exported. The style lingered on after the Restoration of the Bourbons in 1815, for neither Louis XVIII nor Charles X were greatly concerned with decoration. The decline in royal and aristocratic patronage acted as a spur to commercialism, the grandiose furniture of Napoleon's time gradually giving way before demands for greater comfort. In the years between 1830 and 1840 there was a return to naturalism, and carved flowers and fruit and ornament inspired by the East became common. As in England, there was a revival of the Gothic style. The ensuing years saw the revival of other, earlier French styles, but pieces were often

marred by insensitive interpretation aimed at the undiscerning bourgeoisie. The French, like the English, could machine-cut veneers and this was a contributing factor to the poor quality of much of the work. On the other hand great advances were made in upholstery, and new pieces of furniture such as *pouffes*, which benefited from this type of covering, now became popular. By the time of Napoleon III, in the 1850s and 1860s, upholsterers enjoyed a dominant role, eclipsing even cabinetmakers in importance.

Rocking chair made in Boston in the second quarter of the 19th century. American Museum, Bath.

An English papier-mâché sofa made in about 1850, decorated with mother-of-pearl. Victoria and Albert Museum, London.

The poor quality of much of the work led to a reaction similar to that in England. The great International Exhibitions demonstrated the need to end eclecticism and search for improvements in design. As with Morris in England, Comte Léon de Laborde strove in France for a return to true craftsmanship. His organization broke away from historical styles and developed an entirely new one. This was to lead to the style known generally as Art Nouveau, which would dominate an enormous field, including furniture, architecture, painting, ceramics and decoration, from 1895 until about 1910. It was at its most important during the first decade of the 20th century and is discussed in the following chapter.

A few points of interest about other European furniture must be made. The Danish economy was depressed throughout much of the century and this is reflected in its furniture. It might be thought that this would produce pieces of inferior quality; in fact the reverse was the case. Danish craftsmen had to dispense with extravagant ornamentation and were also obliged to rely on local, cheaper woods such as maple, ash and birch. The result was a simple but generally pleasing style, and one which infiltrated much of Scandinavia.

This refreshing plainness in design would have an interesting parallel in the "Utility" furniture of England during the Second World War, when there was a critical shortage of wood. It would seem that furniture design perhaps benefits from interludes when outside influences impose simplicity, and craftsmen must think first of utility rather than ornament.

Italian furniture had, in consequence of Italy's occupation by Napoleon's troops, adopted many of the forms of the French Empire style. Later in the century this influence declined and Italian craftsmen, eschewing the Gothic Revival, turned instead to their own Renaissance themes for inspiration.

Vienna experienced a strong revival of the Rococo and, later, revivals of Renaissance and Baroque styles. Vienna is of particular interest as a centre of furniture production because it was there in the 1830s that the Thonet brothers perfected the process of bending certain woods by the use of steam and thereafter mass-produced a completely new design in chairs, known as "bentwoods". These were produced in Europe in great quantities and may still be had in good condition at a reasonable price.

The eclectic use of different styles, often in ungainly combination, was

Left:
English chair made of papier-mâché and inlaid with mother-of-pearl; c.1860. Victoria and Albert Museum, London.

Below:
English armchair of mahogany with brass inlay, c.1820. Victoria and Albert Museum, London.

the dominant feature of the century until the advent, astonishing in its impact and the universality of its appeal, of Art Nouveau in 1895. Furniture design was, in a few years, to be altered out of all recognition.

American furniture

The transformation in the USA between 1800 and 1900 is one of the most astonishing features of modern times. Not only did the area it covered increase (in 1800 it comprised only the states of New England and the South, while by 1900 it occupied almost all the territory which it does today), but the population increased some 15 times, from roughly four million to about 60 million. It follows that the crucial feature of American furniture during this century is the impact of mass-production.

New York in particular, but east coast cities in general, dominated the manufacture of furniture throughout most of the century. Indeed, it was only those living in the eastern and developed states who could afford to concern themselves with their furniture and tasteful decoration. Other American citizens were either pushing their way westward or struggling to develop homesteads and ranches; their styles were both more simple and more

Left:
Victorian balloon-backed dining chairs, upholstered in the "stuff-over" style.

Below:
French Gothic Revival chairs, in the "cathedral" style of the 1840s. Musée des Arts Decoratifs.

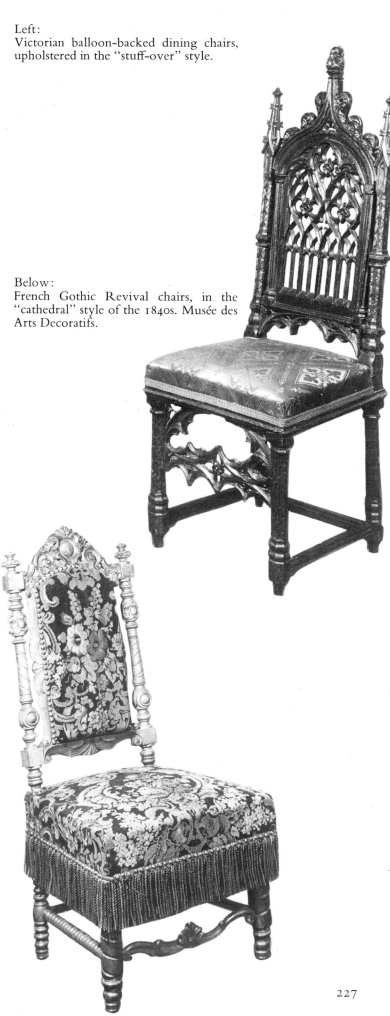

French Empire dressing table. It was made in yew-wood with gilded bronze for the Empress Josephine. Musée des Arts Decoratifs.

brash. There was little time or money for patronage and aesthetic consideration other than in the established, prosperous cities of the eastern seaboard. Styles until almost the end of the century were still imported from Europe, in particular England. Thus the USA experienced the revival of the same earlier styles as did England, and it is arguable that the mixing of styles was even greater there than in Europe. In consecutive order (but with much overlapping) there were, between the years 1830 and 1895, the classical revival known as "Empire", Gothic, Rococo and Renaissance styles. Other influences were also at play, including French styles from the reigns of Louis

XIV, Louis XV and Louis XVI, and further influences from European fashions such as the Egyptian motifs popular since Napoleon's campaign there. As in Europe, the same materials were employed: cast iron became popular for garden furniture and bedsteads, papier mâché for small boxes, trays and light tables.

The most influential American cabinetmaker of the early 19th century was Duncan Phyfe, who worked in New York from 1795 until the 1840s. He produced very personal interpretations of the Empire and Regency styles, and popularized carved decoration. Such pieces of American "Empire" furniture as survive are almost always

found in museums. Today the heavily carved acanthus leaves, the plumes and pineapple motifs and the large animal-paw feet seem curiously inappropriate for the people of a new and developing country. The names to look for when studying American furniture of this style are Alexander Jackson Davis and Andrew Jackson Downing. These men believed, as did their English counterparts of the time, that different styles were suitable for different localities; the Gothic style they found particularly suitable for libraries and places of learning and, inexplicably, bedrooms. Davis's designs were the best of their kind in the USA at the time and his oak "wheel-back" chairs – chairs the backs of which resemble the circular rose-window common to many cathedrals – are of especial value today. The Rococo revival, which lasted roughly from 1850 to 1870, was more widespread and much favoured by the newly-rich. Many pieces of these two decades are notable for their graceful curves, their often attractive carving and their cabriole legs. In the 1870s the Renaissance revival predominated. It affected almost every item of furniture, including sideboards, dressing bureaus, chairs and tables.

As the USA became more prosperous and more of her citizens were able to travel to Europe and elsewhere, so

Opposite:
A mahogany side-chair made in New York by Duncan Phyfe in 1807. H. F. duPont Winterthur Museum, Delaware.

The Great Exhibition at the Crystal Palace, London in 1851: left, the Medieval Court, and, below, designs for pianos in Rococo style. Guildhall, London.

Left:
English pedestal desk made of thuya wood and covered with a leather top; c.1865.

Below:
English credenza (side cabinet, derived from the court cupboard) with walnut inlay; c.1865. Dowell's, Edinburgh.

Right:
English sideboard of 1863; the six panels depict *The Hunting of the Cheviot*. Trust Houses Forte.

Below right:
American hatstand of cast iron and glass, dating from about 1850. Sleepy Hollow Restorations.

there developed a passion for things from the Near and Far East. Moorish and Turkish pieces, most especially tables, were popular, as was bamboo or an imitation of it. The ability to make "bentwood" furniture was also learnt and this type of chair became as popular in the USA as it was in Europe. Curiously, despite the USA's independence from England, its citizens remained fascinated by the British sovereign and, in imitation of the furnishings at Balmoral Castle, Queen Victoria's home in Scotland, they had an affection for chairs made of antlers' horns and for decorating walls with stags' heads.

While the great bulk of American 19th-century furniture was mere repetition, and often inferior repetition, of European styles, one style must be credited as being original, even if it did hark back in concept to the Puritan years of the 17th century. The term "Shakers" or "Shaking Quakers" was first used to ridicule the members of the United Society of Believers in Christ's Second Appearing, and sprang from their emotional and disjointed movements during their religious services. Originally, a few members of this sect had fled persecution in England during the 18th century and, under the leadership of one Ann Lee, rapidly established communities (often made

up of celibate families) on the east coast and later as far west as Ohio. The movement is now virtually defunct but at the time it was an independent, not insignificant sect and today their villages are being preserved as a record of a small part of American history.

The Shakers were extreme in their dislike of ostentation and ornament; furniture design, in their view, originated in Heaven and was translated to earth by angels. Costly furniture was thought to be sinful; plain and simple pieces, often uncomfortable though they were, were all that man could use without offending God. Carving, inlays, veneers – all were considered superfluous. What they sought – and the Shakers made every kind of furniture – was simplicity and utility. However, they also demanded sound construction and perfect workmanship. Only one concession was permitted: different coloured woods might be used and paint employed.

Shaker furniture – as with that of 19th-century Denmark and the "Utility" furniture made in England during the Second World War – is stark and plain but it has a beauty of its own. Pieces are now rare indeed but some may be seen in American museums and there are examples at the American Museum at Bath, England.

In American furniture design and

Left:
American antler chair, made after 1850.
Collection of Miss Elinor Merrel, USA.

Opposite:
An English sideboard designed by Philip Webb in 1862 in the Gothic style. Victoria and Albert Museum, London.

Below:
An escritoire and stand made in 1893 for William Morris and Co. Victoria and Albert Museum, London.

interior design, the last decades of the 19th century witnessed another flourish of revivals. Classic European styles rejuvenated while more exotic and flamboyant designs were imported from Asia and the Far East. As an awareness of other cultures grew, so a greater number of styles were assimilated. At the huge exhibitions, which were so popular during the second half of the century, people were initiated to cultures which were very different from their own. At the Philadelphia Centennial Exposition of 1876 articles were displayed which originated from such distant and disparate areas as North Africa and the Orient, the Near East and the Far East. New possibilities were soon realized. Many drawing-rooms were transformed into Moorish dens, chairs were replaced by mounds of cushions, draperies took over from wall-papers while the air was contaminated with incense. Surprisingly, these interiors were not found exclusively in the houses of the rich. While Moorish rooms, which now reside in museums, were designed for millionaires such as John D. Rockefeller and William H. Vanderbilt, more modest reconstructions were to be found in humbler abodes. The popularity of exotic interiors was almost universal throughout America.

Oriental and Eastern designs did not, however, dominate American furniture during these last two decades. As in England, the Arts and Crafts Movement had considerable impact. Charles Eastlake's *Hints on Household Taste*, which was published in England in 1868, appeared in America in no less than eight editions between 1872 and 1890. In it he advocated a return to medieval methods of craftsmanship, and the application of simple and rectangular forms. Complex contours were excluded from his designs for furniture, though it should be pointed out that ornate decoration was permissible. Some cabinetmakers, however, indulged in quantities of decoration which even Eastlake would have thought excessive. In the last decade of the century the Arts and Crafts Movement, represented by Eastlake, merged into the new flowing style of Art Nouveau. The two most notable cabinetmakers of this phenomenon were Gustav Stickley and Elbert Hubbard.

Left:
A Shaker interior, reconstructed at the American Museum, Bath.

Below:
Mid-19th-century Hungarian wardrobe, made of ash.

Opposite above:
English dining table of walnut, made in about 1860. Victoria and Albert Museum, London.

Opposite below:
A bed in French Second Empire style, made in the 1860s by Manbro the Elder. Bowes Museum, Barnard Castle, Co. Durham.

Perhaps the most influential centre for furniture design in the 1890s was Chicago. There, the architect Louis Sullivan and his pupil, Frank Lloyd Wright, who had established his own practice in 1893, designed furniture which was intended to be an integral part of the interior space. The furniture which Wright produced in the last decade was closely linked organic forms and blended gently into the overall design which itself merged into the natural surroundings. His ideas, of course, made their greatest impact in the 20th century. Nevertheless, they were assimilated in the last years of the 19th century, notably by the Tobey Furniture Company, Chicago's foremost furniture makers.

Chicago benefited from the high quality of Wright's designs but it also managed to display the lowest aspects of commercial eclecticism. While a handful of designers managed to lay the foundations for 20th-century styles, The World's Columbian Exposition in Chicago in 1893 exhibited an enormous range of mass-produced furniture based entirely on the styles of the preceding centuries. This slavish copying of older styles was not, however, restricted to Chicago. Such furniture was manufactured throughout the country.

The last decades also saw a wider variety of materials. Furniture manufacturers, as we have seen, did not fail to exploit cast iron. Improved production processes meant that interchangeable, standardized components could be made and then be assembled into a wide range of articles. This form of manufacture was particularly suited to

Above left:
A late 19th-century mahogany cylinder-front desk.

Left:
English carved oak cradle, which has been painted and gilded; c.1861. Victoria and Albert Museum, London.

Opposite:
A selection of Japanese bamboo furniture; such pieces were extremely popular in late 19th-century England.

Left:
American cast-iron garden chair, with oak-branch decoration. Metropolitan Museum of Art, New York.

Opposite:
French ewer and basin made at Bordeaux in about 1830. Musée National de Céramique, Sèvres, France.

Below:
American fold-away bed made to resemble a piano; c.1870. Collection of Miss Elinor Merrel, USA.

garden furniture and a large quantity of rustic chairs and seats were produced. The manufacturers of these, never keen supporters of plain and honest design, generously decorated them with imitation wooden grain. Bent wire furniture was also produced, but little of this now remains on account of its inevitable lack of strength and durability. Papier mâché articles also exist but few of these are American; most were imported from England. Though the manufacture of traditional styles continued into the 20th century the impact of Wright's designs could not be eradicated. Stickley's Exhibition of Craftsman Furniture at Grand Rapids in 1900 clearly pointed the way into the 20th century.

English ceramics

Ceramics in the 19th century, as with so much else, were affected by the technical innovations of the Industrial Revolution and were produced in such an astonishing variety of styles that all that may be attempted here is a brief indication of the main trends. The century may be conveniently divided at 1851, for in that year the Great Exhibition, the first of several in Europe, was held in London. Large numbers of pieces were on display at all the exhibitions, each acting as a spur to innovation and invention.

First, however, we must look briefly at the years preceding this great divide. As with furniture and other products, the production of ceramics was affected

by the revival of various styles during the century. The classical influence of the early years principally affected the shape of pottery and porcelain; decoration remained largely unchanged. During the 1840s, however, there was a renewal of interest in ancient Greek black- and red-figure vases and imitations, termed "Etruscan", were made in great number. Manufacturers of this ware included Dillwyn of Swansea, and Copeland. Similar work was also produced in Europe. The classical style was followed by a revival of Renaissance forms. The Minton factory produced many pieces in this manner – common designs were creatures such as snakes and snails – but French and other western European potters

were also engaged on similar work. Another earlier innovation, Limoges enamel, was imitated at many potteries, including that at Sèvres.

Throughout the first half of the century underglaze-blue transfer-printed earthenware remained in favour. By the 1830s, however, there had been a change in design, for the *chinoiserie*, the classical designs and country scenes lost favour to idealized and romantic designs to meet the taste of the time. Colours also changed: blue remained the most popular, although after about 1830 it was usually paler, and from the same time other colours make their appearance. Both Copeland and Rockingham were coloured green, and reds and purples also came into favour, as did black, which after 1850 was the most popular of all.

Before turning to the second half of the century, mention must be made of an English product which was popular for some 30 years from about 1830 – the moulded jug. These were decorated in relief and the material most commonly used was stoneware of a pale colour. The range of decorative subject matter was extensive, but country scenes were preferred, with flowers

Above:
English porcelain vase from Coalport, in the Rococo style. It is dated 1830. Victoria and Albert Museum, London.

Opposite:
A Staffordshire china cottage, made in about 1860. Private collection.

242

Above:
Two English jugs in the Gothic Revival style of 1840. Collection of Richard Dennis.

Opposite:
"Grotesque" stoneware bird with a movable head, c.1887. Victoria and Albert Museum, London.

Left:
An English jug made in 1877, with "Japanese" decoration in relief. Victoria and Albert Museum, London.

and trees and graceful animals such as deer. They were made in great number at the time and may still be found.

The Victorian age witnessed a great increase in the manufacture of pottery and porcelain, much of it reproductions of earlier styles not always easy to tell from the original. British ceramics may be dated by their marks. If an object bears a mark which consists of printed initials placed in a circle, often surmounted by a crown, it was made after 1840. If it incorporates a royal arms, this indicates that it was manufactured after 1850. If the firm is described as "Limited", the piece may be as early as 1860 but is more probably later than 1880. The words "trade mark" do not appear until after the Trade Mark Act of 1862. Anything that carries the name "England" is after 1875 at least and more probably after 1891, when the United States government required all imports into America to bear the name of the country of origin. It is worth noting, also, that pattern numbers on Victorian china are no guide to the date of manufacture, since they were used to facilitate the replacement of broken or lost pieces and the same number was therefore used for many years.

Ceramic ware may be divided into two kinds: functional household products and merely decorative objects. Victorian tableware was usually brightly coloured and richly gilded, and the characteristic flower patterns became denser and the gilt heavier as the century wore on. The most popular material was bone china (the common term for standard English porcelain). One of the more unusual pieces of tableware ornamentation was the hen-in-a-nest, which was commonly placed on the lid of covered dishes in the mid-century. Pottery hens were used also as bowls for sweets and money boxes. The Victorian thirst for variety expressed itself in the large number of special-purpose mugs and cups. Toby jugs, like all character jugs (politicians were favourite subjects in the mid-century), showed a marked decline in the quality of modelling and originality of design from their heyday in the 18th century; but many other types of mugs are excellent examples of Victorian taste. Frog mugs (which, when emptied, disclosed a frog seated at the

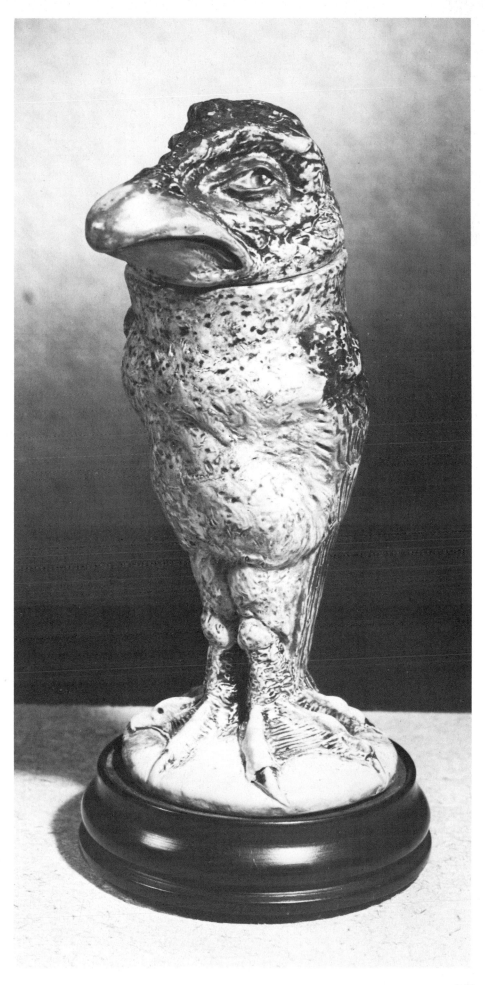

Above:
A moustache cup, made in 1897 and commemorating Queen Victoria's Diamond Jubilee. Collection of Mrs Rita Smythe.

Opposite:
An American Tuckerware porcelain jug. American Museum, Bath.

bottom or climbing up a side) were first made in the middle of the 18th century, but did not fall into disfavour until about 1850, by which time they had become rather heavy and somewhat crudely coloured. Their designs were usually copied from 18th-century models. For men, there were two speciality mugs: the moustache cup and the shaving mug. The moustache cup did not come into general use until the 1890s, although examples of the type can be found as early as the 1860s. It had a ledge inside the rim of the cup on which the moustache could rest while the tea passed, without embarrassment to the hirsute gentleman, through a gap between the ledge and the rim. The shaving mug was made both in pottery and porcelain. It had a perforated lid for holding the soap and a wide, protruding lip to enable the brush to be dipped under the lid into the water. Shaving mugs were usually

decorated in a floral motif, although sometimes they bore transfer-printed views of a holiday resort, the characteristic decoration of gift mugs. Gift mugs themselves were first made in the 1860s. On one side there would be a garishly coloured transfer-print, on the other a gilded (often excessively gilded) motto or inscription. A curiosity of the time, reflecting the new importance of extra-parliamentary pressure groups and public campaigns, were the propaganda jugs, bearing slogans and decorated with relief work and transfer-prints. They came mostly from Staffordshire, the best of them being produced for the Anti-Corn Law League in the early 1840s.

Ceramic ewers, found usually in the bedroom as part of washstand sets, were popular throughout the century. They were often made of fine china and decorated with flowers or landscapes. Common-or-garden kitchen

247

flagons, made of brown salt-glazed earthenware, were, despite their humble habitation, frequently ornamented in relief. More elaborate were the flasks for spirits. They came in many shapes – human figures, animals, mermaids, horns – and were made of stoneware. Those of the highest quality were made at Derby, Vauxhall and Lambeth. Ordinary-shaped flasks were commonly embellished with busts for stoppers and relief images of leading personalities, including members of the royal family. Chamber pots, among the most essential of household objects, ranged from plain earthenware pots for the poor to the ornately gilded and decorated porcelain pots of the gentry. Every Victorian middle-class daughter learned to sew and for her the pottery manufacturers made charming, elegant

pin boxes in bone china. The finest examples were made in Staffordshire between 1850 and the mid-1870s. They were decorated with flowers, birds or landscapes. The rarest kind was in the shape of a miniature bust, often of Queen Victoria or another member of the royal family.

Ornamental ceramics included figures, both in pottery and china, delicate flower pieces, and more fanciful items, like the now much-coveted nursery tableware, china cottages and castles, and the curious, sentimental early-to-beds. The most widely used flowers for ornamental purposes were roses, zinnias and carnations. The finest vase-bouquets came from Derby, the best basket arrangements from the Coalport works. Both types were brilliantly coloured. Figures are difficult to distinguish from 20th-century copies,

but the most handy (though by no means reliable) distinction is that the vent-hole at the bottom of 19th-century figures is smaller than that found in later reproductions. In the 1840s Alfred Singer's Vauxhall works produced some of the century's most engaging and finely-worked figures, small bone china figures in delicate colours, dressed in perforated "lace". The lace was made by dipping real lace into the china slip before firing. China cottages and castles, the most beautiful of them made at the Worcester, Derby and Rockingham works, were occasionally decorated with lithophanes, or "Berlin Transparencies", and those that were are now much sought-after and expensive. In the same vein were the pottery imitations of houses or buildings where notorious crimes had been committed, sometimes known as

Above:
Danish porcelain tureen, part of the so-called Heron service, made at Copenhagen in the late 1880s. Museum of Decorative Art, Copenhagen.

Opposite:
A parian-ware figure of the immensely popular "Greek slave", together with a collection of artificial flowers under glass domes.

"crime-pieces". Early-to-beds were humorous narrative groups depicting scenes from courtship and marriage, exceedingly popular throughout the century.

American ceramics

In the USA the last years of the century witnessed a strong reaction against mass-production. The Arts and Crafts movement, which had made such a crucial impact in Europe, had an equally powerful effect on the development of the decorative arts in America. Small independent potteries employed artists and designers who turned out unique and hand-made articles. The most decisive date in America in the history of this development was 1880. In Cincinnati in that year, Maria Longworth Nichols established the Rookwood pottery. It was not the only

pottery to be founded in that town. Indeed, in the same year no less than five others appeared. The Rookwood pottery, however, was the only one which attained any lasting reputation.

The forms, decorative details and techniques were numerous. Two colour schemes were known as Cameo and Mahogany. These were pink and brown respectively and by the mid-1880s had acquired the generic name of Standard Rookwood. Ingenious glazes such as gold speckled glaze were introduced while some pieces were given silver overlays by the Gorham company. International recognition came in 1900 when the pottery won a gold medal at the Paris Exhibition. What makes these wares particularly popular to the collector is that each one is unique and signed by the artist who was responsible. Early pieces are

Right:
A late 19th-century jug in majolica, the lead-glazed earthenware developed by Mintons. Collection of Richard Dennis.

Above:
An English jug made in Staffordshire in about 1820, with a copper lustre. City Museum and Art Gallery, Stoke-on-Trent.

marked with the words *Rookwood Pottery* while between 1882 and 1886 this was simplified to *Rookwood*. After this the initials *R P* were thought sufficient.

Individual potteries soon sprang up throughout the country. In Colorado Springs Artus van Briggle established a pottery and produced works in the style of Art Nouveau. In 1892 Laura Fry and William A. Long founded the Lonhuda Factory at Steubenville, Ohio. In 1895 this merged with the commercial pottery factory at Zanesville, Ohio, and was renamed Lowelsa.

English glass

The influence of 18th-century glass lasted well into the 19th century but, before we turn to the increased English glassware production after 1851, mention must be made of two types of glass which may be of interest to collectors. The first is the more expensive. Apsley Pellatt, a London glassmaker, took out a patent in 1831 for a refinement in glassmaking which he had learnt in France. This was to encase cameos, decorated in low relief, in clear glass. Distortion during the process of manufacture had been a difficulty but Pellatt overcame this and produced numerous pieces in this manner, known as Crystallo-céramie, including flasks, paperweights, pendants and earrings.

Left:
Porcelain vase made in Copenhagen in 1888. Museum of Decorative Art, Copenhagen.

Above:
A selection of early 19th-century Irish glass. Victoria and Albert Museum, London.

Opposite:
A crystal chandelier made in Venice early in the 19th century.

The second item of potential interest to the collector is the rummer. The word does not, as is often supposed, come from "rum" but from the German *Römer*, and denotes a capacious drinking glass with a short stem. These were common in the late 18th and early 19th centuries and it is thought that they were intended for hot toddy. They are far removed from the elegant table pieces of the time but they have a plain and simple attractiveness (some, however, are decorated) and were essentially tavern glasses. Later examples tend to be heavier and thicker and are more numerous. They may still be found as their toughness has preserved many in good condition, and would make a collection which would undoubtedly increase in value. Once they were little regarded; they have, of course, gone up in price but they remain the least expensive drinking vessels from this period.

Mid-19th-century glassware is most

easily discussed, not by reference to the objects themselves, but by reference to the several kinds of decorative glass which were manufactured, although no account can leave out the principal class of glass objects, namely drinking vessels. First, therefore, let us look at some of the more popular kinds of glass used by the Victorians.

Bristol glass, the name given to coloured glass manufactured in England in the 18th and 19th centuries, was made not only at Bristol but also at Nailsea, Stourbridge and elsewhere. It was used in the Victorian period for a host of items (bottles, jugs, candlesticks, walking sticks) and in a wide range of colours (opaque white, green, dark and pale blue, turquoise). Its most popular use was for pink, tulip-shaped goblets.

Cameo glass was rare and expensive. It was produced by cutting a layer of white opaque glass to expose dark glass underneath. The effect was to create a

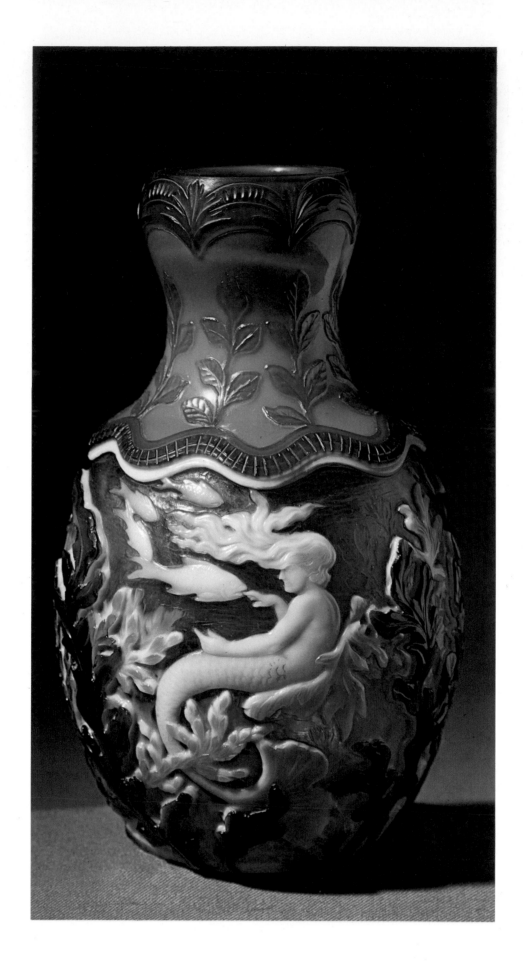

white relief pattern on the dark ground. Although later cameo glass was produced by acid erosion of the white glass, mid-Victorian examples are always hand-cut.

Cased glass, also known as layered glass, was an ornately decorated glass produced by superimposing layers of white and coloured glass on a clear foundation and then cutting the glass to expose the different colours. Cased glass usually bore additional decoration, in the form of gilding and enamelling. Ruskin condemned the cutting of glass as an adulteration of the material, but the mid-Victorians were not swayed by his arguments. Cased glass was hugely popular.

Moulded glass, known to the ancients, was revived in England in about 1850. It was produced by blowing molten glass from a pipe into a mould. It gained its relief decoration from an intaglio (incised) pattern cut into the inside of the mould. Victorian examples are seldom coloured.

Nailsea glass came from the works of that name established outside Bristol in 1788. The firm specialized in novelty items, called "friggers" by the Victorians, done in glass of a greenish hue, often with coloured streaks and spatter technique. Victorian spatter glass itself, derived from Nailsea, was lined with opaque white glass. Its mottled appearance came from the splashings, or spatterings, of green, red, brown and yellow glass.

Pressed glass, made by a machine which pressed molten glass into a cut mould, was an inferior glass, although technical improvements raised its quality after the middle of the century. It was produced in the Midlands and the North of England.

Shaded satin glass is extremely rare. It was a speciality of Thomas Webb of Stourbridge and was made by applying hydrofluoric acid to an opaque

Above:
American pitcher, rose bowl and blown glass bowl made in the last decade of the 19th century. Metropolitan Museum of Art, New York.

Left:
An Australian beaker of about 1815, with the landscape decoration in enamel. Victoria and Albert Museum, London.

Opposite:
Left: a mid-Victorian English claret jug in cut- and engraved glass, and with a silver handle. Right: an American green-glass decanter with a silver case. Private collection.

coloured glass in order to gain a satin-matt appearance. There were various traditional patterns of satin glass, the most notable being a mother-of-pearl finish, a spotted pattern called "raindrop" and, rarest of all, a ribbed design in two tones, known as "cut velvet".

Stained glass, used almost exclusively for tableware, was an innovation of the 1850s. It was made by applying stains to softened glass and then refiring the glass pieces; this was an innovation of the 1860s. And lastly, vaseline glass, most popular colour was a ruby red.

In threaded glass, delicate filaments of tinted glass were woven around glass pieces; this was an innovation of the 1860s. And lastly, vaseline glass, introduced in the early 1860s, was a yellow-green glass which also went by the name of "yellow opaline". It was a clear glass with the unusual effect of appearing brighter at its edges. It was used most often for paperweights, vases and decanters.

Nothing reveals the Victorians' love of variety and grandiose embellishment more than their drinking glasses.

Before the middle of the 19th century the Englishman's drinking glass was most commonly a plain, cut flint glass. By 1845 colours were coming strongly into fashion and at the Crystal Palace in 1851 glasses of every design from the squat and bulbous to the elegant and slender were on display. They were laden with gilt work and profusely etched. Some had feet. The most popular colour was green, followed by ruby red, amethyst and amber. By 1850 dram glasses, the trumpet-shaped glasses on thick, short stems used for

257

Above:
Glass bottle from Dyottville, made in about 1880. It depicts General Taylor and George Washington.

Opposite:
English 19th-century decanter with a silver mounting. Collection of Georgina Pritchard.

drinking spirits, were going out of style. In general, in the second half of the century glasses became more slender, their stems longer. Decanters, too, after the accession of Queen Victoria, became slimmer. The high shoulders and round stoppers of the Regency period gave way to gently sloping sides and ovular stoppers. Cutting was elaborate and fanciful twists and mouldings were in great demand. Claret jugs and water jugs changed their shapes along with the decanters. Early Victorian water jugs tended to have an oval shape; by 1860 the prevailing shape was that of a tankard and a decade later it was that of a pitcher. Throughout the century by far the most common decoration of water jugs was floral or fern engraving.

Now for some oddities: first the scent bottles. Most of these were made of glass, although some were made of porcelain and silver. They were moulded, pressed or cut and they were almost always decorated with mounts of silver or silvergilt. They are easier to date than most glass pieces, because the silver mountings were hallmarked. Especially popular in the 1870s and 1880s were double scent-bottles; really two bottles joined by their bottoms. One was used for smelling salts and was ordinarily fitted with a hinged top; the other was for perfume and had a screw top. Witch balls, also known as wish balls, were in fashion between 1820 and 1865; they were filled with holy water and were hung in windows to fend off evil. The most popular ones were made of silver lustre, although Nailsea glass ones, early in the century, came in several colours. Walking sticks, in all colours and designs, were the most popular of all Victorian glass curiosity pieces or novelties. They were often filled with sweets and sold at holiday resorts as souvenirs. The heyday of glass busts was the 1850s and 1860s. They were portraits of famous public figures, royalty, military heroes, politicians and writers. Like walking sticks, they are now very rare.

American glassware

The most important innovation in American glassmaking at the beginning of the 19th century had been the invention of pressed glass; in the following decades this was made in a wide

range of colours by most American manufacturers. The period between 1840 and 1890 was particularly notable for the great production of pictorial flasks and bottles. These were often decorated with portraits of American statesmen, soldiers and foliated ornamentation. The two principal glassworks which produced these flasks and bottles were those at Dyottville, Philadelphia, and Lockport in New York.

The most unusual and inventive forms of American glass were those of the art glass type which were produced at the end of the century. Louis Comfort Tiffany began manufacturing glass in 1879 and the company which he established continued under various names until 1938, five years after Tiffany's death. Tiffany has now become a well-known name in the history of American applied arts and his influence has been extensive. In addition to glass, ceramic and enamel works were in part or wholly fashioned by hand and made under his personal supervision. These he termed favrile.

Above:
A group of cut- and pressed-glass bottles, including a number of double scent bottles in the foreground.

Right:
American free-blown pitcher of about 1850. Corning Museum of Glass.

Opposite above:
A selection of Nailsea glass, very popular in Victorian England. Collection of Mrs Jane Renn.

Opposite below:
American decanter of pressed glass, intended to resemble cut glass. Second quarter of the 19th century. Victoria and Albert Museum, London.

Left:
English blue glass mug of Bristol glass. It is inscribed with the word "friendship". Torre Abbey Museum, Torquay.

Tiffany glass is found in diverse and original forms and colours. Essentially, there are 13 separate types of Tiffany glass and include such examples as the monochrome irridescent pieces, agate and marbled glass and glass which was variously decorated with heavy gold lattice work and *mille-fiore* decoration. Among the most well-known pieces are Tiffany stained glass panels and glass and bronze lamps, particularly the one known as the Wisteria lamp.

The other two major glass companies which produced art glass were the New England Glass Company and the Mount Washington Glass Company. The former was particularly associated with Amberina, a type of glass of clear yellow shading to red. At the Mount Washington Glass Company Burmese glass was produced. This was predominantly yellow shading to salmon pink. These two companies employed various forms of decoration.

Some of their motifs are reminiscent of Islamic art. The quality of American art glass equals and in many cases surpasses contemporary European work and Tiffany's work can be compared with the finest of Emile Gallé's works in France.

English silver and metalware
Silverware of the first half of the 19th century followed the revival of styles in much the same way and in the same order as did other products. Silver was relatively cheap, demand enormous; moreover, new techniques enabled manufacturers to mass-produce pieces, with tea- and dinner-table silver especially popular. For those who could not afford silver there was always Sheffield plate (although this was slowly going out of production) and soon there would be electroplating.

Perhaps never had there been such opportunities for the silversmith, but unhappily the results were for the most

Right:
English silver hot water jug of 1805.
Victoria and Albert Museum, London.

Below:
English silvergilt teapot, made in 1806.

264

Right:
A design for an electroplate salad stand, produced in England in 1852.

Opposite above:
English King's Pattern cutlery service (with modern knives). The service dates from the 1820s. Mappin and Webb Ltd, London.

Opposite below:
Silver gilt desk stand made by Philip Rundell in 1821. Private collection.

part inferior. The revival of styles – Renaissance, Gothic, Rococo, Baroque and Louis XV – served only to confuse design, since pieces were often made of more than one style. It is common, for example, to find the body of a pot and its spout in conflict. Moreover, decoration now became extravagant. Napoleon's expedition to Egypt, for example, had led to a fascination in sphinxes and Middle-Eastern motifs in furniture and elsewhere, and the same ornamentation was now added to silver. Many European countries, in particular England, now had colonies overseas to which they looked for trade and aesthetic inspiration, so that Indian, Chinese and African figures abound at this time. A bizarre but recurring result of this love of over-ornamentation was a taste for humorous or grotesque silver products, which took the form of animals, birds and figures, distorted in

both proportion and appearance, which were made into jugs, pots and so on.

A further cause of the lapse in taste which obtained throughout most of the century was the gradual disappearance of the discerning patron. The full effect of this would not be felt until the 20th century, but the process had already begun by 1815. The new patrons – the successful manufacturer or financier – considered that size displayed his new wealth best. Pieces became of enormous proportions, wholly out of keeping to their use. Table centrepieces might be as much as three feet long; ponderous, often heavily ornamented in a variety of styles, they are the antithesis of the supreme elegance of mid- and late-18th-century silver.

There were, however, exceptions. Albert, the Prince Consort, who sought to combine art and industry, tried to reinstate the craftsmanship of earlier

years but his efforts met with limited success in the field of silver. Mention must also be made of Sir Henry Cole (1808–82), who sought to "promote public taste" by commissioning artists to design household goods, but the products of this attempt to return to naturalism seem today to be too "artistic" and in any event the movement was to be overwhelmed by the Great Exhibition of 1851.

The mid-Victorians were mad about silver. No other metal came close to it, for tableware or ornamental pieces, in their esteem. Copper and brass continued to be used, of course, but pewter, although cottagers continued to be supplied by the work of fine rural craftsmen, was so unfashionable that the Victorians melted down a great deal of old pewter to use it as solder. For the collector who is weary of Victorian flamboyance, the simple pewter

Opposite:
Two Sheffield plate candalabra of the Regency period.

Below:
English candlesticks and inkstand in silver; 1830s.

Right:
Victorian silvergilt vase made in 1849, in the Rococo style.

pieces of the country poor and the kitchen provide a restful contrast. But silver ruled the day. It was the most obvious status symbol of the mid-Victorian middle classes. To display silver on a sideboard or in a cabinet was to demonstrate, not simply that you were prosperous, but also that you lived a life of refinement.

The great demand for silver meant that manufacturers catalogued their wares in two classifications: firstly expensive display pieces for public use and the very rich, and secondly more modest household goods, table services and tea and coffee sets. The household goods were themselves divided into the better-quality, hand-worked pieces

and the cheaper mass-produced ones, the latter in silver, Sheffield plate or electroplate. By 1855 the electroplating process had spread throughout the country and Sheffield plate had become rare. Electroplating was looked upon as one of the marvels of the age. The exactness with which it was able to reproduce natural details

267

American tea and coffee service of about 1828. The Brooklyn Museum, New York.

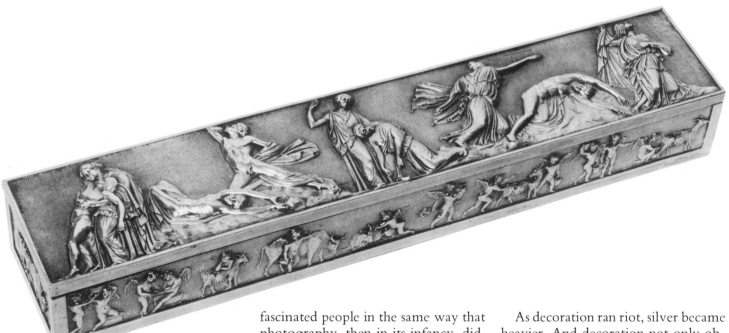

English pencil box, electrotyped and silvered; c.1854. Victoria and Albert Museum, London.

fascinated people in the same way that photography, then in its infancy, did. Obsessed with naturalistic detail, the Victorians, especially after the Great Exhibition had revealed to them the fantastic shapes in which silver could be worked, paid little attention to form and proportion. Restraint was eschewed as silver items became burdened with massive encrustings of flower-blooms, vines, animals and arabesques. Fish servers were shaped like fish and decorated with fish. Spoons for tea caddies were given handles in the form of tea plants. And where the electroplaters led, the silver masters, to keep pace with popular fashion, followed.

As decoration ran riot, silver became heavier. And decoration not only obscured form, it drove away the distinction between styles. Victorian Rococo was really a strange blend of Rococo, Regency and naturalistic elements. The Rococo element itself was, it is true, strong: teapots and jugs carried scroll and shell work until the end of the century. But the symmetrical arrangement of classical motifs, especially the acanthus leaf, gave way to an asymmetrical, naturalistic treatment of leaves and flowers. Classicism itself had a revival in the 1840s, thanks to the ability of electroplating to reproduce exact copies of Roman models. But no style was able to assert dominance over the others. *Chinoiserie*, the craze of the latter part of the 18th century, returned. The Gothic revival was carried into silver work: table sets and decanters, tea pots and caddies were decorated with Perpendicular tracery. Gothic wine flagons were immensely popular.

The public measured a silversmith's work by his originality, and by originality the public meant a hitherto unknown conjunction of styles and motifs or an even more elaborate massing of naturalistic details. Novelty was praised before everything else, because it was novelty that best demonstrated the new technical mastery of the silver plater.

Dating English silver is a relatively simple matter, since all silver was hallmarked. Two marks, however, deserve notice. The mark "EPNS" appears after about 1840 on pieces of nickel alloy electroplated in silver. The mark "EPBM" appears at about the same time on objects of "Britannia metal" electroplated in silver. "Britannia metal", first produced in the last third of the 18th century, was a soft alloy of tin, copper and antimony. It got its name from its manufacturer, John Vickers of Britannia Place, Sheffield. It was also known as "French metal" or hard pewter, its silver-bluish tinge giving it the appearance of pewter. Pewter collectors should guard against mistaking it for the genuine thing.

Tableware and tea sets are the pieces by which Victorian silver work is principally to be judged. But some smaller objects and some less ordinary items of other kinds of metalwork may be of interest to the collector.

"Billies and Charlies", which were sold in the second quarter of the century, were faked ancient medallions, pendants, seals and the like, claimed by William Smith and Charles Eaton to have been recovered from the bed of the river Thames. They were made of a cheap lead alloy. Silver caddies especially became more elaborate in their design and ornament as the century wore on. So did caddy spoons, which before 1850 were often charmingly light and restrained pieces. Caddy spoons were sometimes called "caddy shells" from their shape. After the 1850s, cigar cases were most commonly made of silver or leather. Door stoppers, on the other hand, were almost always in cast iron. They were pro-

duced in a great variety of shapes. The most popular were cast as animals or as likenesses of contemporary celebrities.

Fenders, cast iron, brass or polished steel, became heavier and more elaborate as the century wore on. Often decorated with animal scenes and scroll work, they provided Victorian craftsmen with scope to indulge the current taste for large, sweeping curves.

Inkstands were made of almost every metal – iron, gold, silver, pewter, brass and copper. Despite the mid-Victorians' delight in mass production, it is rare to find two that are alike. Brass inkstands were the most common.

Posy holders, shaped as funnels, trumpets or cups and joined to a long

English electroplated eggframe, made in Sheffield in about 1870. Private collection.

269

Above:
Victorian tea-set in parcel gilt, and decorated in the Japanese style, with matching porcelain cups and saucer; about 1875.

Below:
Late Victorian novelty condiment sets, in electroplate.

Opposite:
Late 19th-century French inkwell in gilt bronze. It is in early Art Nouveau style. Private collection.

handle, were first made in the 1820s. Between 1850 and 1874 no fashionable woman appeared at a ball without one. They were made of silver and, much more rarely, gold. They were frequently inlaid with jewels and mother-of-pearl.

Vinaigrettes, originally made in the 18th century, continued to be produced throughout the 19th century. They were small boxes, meant to fit into pockets, with a hinged lid and an inner perforated lid. They carried a sponge filled with vinegar to blot out unpleasant smells.

American silver and ceramics
The foremost American silversmiths in the last decades of the century were undoubtedly the Gorham Company and Tiffany's. It was these two companies which pioneered the Japanese style which came to dominate European and American silverware at this time. Much of the ware was actually made by Japanese metal workers who had emigrated to the USA. The workmanship was undoubtedly of a high standard and at the Paris Exhibition of 1878 Tiffany's were awarded a gold medal for their highly ornate articles which were modelled in the Japanese manner. It would be true to say that American silverware, which for two hundred years had been influenced by European styles, now itself exerted an influence on English and Continental silversmiths.

This style, though, was not the only one which appeared. Indeed the range of decorative motifs and the styles which were employed was almost limitless. Silversmiths harked back as far as the Middle Ages; Baroque,

Louis XIV, Queen Anne and the Rococo were drawn upon, while both East Indian and American Indian styles were used. In the very last years of the century Art Nouveau made itself felt and the flowing forms which were produced by the Gorham Company amounts to the most important silver which was produced at this time.

Clocks

During the last decades of the 18th century large clocks were made for inns. They were weight-driven and, like long case clocks, had a long pendulum; they are easily identified by their huge dials, which may be as much as three feet across. These dials were made of wood and are uncovered. The inn clock's contribution to the history of clockmaking is, however, largely a negative one. In 1797 a tax was imposed on clocks and watches; many

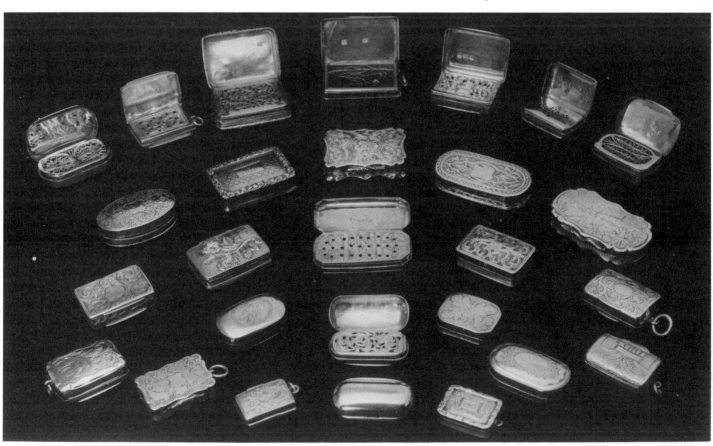

people stopped buying their own pieces in consequence and relied instead on inn clocks. In the short time that the tax lasted (it was repealed in 1798) the clockmaking industry in England was nearly destroyed. The industry cannot be said to have recovered until the middle of the 19th century, when it was to suffer a further reverse in the shape of strong foreign competition.

Several new clocks, or the cases which enclosed them, appeared in this century. Modifications were also common; for example the bracket clock was produced with a round rather than a square dial after about 1850. Balloon clocks (so-named from their resemblance to the shape of a hot air balloon) appeared, as did Gothic-shaped lancet clocks. Another English clock of the Victorian years was the "English dial"; it was hung on a wall, usually in a kitchen or office and its spring-driven and pendulum movement behind the dial made it appear to be no more than a white dial with hands. Another favourite was the musical clock.

In direct contrast to the "English dial" was a clock with a skeleton frame, usually mounted on a marble base and protected by a glass dome which could be removed when the clock needed rewinding or attention. All the movements might be seen, a virtue being made of the mechanism in contrast to its disguise in "English dial" clocks. These had been made in France since the middle of the 18th century but the great popularity of this form of exposed mechanism clock came later in one form as what are commonly called carriage clocks. Their origin lies with Napoleon, who wanted reliable travelling clocks (*pendules de voyage*) for his officers. A.-L. Breguet, a Paris clocksmith, produced them in small cases made of glass and brass, with a handle on top. Later they developed into carriage clocks, which have a brass base and top with handle, connected by four upright columns, one at each corner. The rest of the frame was made of glass, so that the mechanism might be seen. Often, elegantly decorated

French ormolu and brass clock, in the Empire style. Lady Lever Art Gallery, Port Sunlight, Cheshire.

Above:
Two French carriage clocks; the one on the right has a repeater mechanism. Most carriage clocks are not so elaborately ornamented.

Left:
An English "farmer's" watch, mass-produced in England in the 19th century.

Opposite:
An "acorn" clock of about 1850, with acorn decorations on the front panel. British Museum, London.

china was used in place of glass and some had quite extensive decoration, but the plain variety is the most typical and the type most likely to be found. A refinement was a "repeater" mechanism: a stud at the top, when depressed, enables the chiming mechanism to repeat the number of chimes it last made. This enables a person to verify the time in the dark if he suspects he had at first miscounted.

Carriage clocks are valuable if in good condition and, as with clocks in general, have recently risen steeply in price. However, they represent a sound investment and no collection of clocks could be considered complete without one. Collectors must be warned, however, that they have recently been reproduced in great number. This does not in fact pose much of a problem, for even an untrained eye can quickly detect the difference between an original and a reproduction carriage clock. The reproduction versions may become valuable in time but they should never be purchased at a price more appropriate to an original.

The English industry, which had barely recovered from its setback arising from the clock tax at the end of the previous century, was again badly hit, this time by an assault on the market in the middle years of the century and later by cheaper American and German products. These clocks were in general ill-designed, made of inferior materials and unlikely to have a long working life. Some, however, have survived and may be found on occasion, often for a reasonable price.

The further points need to be made about the clocks of the 19th century. The first is that (except in the case of obviously inferior pieces) the Victorians achieved a quite astonishing degree of accuracy in their timepieces. Collectors, therefore, should never tolerate inaccuracy in their clocks and watches of this period. Earlier pieces may not always have had a high degree of accuracy but by the 19th century they regularly attained this and the technically-minded collector should almost always be able to restore clocks of this period to their original level of efficiency.

The second point which may be of interest to the collector is the great abundance of novelty clocks. As we

Opposite.
A "dwarf tallcase" clock, made in Massachusetts in about 1815 by Joshua Wilder. Old Sturbridge Village, Massachusetts.

Above:
A verge watch of about 1830, painted with a rural scene.

Above:
American lyre clock of the early 19th century; these are very similar to banjo clocks.

have seen in so many areas, the Victorians, and their Continental and American contemporaries, were a highly inventive people and delighted in innovation and in oddities of all sorts. Novelty clocks are an interesting area in which to make a collection, which might include clocks made in imitation of steam engines and lighthouses; ticket machines were another favourite shape and there were numerous "mystery" clocks which sought to baffle the viewer. An example of this is a figure which holds a pendulum in an outstretched hand, but there were many more. They are by no means easy to come by and a collection would probably take many years to complete, but it is a rewarding pastime since each new addition adds enormously to the value and interest of the whole.

Above:
French clock of about 1875; these were produced in factories but were soundly made.

Opposite:
A selection of Victorian jewellery, in which diamonds tended to figure prominently.

Jewellery

Until the 18th century jewellery was beyond the means of all but the richest. From then onwards attractive but less expensive pieces were made and during the 19th century, with its technical expertise born of the Industrial Revolution, production increased dramatically. A contributory factor to this increased production was the advent of a prosperous middle class, which could afford to ape the upper classes in this as in many other ways. Much 19th-century jewellery is of fine quality, but the collector must be wary of the inferior factory-produced pieces which were mass-made after about 1850. These, which were made for those who could not afford genuine stones, had their settings stamped out in metal and were then set with coloured paste.

It has elsewhere been noted how world events affect the nature of antiques. Of no area is this more true than jewellery. Thus, the development of gold mines in the USA and Australia and the discovery of diamonds in South Africa affected both the appearance and nature of jewellery. Excavations in Italy and Greece during the 18th century gave rise to a new interest in classical design while Napoleon's military expedition to Egypt inspired an interest in scarabs and sphinxes. Mourning jewellery also became widely used, partly in consequence of Queen Victoria's long widowhood, partly from the casualties suffered during the Crimea War. These and other influences were all important in the development of the styles of 19th-century jewellery.

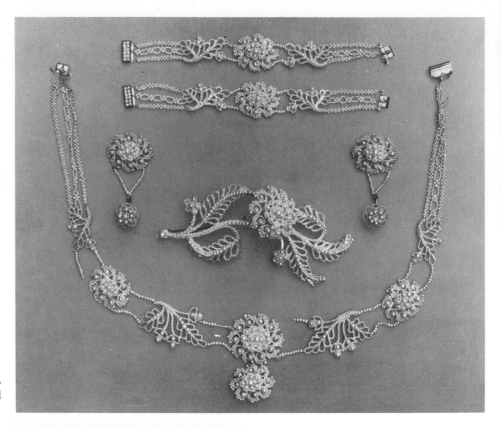

Above:
American seed-pearl jewellery of the second half of the 19th century. Metropolitan Museum of Art, New York.

Below:
Victorian costume or "secondary" jewellery, made of shell and glass. Victoria and Albert Museum, London.

Opposite:
English necklace and cross made of enamelled gold set with garnets and pearls. It was designed by A. W. N. Pugin in about 1848. Victoria and Albert Museum, London.

One reason for the increased production of jewellery during the 19th century was the important role it played in social life. Even a modest middle-class home would include at least two servants; the mistress of the house was thus at liberty to follow a busy social life and to modern minds the number of her engagements – family parties, tea parties, social calls, theatre and dinner engagements – seems astonishing. Clothes were changed often during the day and jewellery with them. Many middle-class ladies had what was called "secondary" jewellery, attractive but informal pieces, usually made of gold or silver and set with semi-precious stones, which they wore during the day. Evening jewel-

lery was naturally more elaborate and costly. Pieces were often made into matching sets, which might comprise a necklace, earrings, a brooch and possibly a bracelet, usually made by the same designer.

Jewellery was often given as gifts and as tokens of love or esteem. It was a 19th-century custom, for example, for a bridegroom to give his bride a small casket of jewels on their marriage. These would be pieces of coloured stones in intricate settings. Age also played its part, for it would seem that to the Victorians coloured stones were entirely suitable for young girls, while diamonds might be worn with propriety only by married women and were given a more mature setting.

To present-day generations the Victorians seem to have been preoccupied with death and mourning jewellery was abundant. Mourning jewellery was not a new concept (it had been known as early as the 16th century and rings in remembrance of Charles I were common in the 17th century) but the Victorians indulged in it to an almost morbid degree. Many of these pieces took the form of hair-work jewellery, intricate designs incorporating some of the hair of a deceased relative. This form of ring or brooch is hardly made today. The 20th century seems less concerned with symbols of grief; furthermore, the process of threading hair, knotting and plaiting it is extremely time-consuming and

though it was an economic proposition in the 19th century, with plentiful and cheap labour, it would be too expensive to produce today.

Jet was especially popular in the 19th century, particularly in Britain where it was favoured by the Queen as proper adornment for a widow. Its production was greatly increased when a considerable quantity of jet was found in cliffs and beaches near Whitby, in Yorkshire. It was of extremely high quality and although found elsewhere in Europe the jet at Whitby remains the most pure and the most expensive for the collector.

To leave the impression that the Victorians were entirely without pleasure in life would, however, be misleading. They were equally unrestrained in displaying their affection and in celebrating, not only funerals, but marriages and births. Of these the largest category is the love token. A popular and rather appealing device of the time was a ring or brooch with stones set in a "message". This was achieved by selecting different stones and setting them in a sequence, the first letter of the name of the stones together forming a word. Thus a diamond, followed by an emerald, then an amethyst, ruby, emerald, sapphire and topaz reads as "dearest". Jewellery in the shape of hearts and flowers were also popular.

As in other countries, the wearing of jewellery was not the prerogative solely of women. Men also wore adornments, usually sober but attractive in design. A watch-chain worn across a waistcoat was almost compulsory wear; at one end of the chain would be a watch, secreted in a pocket, and at the other a gold locket, lodged in another pocket. A sovereign purse made of gold or silver was also carried to house gold sovereigns, legal currency at the time. Cuff-links, often ornate, were worn, as were rings and tie-pins. At dinner men would wear pearl studs with their evening dress.

Different stones and settings went in and out of fashion during the century. One of the most abiding forms of jewellery, however, was the cameo. The craft of cameo-making goes back to Roman times but cameos again became popular in the late 18th century. They first reappeared in France during the reign of Napoleon, largely because they were among the Empress Josephine's favourite adornments. The fashion spread from France to Britain and elsewhere and demand rose dramatically. Many were carved in gemstones – amethyst and turquoise were popular, as were shell cameos. They were made into brooches, earrings and necklaces for "secondary" jewellery and sometimes set with precious stones for evening wear.

Coral was also popular and during the middle years of the century it was often set with diamonds or pearls. Coral, which may be in any shade from palest pink or white to bright red, had long been thought to ward off evil and was a popular gift for godparents to give their godchildren.

Naturalism returned to favour in the middle years of the century and diamond jewellery designed on natural forms and often of great beauty was produced. Popular emblems in a

Left:
An example of Whitby jet jewellery – a hair comb and watch-chain; c.1870. Private collection.

Below:
A drum of the American Civil War period,
belonging to the Ninth Regiment of
Vermont Volunteers.

natural shape included moons and stars, bees (Napoleon's emblem), butterflies and numerous birds. Necklaces and bracelets in the form of a serpent were also popular and many fine representations of the spider's web were made in gold. Another popular device was a spray of diamond "flowers" attached to tiaras and brooches, so made that they trembled with the wearer's movements.

There was an abundance of gold in the Western world in the mid- and late 19th century and this metal was frequently used to make brooches; these were commonly in a sporting motif, usually connected with hunting (foxes, whips, spurs and so on), but also of sports which had recently become popular, so that bicycles and golf clubs were common motifs.

Silver, too, was much used in the

production of jewellery, with lockets, necklaces, brooches and chains being among the most popular. It was also a favoured metal for religious emblems, which were produced in great numbers during the 19th century. Crosses were especially plentiful and scarcely any "respectable" woman was without one.

Great social changes towards the end of the century had their effect on jewellery, as on so much else. Social mores changed particularly for women, who were beginning to pursue their own careers, were struggling to secure the vote and anxious to discard the emblems of their "slavery" to men. It may not be too much to say that a revulsion against all things Victorian set in at the end of the century and it was not until the 1950s and later that dealers and collectors looked once again at the

Above:
American toy oxcart. It was carved by a father and his son in about 1860. Essex Institute, Salem, Massachusetts.

Opposite left:
A Pennsylvanian punched-tin coffee pot made in about 1835. Index of American Design.

Opposite right:
A late 19th-century cast-iron American bootjack, designed as a grotesque beetle. Index of American Design.

Victorian jewellery and admired its fine workmanship and the great variety of its execution and invention. During the 1960s and 1970s prices rose but the 19th century still remains the most productive area for the collector of jewellery, its sheer quantity providing him with an unparalleled choice. The quantity may at first seem daunting but numerous specialized books are available and collectors of this period have the advantage of being able to study photographs of the time, show-ing what pieces of jewellery were worn and in what combination. There are also, of course, outstanding collections in museums and elsewhere. Specializ-ing in this field is as desirable as it is elsewhere, but since the individual pieces remain reasonably priced a col-lection of 19th-century jewellery will be easier and quicker to make than one from any other period.

Americana
The first half of the 19th century was a period of vigorous exploration in the USA, the settlers pushing the frontier farther and farther west until the vast interior regions and the west coast were occupied. Settlement was made by following various trails – the Oregon Trail, the Santa Fé Trail and others – from which secondary trails branched out. It is often assumed that the arte-facts of this hard period were entirely utilitarian, that the collector can find only pieces such as saddles, spurs, cooking pots, home-made blankets

and so on. The truth is otherwise. Despite the frugality of their daily lives, the frontier settlers none the less found time to make ornaments and decorations for their modest log homes. These pieces are now scarce but some are available and have a charming simplicity of their own. There was much for the settler to do but little he could accomplish after nightfall. The long winter evenings were filled, not merely with making useful artefacts but in decorating them to make them more attractive. Indeed even women travelling the trail in covered wagons passed the time by knitting or making embroidery. Since the journey might take many months, embroidery was usually intricate and often of attractive and original design.

How can the collector differentiate between genuine American pieces and those imported from England in the early days? According to the regulations governing the original colonies, many industries were banned amongst the colonists, so as to protect the manufacturers at home; therefore as a general guide, it might be said that Americana comprises those categories which the

Below:
An American hooked rug, incorporating the Star of Bethlehem design.

Opposite:
A saddle blanket made towards the end of the 19th century by a North American Indian in California.

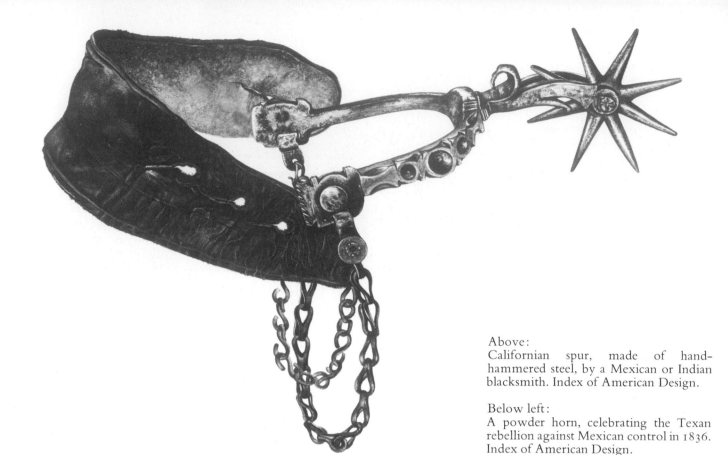

Above:
Californian spur, made of hand-hammered steel, by a Mexican or Indian blacksmith. Index of American Design.

Below left:
A powder horn, celebrating the Texan rebellion against Mexican control in 1836. Index of American Design.

English did not ban the original colonies from making. This, however, can easily lead to wrong attribution, since the settlers were an independent breed and often made pieces whether they were forbidden to do so or not. A more accurate guide is the appearance of the piece: genuine Americana is typically simple, devoid of ostentatious ornamentation and gives the appearance of utility, naturally considering that a wagon or a plough was of greater moment than elegant tableware. Nevertheless, many settlers found time to improve the appearance of their possessions and in this respect one of the most rewarding areas for the collector of Americana is painted tinware. The settlers often decorated their trays, coffee pots and so on with floral, animal and other designs, often with great skill. Collectors of metalware can also find interesting pieces, since the settlers were always seeking improvements in their farm tools, and improvements often meant that earlier pieces were abandoned. Implements which had hardly changed for centuries – knives, saws, axes and so on – were now re-shaped. Weapons are also a fruitful area, since the settlers were in some measure dependent on game for their survival.

Treen, or household ware made of wood, is perhaps an especially good field. Wood was free and was thus turned into all manner of items, such as bowls and platters. Embroidered linen samplers, often depicting religious or domestic scenes, were made in great number, as were shawls and intricate bed quilts. Recently there has been renewed interest in Americana and such pieces are in general scarce, but other areas to which a collector might give consideration are bottles, domestic cooking items (cauldrons, pans, kettles), pewter and pieces connected with farming, the gold rushes and the development of the railways. Toys, as in other countries, make fascinating collections, as do watercolours, sketches and drawings, but unfortunately these are all now extremely scarce and expensive.

Collecting items of North American Indian work is a specialized field but the central and western States still afford opportunities to acquire such items as Indian shawls and saddle rugs. The collector must be warned, however, that it is not always easy to distinguish between those pieces made when the Indians roamed America and those made today for tourists by Indians in reservations. Traditions have been handed down over the generations and it is easy for an unscrupulous dealer to give a modern saddle rug the appearance of age. The collector should always remember that the great majority of Indian pieces extant are of modern production.

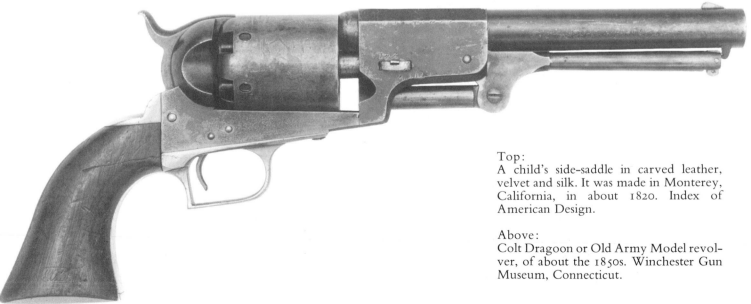

Top:
A child's side-saddle in carved leather, velvet and silk. It was made in Monterey, California, in about 1820. Index of American Design.

Above:
Colt Dragoon or Old Army Model revolver, of about the 1850s. Winchester Gun Museum, Connecticut.

Rice.

S' INN.

A painted wood tavern sign of
about 1830.

Left:
American dolls' house of 1879. Lyme Historical Society, Connecticut.

Below:
Some English toy soldiers, made of lead. Late 19th century.

Opposite above:
Simple Victorian jigsaw puzzles. Museum of London.

Opposite below:
A clockwork walking figure, whose head turns from side to side. Tunbridge Wells Museum.

Toys

Children down the centuries would seem to have liked the same playthings, but they have preferred them to be of contemporary design. Toy soldiers, for example, have always been popular, but whereas in the 19th century they were made of lead and with appropriate colouring, both infantry and cavalry, they are today made of plastic and are equipped with modern weaponry. Toy soldiers were especially popular in the 19th century. In 1848 a scale called the "Nuremburg scale" was introduced, stipulating that toy soldiers should be one and a third inch in height per man; not all manufacturers adopted this but it is from that date that toy soldiers became of interest not merely to children but to adult collectors, since the process of making a collection was greatly simplified. Soldiers were not always made of lead, of course; many substances were used, including card and papier mâché. Other favoured toys of a warlike nature were pistols and guns.

Puppets were much in favour in the 19th century and numerous illustrations, drawings and photographs of the period testify to the popularity of Punch and Judy shows.

Wood remained a favourite substance for toymaking, wooden horses and farm animals, building blocks and painted dolls all being in common use. However, the 19th century saw the advent of metal for toys. The children of the rich of other centuries had indeed played with toys made of silver but metal now became general for the first time. Thus, while some toy trains were still made of wood, metal was clearly more lifelike and was preferred. After about 1850 many toy trains were self-propelled and were often of some sophistication: some had whistles and a popular refinement was a smoking device which would emit puffs of smoke. The enormous popularity of of the toy train in the 19th century was no doubt partly due to the fact that trains were themselves new but partly also because they satisfied the child's liking for toys with movable parts. Indeed, there was a craze for mechanical toys of all sorts from about 1840 onwards.

Balls had always been popular but became more so with the discovery of

rubber. Kites and hoops were common playthings for outdoor play, while indoors jig-saw puzzles, card games and toy theatres were favoured.

Outstanding among 19th-century toys is the doll. They were produced in numerous materials, including china, rubber and wax, and were often of exquisite design. For the first time, too, the baby doll appeared; previously all dolls had been miniature representations of adults. Why it had taken so long for the baby doll to be produced is one of the minor curiosities of social history. We have seen how the price of 19th-century dolls has risen dramatically and this must be considered before beginning a collection. It is, however, a fascinating field and a collector of dolls is in fact preserving a small but valuable aspect of social history.

Opposite above:
An English porcelain doll of about 1855;
the sofa is of a later date. Blaise Castle
House Museum, Bristol.

Opposite below:
Some of Queen Victoria's dolls, and her
music box; early 19th century London
Museum.

Right:
A Victorian collage picture, decorated
with shells. Private collection.

Below:
An engraving by the American artist
Thomas Birch, of an incident in the War
of 1812 between Britain and the USA.

Bottom:
The covers of a Victorian engagements notebook; it is decorated with tortoise-shell and gold; *c.*1830. Victoria and Albert Museum, London.

Below:
A selection of 19th-century *netsuke*: small Japanese carvings of ivory or enamel worn as a toggle attached to the belt.

Oddments

The 19th century offers many attractions to the collector. It is not merely that pieces are in general cheaper than those of other countries; it is their great abundance which gives the collector such scope. Moreover, many interesting items are small, an important consideration when making a collection.

Apart from the main groups – furniture, silver, toys, jewellery and so on – there are countless small objects of real merit which might be considered by a collector. Animal and human ornament figures were made in great numbers; specializing might take the form of collecting, say, figures of dogs, which were popular at the time, or pieces by a particular manufacturer. Commemorative ware is also plentiful, mugs, plates and jugs being still readily available. Cooking utensils, brass fire irons, copper moulds and kettles, horse brasses, watches and clocks, butterfly specimens, picture frames and fans – the list of possible areas for collecting is almost without limit. Printed matter, such as invitation cards and valentines, is always rewarding and takes up little space.

If the collector decides to specialize in the 19th century, he might give thought to choosing something particularly Victorian. Intriguing collections have been made of such items as smoking tools, comprising pipes, cigarette cases and cards, smoking cases, lighting devices and so on.

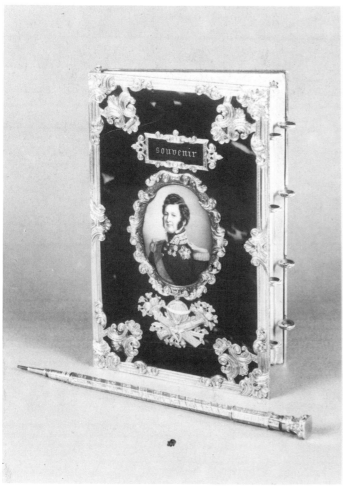

The 20th Century

Introduction

As mentioned at the start of this book, no piece made in this century, whether furniture, jewellery or glass, may properly be termed an antique since it is not yet 130 years old. For a number of reasons, however, a short chapter taking the reader up to the end of the Second World War is desirable. In the first place, it will bring the account of trends and fashions up to date. Moreover, within the space of a lifetime pieces made at the beginning of this century will have reached an age at which they may properly be termed antiques. Nor can collectors be expected to omit pieces simply because they are of recent production. Lastly, and perhaps most important of all, pieces from the early years of the century are often attractive, usually readily available and on the whole less expensive than older items. Their value in strictly financial terms is likely to increase disproportionately quickly.

Two points of social history should first be understood when considering the early, or "Edwardian" years. In England especially, but also in western Europe and the USA, the years of Edward VII's reign and up to the First World War saw perhaps the greatest inequality of wealth in modern times. Aristocratic households comprised numerous servants, often running into hundreds; entertaining was on the most lavish scale, scarcely equalled since the Middle Ages; for gatherings at the great houses trains with many carriages would sometimes be employed to carry guests, their servants and trunks to the local, often private, railway station. When we speak of the "taste" of this period we are therefore speaking of the taste of the rich and the middle class, for the poor were poor indeed and could afford little beyond the barest essentials for living.

This great wealth had been earned by the Victorian generations. The image

Opposite above:
Two early 20th-century German cigarette cases, of gold, silvergilt and enamel.

Opposite below:
An English Edwardian interior, decorated in the Arts and Crafts style of Charles Annesley Voysey. Geffrye Museum, London.

Right:
Art Nouveau fire screen, made by Emile Gallé of ash in 1900.

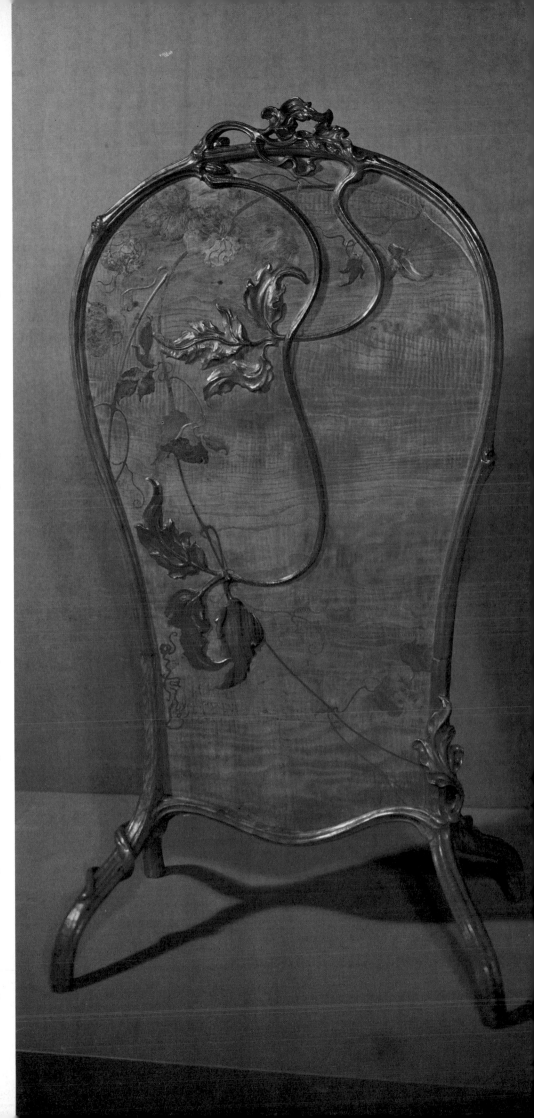

of the Victorians which lingers in the mind is of a hard-faced, money-conscious industrialist. With the death of Queen Victoria, however, this image changes. Solemnity is discarded; splendour and extravagance become the order of the day, which the massive, accumulated wealth enabled the upper classes to indulge. With this pomp went a contrasting yearning for the supposedly wholesome era of medieval chivalry, as witnessed by recurring themes. Thus, the repeated use of medieval knights in honourable and victorious battle contrasts as a motif with the equally frequent use of the strutting peacock, not only in book illustrations and on glass and silverware but often with whole rooms decorated with a peacock motif.

The early years of the century were dominated by the style known as Art Nouveau, which had its beginnings in the last decade of the 19th century. Its origins are controversial but it is generally considered to have been a fusion of a number of influences, including William Morris's Arts and Crafts movement, the Japanese print, the aestheticism of Beardsley and Wilde and the paintings of such as Toulouse-Lautrec and Gauguin. The name itself was probably derived from the name of Samuel Bing's Paris shop, Maison de l'Art Nouveau, where Japanese prints were offered for sale. The shop was later expanded into a permanent showroom for Art Nouveau designs. Art Nouveau is, however, only one of the names by which the style is known. In Germany, for example, it is called *Jugendstil* (youth style), in Spain *Modernismo* and in Italy *Stile Liberty*, after the London store which enthusiastically embraced the new style. It was in favour from about 1895 until 1910 and ceased altogether with the advent of the First World War. However, it returned to favour in the 1960s and has remained popular in various forms ever since.

Art Nouveau is instantly recognizable for its fluid, undulating lines, to which forms and even colours are subservient. It is often referred to as "whiplash" in appearance since, like a snake, its lines seem to turn back on themselves, often at unexpected points. It represented a rejection by contemporary artists of much of the art of the previous 50 years and was a conscious attempt to devise something entirely original. In essence, it took one of two forms, although these were often combined. One form, as in Beardsley's drawings, was reminiscent of writhing plants of sinuous linearity, while the other, as in the architecture and interior designs of Charles Rennie Mackintosh, was severely geometric and with sparse decoration.

Art Nouveau had an astonishing impact on the design of the period. Within a few years it had spread across Europe and to the USA and had come to dominate virtually every art form, including furniture, jewellery, typography, sculpture, painting and architecture. For some 20 years it had no rival in the Western world; then production abruptly ceased and, until its return to popularity half a century later, became indeed an object of derision. It affords a pleasing area for the collector, since many of the pieces have an intrinsic beauty of their own and a great many are extant. Twenty years ago an Art Nouveau item could have been acquired for a modest outlay; today, however, prices are high and making a collection cannot be embarked upon lightly.

The Edwardian era, both in England and the USA, saw the zenith of the great department stores, which cut costs by being their own manufacturers. These stores were not as we know them today. There was no raucous advertising; indeed, they prided themselves on their genteel conduct of business. The Army and Navy Stores in London, for example, was a strictly "members only" establishment. These stores could produce pieces such as furniture cheaply and in great number, so that with the post-war years and greater financial and social equality the era of mass-produced furniture arrived. After 1945 the character of the great stores changed again: the combination of intimacy and opulence went, and instead they catered almost wholly for the ever-growing number of newly prosperous.

Although Edward VII died in 1910, the Edwardian era may be said to have ended only with the First World War. The ever-lengthening casualty lists and ever-increasing taxation, together with the national disbursement of western Europe's accumulated wealth during hostilities produced an altogether different social climate after 1919. A new

Early Art Deco design coffee pot of porcelain, made in about 1910.

class emerged, one which could for the first time buy things which hitherto it would have regarded as extravagances wholly beyond its means. A new style emerged, typifying the changed mood of the times.

Art Deco derives its name from the great 1925 exhibition in Paris entitled "L'Exposition Internationale des Arts Décoratifs et Industriels". It had originally be scheduled for 1915 but was postponed for ten years because of the First World War. The style reflected the changed circumstances of the postwar world and was to dominate western decoration throughout the 1920s and 1930s. Huge cities, fast cars, the cinema and jazz music had replaced the more leisurely Edwardian years. Artists embraced this new world and sought to create for mass-production sleek, linear, decorative and industrial designs which made use of modern technology. Glass, semi-precious stones and man-made materials such as concrete and plastics, were used.

Essentially, Art Deco decoration comprises geometric patterns and zigzags, circles and curves, executed in strident colours. It rapidly found its way into almost every area of life, in architecture, in furniture and decoration, in silver and glass. Lighting fixtures, book bindings and jewellery were all made in this style. Most notable, perhaps, were the large buildings, especially the many Odeon cinemas built at the time and the Radio City Music Hall, New York, designed by Donald Deskey. At its most perfect it could be seen on the great Atlantic liners, especially the *Normandie*, but also in the decoration of cocktail bars, clubs and the many Berlin cabarets. It was also in evidence at the ballet, in Erté's stage and costume designs, in ceramics, screens and in erotic figurines.

Art Deco ceased with the Second World War but has undergone a resurgence of popularity in the 1970s and now provides the collector with an interesting and extensive field. A collection might be made of Art Deco glass, or figurines, or lamps and lighting fitments; pieces are readily available although their price is rising steeply. Alternatively, the collection might cover the full range of the style, possibly to furnish part or all of a home.

A French bed in Art Nouveau style, made of oak and mahogany and decorated with marquetry. Victoria and Albert Museum, London.

301

Furniture

Furniture up to the middle of the 20th
century may most conveniently be
considered in two periods: 1900 until
the end of the First World War and
1920 until the outbreak of the Second
World War. During the early years of
the century the Art Nouveau style remained dominant, only losing favour
from about 1914 onwards. Comfort
was essential: furniture was often large
and heavy, rooms, especially those of
the upper classes, were often con-
gested. It was not that pieces were always ornately decorated; it was rather
that people felt the need to have a great
many little things about them. This
abundance of pieces was in part the
consequence of the development of
new machines. The gramophone, for
example, began to be produced in large
numbers and would often be enclosed
in a cabinet, thus becoming another
piece of furniture. Other items such as
electric fans, could not be so disguised

but added equally to the general impression of clutter. A typical piece of
the period was the chesterfield. A large
upholstered settee, it was covered in
leather or corded velvet and had deep,
square cushions. It was usually accompanied by heavy armchairs, standard
lamps, screens and numerous small
tables.

The middle-class home, on the other
hand, tended towards simplicity, apparently by preference rather than
economic necessity. In passing, it may
be noted that metal lost much of its
popularity at this time; the iron or brass
bed, for example, was generally replaced by a simple wooden one, most
commonly made of mahogany.

Another feature of the period was
the enormous output of reproduction
18th-century furniture, mostly "Sheraton". Just as the Morris school had
feared, manufacturers met the increased demand from the undiscerning
mass market in this way, turning out in

Far left:
Mahogany chair with leather upholstery, made for the Paris shop of Samuel Bing in 1895. Musée des Arts Decoratifs.

Left:
An English dining chair designed by Roger Fry for the Omega Workshop in about 1914. Victoria and Albert Museum, London.

Below left:
English bookcase made in 1905 by Ambrose Heal. It is mahogany with mother-of-pearl inlay. Victoria and Albert Museum, London.

Opposite above:
A settee by Charles Rennie Mackintosh. National Museum of Antiquities of Scotland.

Opposite below:
Three chairs by Charles Rennie Mackintosh, typical of his geometrical style.

addition to 18th-century imitations, chairs in mock-Tudor and Stuart designs. These were for the most part of inferior construction and materials. Nevertheless, some manufacturers resisted the temptation to debase furniture production in this way. Outstanding in this respect was Ambrose Heal, who was himself a product of the Arts and Crafts Movement. He produced commercial furniture for his London store but it was reasonable in price, well-designed, usually simple in appearance and of sound construction. In general, however, a notable change was taking place in the production of furniture: the general wish was for newness, for novelty in design in contrast to the hitherto predominate demand for durability. A somewhat different development was taking place in the USA. Americans had as yet little culture of their own on which to fall back; until this time their styles in furniture and much else had been broadly copied from European, especially English, styles. They now tended to break from this and, in order to establish an individual style, turned rather to the Near East and to ancient Greek, Roman and Byzantine models for their inspiration.

In Europe a remarkable change was to occur in the 1920s. As we have seen, profound social upheavals had been wrought by the First World War and innovation now became of the essence. The main centres of production were based in France, Holland and Germany. A number of artists called the de Stijl group, a name derived from the title of the magazine they published, rejected traditional styles and instead adopted abstract geometric forms, heavily influenced by Cubism. These ideas were amplified in the Bauhaus design school in Germany, where innovations included the use of chrome tubing, used not only for chairs (Marcel Breuer had in 1925 produced a design for an armchair composed of light chromium-plated steel tubing and canvas) but for all manner of furniture, standardizing the elements so that different parts could be constructed in a variety of ways. The Bauhaus and its artists were also important in the development of modern American design. The Bauhaus was detested by the Nazis, and on coming to power in 1933 they immediately closed it down. Many of its leading members fled to Britain and a great number then crossed to America, taking with them the new European theories and adapting them to the American environment.

Architects again played a considerable part in developments in furniture design. In France, for example, Le Corbusier produced furniture as an integral part of his interiors, but standardizing them so that any piece could be placed with equal effect in any of his buildings. Frank Lloyd Wright adopted a different view, for he held that every house was an individual construction and that new designs in furniture were necessary for each new building.

Scandinavian designers were prominent, although they did not always reject the past, especially in the materials they chose. They often adapted historical styles of different countries and other centuries but the sparse forms of their furniture and its clean lines stamp it as "modern". Danish and Swedish designers were particularly influential in the 1930s and 1940s. "Utility" furniture was a development of the Second World War, introduced by the British government to meet the

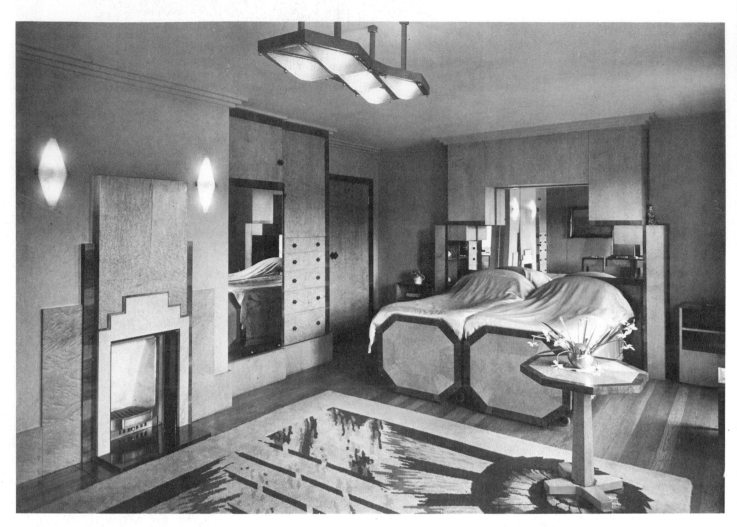

timber shortage. It was controlled in price and was inevitably austere but almost all of it, especially the chairs, were of good proportions and excellent construction. It had the happy effect of introducing the mass market to the attractiveness of plain surfaces and clean lines, but the effect was short-lived for with the end of the Second World War manufacturers again produced ornamented and eye-catching mannerisms.

The 20th century has seen not only changes in style but also in the materials used and the pieces made. Some items are no longer produced (the bedroom washstand, for example, was not made after the First World War) while others have taken a different form (in small houses wardrobes have lost favour to the fitted cupboard). Perhaps, however, the most significant development has been the use made of newly invented materials: plastics, foam rubber and new metals were all used in the manufacture of furniture as soon as they were discovered, as no doubt new materials will be in the future.

Right:
An armchair of chromium-plated steel and canvas, designed in 1925 by the Hungarian-born architect Marcel Lajos Breuer.

Below:
Frank Lloyd Wright's interior of the Kaufmann House, designed in 1936.

Opposite above:
A bedroom of the 1930s, in Art Deco style. Ide Hill, England.

Opposite below:
Table with drawers of Cuban mahogany, a typical Danish piece of the early 1930s.

Right:
Dining table of about 1940 by the Swedish designer Karl Bruno Mathsson. In the 1930s he had experimented with bentwood furniture.

Below:
A set of stacking stools by the Finnish architect Alvar Aalto; late 1930s.

Silver

By the end of the Victorian age the quality of English silver production had deteriorated. The great centres, in Birmingham, Chester, London and Sheffield, mass-produced items of silver and plate, plagiarized from earlier styles with little or no invention. Although these pieces formed the great bulk of silverware in the early years of the 20th century, a younger generation of silversmiths was emerging who were to produce imaginative and original pieces. Their work is characterized by a bold use of plain surfaces combined with decorative detail. Warmth and softness were enhanced by hand-hammering. These silversmiths were adept at adding colour to their silver and almost all used enamel at some time or another. The most popular colours for enamel were turquoise, blue and green; another favoured colour was orange. Many designers in fact included entire allegorical or landscape scenes into their silverwork in this way. Romantic motifs were also much in evidence, especially roses and the ubiquitous galleon.

Some of the most attractive silver produced in the early years of the century were manufactured by Liberty & Co, the London store. Their "Cymric" range, so named in acknowledgement of the Celtic inspiration of many of its designs, such as the Book of Kells, was especially distinguished.

While Art Nouveau was the dominant influence in English and Continental silver, it was otherwise in the USA. As with furniture, American

Right:
Furniture of the "Utility" style of Britain of the 1940s. Geffrye Museum, London.

Below:
A chess set designed in 1927 by the Surrealist artist Man Ray. Museum of Modern Art, New York.

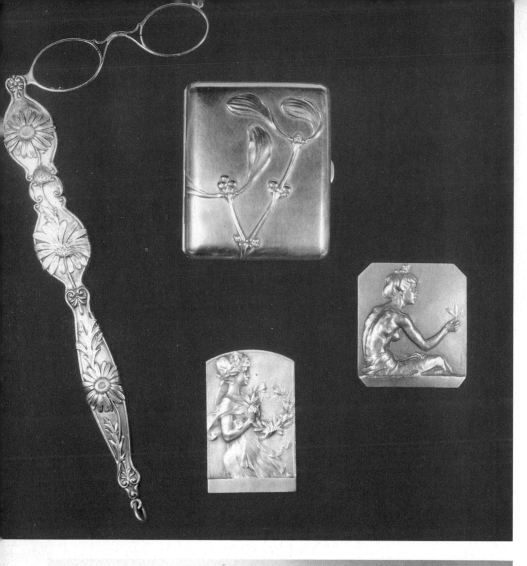

craftsmen of the time were principally concerned with evolving a distinctive national style of their own rather than merely aping European experiments. American silver, therefore, shows none of the influence of the Arts and Crafts Movement but rather influences from the Middle East and earlier European styles, such as Neoclassicism.

Glass

Glass, on the other hand, enjoyed a rich period in the early years of the century. In France Emile Gallé, considered by many the greatest craftsman in glass of the time, was at the height of his powers, while in the USA Tiffany (he was to have many imitators) was internationally known. He had visited Spain and Algeria as a young man and had become fascinated by Moorish and Islamic art. He had also studied the mother-of-pearl effect produced by oxidization when glass had been buried for many years. The pitted surfaces of old glass also appealed to him and he sought means of producing glass with similar effects, but produced deliberately and under his strict control. He also deliberately produced vases which were slightly asymmetrical. He refrained from superimposing further decoration or colouring, believing that these should instead be integral parts of the piece.

Tiffany was quick to adapt his glassware to the newly invented electric light systems, producing perhaps his most popular pieces – floor and table lamps in which the shade incorporated pieces of coloured glass and was supported on a bronze stem. Most of these lamps had floral motifs (rambling roses, daffodils and tulips were particularly popular); one of his greatest successes was a shade decorated with dragonfly designs.

Above left:
Art Nouveau silverwork of about 1900.

Left:
Art Nouveau glass; the pieces on the left and in the centre are by Emile Gallé; the others by the brothers Auguste and Antonin Daum. Private collection.

Opposite:
A peacock vase in "favrile" glass (hand made irridescent glass), made by Tiffany in about 1896. Metropolitan Museum of Art, New York.

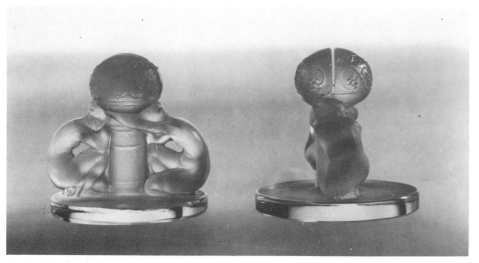

English glass, by contrast, was in a period of decline, although there were exceptions, notably "Clutha" glass (Clutha being the Scots' word for cloudy) produced by the Glasgow firm of James Couper and Sons. Some of their pieces were derivative but essentially they tended towards novelty, with spiralling ripples, areas of different tone and patches which included silver powder or copper crystals. As with silver, and indeed all decoration, the Art Nouveau style gave way to that of Art Deco between the two World Wars, reflecting the interests and life-style of the new generation.

Toys

The years 1900 to 1914 were a golden age for children. J. M. Barrie's creation of Peter Pan in 1904, a boy who was never to grow up because adult life was much less pleasant, typifies the change in attitude to children from that of the Victorian dictum that they should be "seen and not heard". It is hardly surprising, therefore, that the production of toys increased and diversified. One English manufacturer of toy soldiers was producing 20 varieties in 1895; by 1905 he was casting five million soldiers from more than a hundred moulds. Mechanical train sets were also popular and working model aeroplanes appeared shortly after the actual first flight.

The market was not aimed exclusively at boys, however. Many attractive dolls were produced, either of wax or with a porcelain face above a body stuffed and covered with soft leather. At the same time dolls' houses became mass-produced. They were relatively cheap and pieces of furniture could be bought separately, so that the house could be furnished over a period of time.

In England, with her great navy and nautical traditions, model ships and anything to do with the sea were popular; many English children of the time were even dressed in sailor outfits. Other toys were of more universal appeal. The Golliwog (one of the first soft toys to be given a name) made its appearance in 1895, followed in 1903 by the "Teddy" bear, so named from a cartoon made from a photograph of President "Teddy" Roosevelt on a bear hunt. To accommodate all these play-

things children in rich families were given rooms of their own, usually at the top of the house, comprising nursery, bathroom and playroom.

With the end of the First World War there was a natural reaction against war toys and emphasis was placed instead on items such as animals, zoos, vehicles and farm workers.

By this time modern methods enabled manufacturers to produce toys far more cheaply so that they were within the financial reach of all. As we have seen, toys have been known since the earliest times but now that they were universally available teachers and parents began to ask which were the best toys to give to children. The Victorian belief that a toy should be something edifying gave way to the belief that toys should be an aid towards the child's approach to adulthood, and it is from this time that "educational" toys came into prominence. "Meccano" sets teaching the principles of engineering had been made since the first decade

of the century, but during the inter-war period many similar toys were produced. One example is a simple toy train made of wooden blocks which the child had to fit together in logical order. In the 1930s, as the world began to re-arm, war toys again became popular, and manufacturers produced more sophisticated versions than before to match the advanced weaponry of the time.

Collecting toys can be a rewarding pastime but would-be collectors should be aware that they are not, as might be supposed, entering an inexpensive field. In about 1970 it was estimated that, of all antiques, dolls had increased most in value in recent decades. Lead soldiers (today toy soldiers are almost all made of plastic) have also risen steeply in price, as have toy vehicles made of lead. Moreover, it must be remembered that toys were, after all, originally playthings and so the likelihood of finding one in perfect condition is slight. However, with the exception of

Above:
An Edwardian toy fort with lead soldiers of various regiments and periods. Museum of London.

Opposite above:
Glass card-holders made by the Frenchman René Lalique. Victoria and Albert Museum, London.

Opposite below:
An English green glass and silver decanter, made by the Guild of Handicrafts in 1904. Victoria and Albert Museum, London.

dolls and dolls' houses, pieces are cheap individually and as the collection grows their combined value is virtually certain to increase.

Clocks

To the collector the 20th century is the least interesting period in the history of traditional clocks and watches. This was not in consequence of a dearth of invention among clockmakers; rather it stems from the fact that, until the development of electronics in the 1960s, there was little of importance still to invent. Fashions such as Art Deco altered the appearance of clocks and watches but the fundamental mechanics remained unchanged. Automatic watches, calendar watches, stop watches, alarm clocks; all had been invented many years earlier. The only significant development was the popularity of the wristwatch in preference to the pocket watch; this, it is believed, was brought about by the First World War when they were more convenient for fighting men and less likely to be lost. Electric clocks made their appearance, but they are in reality little more than an electric motor with gearing. In 1920 certain nickel–steel alloys were discovered which were impervious to temperature changes and they immediately superseded earlier methods for temperature compensation, but this can be considered no more than a fringe invention. Many fine watches are produced nowadays, but in many ways a modern mechanical watch (unless it be highly expensive) is not likely to be greatly superior to a good-quality 19th-century example.

By way of comparison there are many other areas where a modern piece will be as interesting, although probably not so immediately valuable a member of a collection as older items. Thus the stamp collector, unless he is specializing in a particular, earlier field, will wish to buy examples as they are produced. So, too, may the collector of such small items as tins and boxes. In

Left:
An early 20th-century dolls' house from America, furnished with pieces from other periods. Shelburne Museum, USA.

Above left:
"Maggie and Jiggs"; dolls based on a popular cartoon strip of the 1920s, by Schoenhut.

most cases, however, the interest is in finding something representative of a modern style. It is also a matter of judgment and speculation. Chess sets, for example, are today produced in a variety of materials and with sometimes startlingly original motifs. A collector may feel that a modern set will embellish his collection; whether the set and its design stands the vagaries of time will be a test of his discernment.

Other areas where present-day items are helpful in keeping a collection complete are coins, orders, medals and decorations. On the other hand a collector of, say, snuff boxes would find little to interest him in this century; production has been in decline for many years and much of what is now produced is aesthetically undistinguished.

An Art Deco "mystery" clock, made in Geneva in about 1930. Mr Chiu, London.

The future

It is difficult, although by no means fruitless, to speculate on which present-day products may become valuable antiques in the future. Little is certain for tastes change and often, as we have seen, for reasons unrelated to aesthetics. Certain premises, however, may be accepted as valid. In the first place, ephemera, paradoxically by virtue of the great numbers in which it is produced, quickly becomes scarce. That which we do not prize today is readily discarded, so that in a relatively short space of time it becomes scarce and, regardless of its artistic merit or otherwise, acquires a rarity value of its own. Thus in the USA Coca-Cola was at first sold in green bottles; although the bottles were manufactured in great numbers they were later superseded by cans, and they are now rare and collectable. Likewise in England, private telephones were, until about the 1940s, generally of upright design, comprising a stem, at the top of which was an aperture into which the telephoner spoke, and an earpiece which was attached to a hook on the side of the stem when not in use. These were produced in many millions but when more advanced and efficient designs were developed they ceased to be of use and could be bought from the Post Office as scrap for almost nothing. Who could have guessed that a mere 20 or so years later they would become popular as lamp stands in public houses, so popular that reproductions are made and fetch a high price. No collector should shun an object because it has been made in large numbers, nor should he disregard items simply because they no longer serve the purpose for which they were produced.

How, though, can the collector judge the taste of future generations? The golden rule is to stick to what he admires himself rather than try to guess what others may come to admire. He should use his accumulated experience and knowledge to select that which he himself finds pleasing. He may not be proved right but he is more likely to be right by this than any other method. Secondly, he should look for intrinsic quality. Styles almost inevitably go out of favour for a time but styles of real merit usually enjoy a return to favour. In this century, for example, Art Deco enjoyed an almost total dominance for some 20 years, and then for nearly 30 years had few supporters; in time its inherent merits were again appreciated and it returned to favour. Although this is a common cycle it occurs only when the objects in question have real merit in design, materials and construction. Trash remains trash and must rely on rarity or curiosity to enhance its value.

Durability is another consideration for much of today's mass-produced matter is designed for but a short working life. Mahogany chairs of the 18th century, for example, were built to last; the craftsmanship was good and mahogany is a durable wood. Many chairs of the present day, however, are fragile by comparison.

In this respect metalware is particularly attractive. Tins of gramophone needles, for example, were made in great number in the 1920s and 1930s and may still be in good condition. They have increased in value and make a useful addition to any collection related to communications. Other small items of metalware which might make an interesting collection in the future would include tin lapel badges or buttons, so popular in the 1970s. Bigger and more expensive items include typewriters. Machines of the early years are already valuable and, with new technology, new styles and mechanisms are frequently developed. The manual machine, for example, is already losing favour to the electric machine and at the present time a new shape for the traditional keyboard is being designed.

More vulnerable pieces must, of course, be preserved by the collector. Clothing, for example, is of great interest in social history and can be preserved with little difficulty. Thus the so-called "demob suit", a suit of somewhat coarse material and uninspired design given to every British serviceman on his demobilization at the end of the Second World War, is now, if in good condition, of much greater value than at the time of its manufacture. Fashions change so rapidly today that forming a large collection, given sufficient storage space, is a relatively simple process. The collector is nevertheless advised to specialize, and form a collection of, say, Second World War uniforms. These, however, have recently risen steeply in price and are becoming rarer.

Two further points should be mentioned. One area where a collector might speculate is in searching out pieces which are evidently going out of fashion. It would seem, for example, that the simple receipt as we have known it for many generations – an itemized list with total sum paid, stamped and dated – is losing favour to a more general form of receipt from a cash machine or computer. Receipts from the 19th century are already fascinating social documents and those of today will probably shortly become so. The fountain pen, once a prized possession, is also in decline. Many examples from the earlier years of the century are available at reasonable prices, often extremely well made and finely decorated. It would be reasonable to speculate that such a collection could not but increase in interest and value.

The second point worth considering is that of making a collection of items which, although often quickly discarded today, would provide future generations with a useful insight into present-day life. Printed material is especially rewarding in this field. High-class magazines fall into this category (a complete set is considerably more valuable than an incomplete one) as do children's magazines and annuals. Smaller and cheaper items include theatre and cinema programmes, menus, railway timetables and so on.

The possibilities are virtually limitless. Provided the collector selects a field in which he is genuinely interested, specializes sensibly and is prepared to spend time, sometimes much time, searching for additional items, he will have provided himself with a fascinating pastime and one which can last throughout his life. With growing experience and knowledge he will also have provided himself with a good investment.

ACKNOWLEDGEMENTS

Photographs
The illustration on page 161 bottom is reproduced by gracious permission of Her Majesty the Queen.

Norman Adams 130 top; Alinari, Florence 79 bottom; Alinari/Mansell 57; American Museum in Britain, Bath 23 top, 35, 146 bottom; And So To Bed 222 top; Artek, Helsinki 308 bottom; Ashmolean Museum, Oxford 18, 161 top; B.P.C. Picture Library, London 302; Baltimore Museum of Art, Maryland 148 bottom, 220 top; John Bethell, St Alban's 218–219; Bibliothèque Nationale, Paris 56, 216 top; Board of Regents of Gunston Hall 145; Bowes Museum, Barnard Castle, Co Durham 236 bottom; British Museum, London 29 top left, 62, 63 top, 63 bottom, 111, 175, 178, 194, 275; Brooklyn Museum, New York 268 top; D. Celesta Cabral, Evora 74 top; Caisse Nationale des Monuments Historiques, Paris 134 left; Christie's, London 11, 76 top right, 116 right, 160, 162, 208 bottom, 254, 277 left; City of Manchester Art Gallery 94 top; Civici Musei, Veneziani 172 top; Colonial Williamsburg Foundation, Virginia 140; Connecticut Historical Society 144 top right; Cooper-Bridgeman Library, London 21 top, 38, 50, 54 top, 54 bottom, 58 right, 67, 71, 79 top, 91, 98, 167, 179, 183, 187, 198 top, 230 top, 230 bottom, 231 234 bottom, 235, 243, 247, 255, 262, 282, 295 top, 298 bottom, 315; Cooper-Bridgeman Library/ Christie's 59, 112, 298 top; Corning Museum of Glass, New York 170, 171, 261 bottom; Country Life 17, 24, 72 bottom, 73, 123 bottom, 125 right; Dowell's, Edinburgh 232 bottom; Dithmarscher Landesmuseum, Meldorf, Holstein 53 bottom; Frank Dobson 214 top; G. W. Elliott 27 bottom, 96 top right; S. Elliott, Stoke-on-Trent 250 left; Essex Institute, Salem, Massachusetts 284; June Field 210 top; Financial Times, London 16; Fitzwilliam Museum, Cambridge 60 left, 190; Raymond Fortt 126, 130 bottom, 212 bottom; The Frick Collection, New York 49; Garrard & Co. Ltd., London 7, 274 top; Geffrye Museum, London 309 top; Gemeentemuseum, The Hague 176 bottom; Photographie Giraudon, Paris 220 bottom, 303; Hamlyn Group Picture Library 9 left, 10, 13, 18–19, 22 top, 22 bottom, 26 top, 28 top left, 28 bottom, 31, 32 top, 32 bottom, 34 top, 34 bottom, 37, 40 bottom, 40–41, 42, 44 bottom, 45, 51, 53 top, 65 right, 66, 68, 72 top, 84 top right, 87, 89 right, 91 bottom left, 91 bottom right, 92, 100 bottom, 106 top, 107, 115, 116 left, 117, 118 bottom, 120 right, 121 bottom, 124, 125 left, 127, 129 top, 129 bottom, 132 left, 132 right, 151 bottom, 156, 159 top; 159 bottom, 163 top, 164 top, 164 bottom, 166, 177 left, 180, 182, 185, 186, 188 top, 191, 195, 201, top, 202 left, 202 right, 203, 204, 205, 206 top, 207, 209, 212 top, 222 bottom, 223, 226–227, 237 top, 237 bottom, 239, 241, 242, 248, 250 right, 252, 257, 259, 260 bottom, 261 top, 264 bottom, 265, 266, 267 top, 267 bottom, 268 bottom, 269, 270 bottom, 271, 272 top, 277 right, 278, 279, 292 bottom, 293 bottom, 295 bottom, 296 top, 299, 305 bottom, 306 top, 306 bottom, 308 top, 310 top, 310 bottom, 314 top; Hamlyn Group Picture Library: A.C. Cooper 52 top, 151 top; Hamlyn Group Picture Library: John Freeman 48 right, 103 bottom, 110; Hamlyn Group Picture Library: Gilchrist Photos, Leeds 96 top left; Hamlyn Group Picture Library: Hawkley Studio Associates 154, 208 top, 229 bottom, 263 top, 272 bottom; Hamlyn Group Picture Library: A. F. Kersting 214 bottom; Hamlyn Group Picture Library: Mae McDermott, Godfrey Argent Studio 126 bottom; Hamlyn Group Picture Library: Peter Parkinson 157; Hamlyn Group Picture Library: John Webb 58 left, 206 bottom, 221, 244 top, 250 top; Henry Ford Museum, Dearborn, Michigan 144 bottom left; Henry Francis du Pont Winterthur Museum, Delaware 9 right, 139, 141 bottom, 146 top, 211, 231; Hispanic Society of America, New York 74 bottom; Jacqueline Hyde, Paris 196, 229 top; Index of American Design, National Gallery of Art, Washington 15, 82 top, 134 right, 135, 143, 147, 210 bottom, 215, 283, 285 left, 285 right, 286, 287, 288 top, 288 bottom, 289 top, 290–291; Jagdmuseum, Munich 102–103; Lady Lever Art Gallery, Port Sunlight 120 left, 273; T. R. G. Lawrence & Son (Fine Art), Crewkerne 26 bottom, 238 top; Livrustkammaren, Stockholm 69; Lyme Historical Society, Connecticut 292 top; Mallett & Son, London 119, 122–123; Mappin & Webb, London 264 top; Marcel Breuer & Associated Architects, New York 307 top; Miss Elinor Merrell, New York 234 top, 240 bottom left, 240 bottom right; Metropolitan Museum of Art, New York 65 left, 84 top left, 163 bottom, 240 top, 256 top, 311; Musée Nissim de Camondo, Paris 138 top, 138 bottom; Musée de Lyon 52 bottom; Musée des arts Decoratifs, Paris 21 bottom right, 27 top, 55, 78 bottom left, 80, 136 bottom, 193, 227 top, 227 bottom, 228, 304 top left; Musées Nationaux, Paris 81 bottom, 181; Museum für Kunst und Gewerbe, Hamburg 64 right, 104 left; Museum of Decorative Arts, Copenhagen 249, 251; Museum of Fine Arts, Boston 83, 89 left, 148 top, 200; Museum of London 12 top, 165 left, 201 bottom, 293 top, 294, 313; Museum of Modern Art, New York 309 bottom; Museum Roseliushaus, Bremen 64 left; National Maritime Museum, London 40 top; National Monuments Record 123 top; National Museum of Antiquities, Edinburgh, Scotland 305 top; National Trust 75 top right, 192 left; National Trust: Waddesdon Manor 184 top; Old Sturbridge Village, Massachusetts 276; Phillips, London 25 right, 28 top right, 75 bottom, 82 bottom, 128, 137, 142 top, 213; Pilkington Museum of Glass, St Helen's 169; Rex Features, London 14; Mrs Jane Renn 260 top; Rheinisches Bildarchiv, Cologne 104 right; Rijksmuseum, Amsterdam 84 bottom, 99, 136 top, 141 top; Royal Academy of Arts, London 76 top left, 76 lower left, 77 right, 78 top, 78 bottom right; Scala, Florence 46–47; Shelburne Museum, Vermont 314 bottom; Sleepy Hollow Restorations, Tarrytown, New York 233 bottom; Society for Cultural Relations with the USSR, London 152; Sotheby Parke Bernet & Co, London 8, 12 bottom, 85, 106 bottom, 153, 155, 165 right, 258; Sotheby Parke Bernet & Co., New York 39, 42 bottom; Sotheby's – Belgravia 270 top, 297, 300; Spink & Son Ltd., London 33; Staatliche Kunstsammlungen, Kassel 95 left; Tass 101; Trust House Forte, Hayes 233 top; Victoria and Albert Museum, London 20, 21 bottom left, 25 left, 29 top right, 30 top, 30 bottom, 36, 44 top, 48 left, 60 right, 61, 75 top left, 77 left, 88, 90, 93, 95 right, 96 bottom, 97, 100 top, 105 top left, 105 bottom left, 105 right, 108, 113 left, 113 right, 114, 118 top, 121 top, 133, 150, 154, 168 left, 172 bottom, 173, 176 top, 177 right, 183 bottom, 184 bottom, 188 bottom, 189, 192 right, 197, 216 bottom, 217, 224, 225 top, 225 bottom, 236 top, 238 bottom, 244 bottom, 245, 253, 256 bottom, 281, 296 bottom, 301, 304 top right, 304 bottom, 307 bottom, 312 top, 312 bottom; Wallace Collection, London 131, 198; Wark Collection, Jacksonville, Florida 174; Wilsdorf Collection at Rolex Watches, Geneva 274 bottom; Winchester Gun Museum, Connecticut 289 bottom; The Worshipful Company of Goldsmiths, London 86, 158; Yale University, New Haven 149; Zwinger Museum, Dresden 109.

Index